MORALS FROM MOTIVES

MORALS FROM MOTIVES

Michael Slote

OXFORD
UNIVERSITY PRESS

2001

OXFORD
UNIVERSITY PRESS

Oxford   New York

Athens   Auckland   Bangkok   Bogotá   Buenos Aires   Calcutta
Cape Town   Chennai   Dar es Salaam   Delhi   Florence   Hong Kong   Istanbul
Karachi   Kuala Lumpur   Madrid   Melbourne   Mexico City   Mumbai
Nairobi   Paris   São Paulo   Shanghai   Singapore   Taipei   Tokyo   Toronto   Warsaw

and associated companies in
Berlin   Ibadan

Copyright © 2001 by Michael Slote

Published by Oxford University Press, Inc.
198 Madison Avenue, New York, New York 10016

Oxford is a registered trademark of Oxford University Press

Library of Congress Cataloging-in-Publication Data
Slote, Michael A.
Morals from motives / Michael Slote.
p.   cm.
Includes index.
ISBN 0-19-513837-6
1. Virtue.   2. Ethics.   3. Agent (Philosophy)
4. Caring—Moral and ethical aspects.   I. Title.
BJ1521 .S577 2000
171—dc21   99-088072

1 3 5 7 9 8 6 4 2

Printed in the United States of America
on acid-free paper

For Rosy

PREFACE

Till very recently, most of the contemporary revival of virtue ethics has led in the direction of Aristotle. But in the past few years, Stoic ideas have started to have an influence on current debates, and the moral sentimentalism of Hume and Hutcheson has also begun to be related to the themes and methods of virtue ethics.

The present book deliberately avoids patterning its ideas on Aristotle. Although my earlier book, *From Morality to Virtue*, works in a neo-Aristotelian vein, the historical Aristotle seems irrelevant to some of the most important problems of contemporary ethics, and neo-Aristotelian virtue ethicists have to take Aristotle in some unaccustomed new directions if they wish to make that approach completely attractive. Let me be a bit more specific.

It has long and often been said (e.g., by Grotius) that Aristotle's doctrine of the mean has no way of dealing with virtues like truthtelling and promise-keeping, and though I by and large agree with this criticism, I believe there is a deeper problem with Aristotle's (own) ethical views. Although Aristotle mentions the fact that we tend to praise lovers of humankind, his *theory* of morality doesn't seem to require a concern for human beings generally, and for any moral philosophy seeking to deal with the increasingly connected world we live in, this lack is very telling.

The moral philosophies that today dominate the philosophical scene, (utilitarian) consequentialism and Kantianism, are both ready with answers as to why we must be concerned, at least to some extent, with all other human beings. And it has become difficult to accept any overall moral philosophy, like Aristotle's, that offers no defense of generalized concern for (other) people. Such a moral philosophy now strikes most philosophers as retrograde, and, more particularly, it seems to be unhelpful in regard to one of the great and central moral issues of contemporary (or modern) life, namely: how *much* concern or help do we owe to those, half a world away, whose troubles or sufferings we hear about and can do something to relieve. (However, the difficulty for Aristotle here also lies partly in the fact that he lacks our modern notion of supererogation: never distinguishes between what it would be morally good for us to do for others and what we actually have an *obligation* to do for them.)

Mainly for the reason(s) just mentioned, therefore, a reviving Aristotelianism can seriously compete with consequentialist and Kantian approaches to ethics and politics only if it offers some way to defend obligations to human beings generally, and some recent neo-Aristotelians—e.g., Philippa Foot and Rosalind Hursthouse—have indeed moved in this direction. In any event, historical Stoicism very clearly does assert a general concern for humanity on a rational(istic) basis that to some degree anticipates Kant's arguments for such concern. So a reviving virtue ethics might well think of looking to Stoicism for contemporary relevance, and some recent virtue ethicists, notably Julia Annas, Lawrence Becker, and Martha Nussbaum, have been doing just that.

However, there is another possibility, another way to make virtue ethics relevant to and promising for current-day ethical theory. Rather than follow, or try to update, Aristotle or the Stoics, virtue ethics can look for inspiration to eighteenth-century British moral sentimentalism. For both Hume and Hutcheson speak about and defend generalized forms of benevolence, and Hutcheson in particular does so by reference to a motive, universal benevolence, conceived as admirable and morally ideal *independently of its consequences*. This is more like virtue ethics than like utilitarianism or consequentialism more generally, and the idea of an agent-based virtue ethics that grounds its evaluations of actions in (evaluations of) sentiments that reflect a general concern for humanity has recently seemed to me to be a very promising way of reviving virtue-ethics into contemporaneous relevancy. Moral sentimentalism offers virtue ethics some splendid opportunities it has previously, to a large extent, neglected, and it will be my primary aim in what follows to make good on this claim. Thus the present work will focus less on criticisms of other (virtue-ethical) views than on the attractive features of a sentimentalism-inspired virtue ethics (and on the answers that such an approach can give to criticisms directed at *it*).

But the book's reliance to some extent on eighteenth-century sentimentalism also relates to a more recent development, the so-called feminine ethic of caring. For like benevolence, caring is a natural motive in Hume's sense, one not presupposing any form of self-conscious or explicit moral conscientiousness (or rational argument). It early on struck me that the morality of caring is like sentimentalism in the way it emphasizes and values motives, but that it is in fact best understood or at least best defended as a form of agent-based virtue ethics.

Via arguments to be advanced in later chapters, I have also become convinced that an ethic of caring can take the well-being of all humanity into consideration just as easily as an agent-based virtue ethics grounded in universal (i.e., impartial) benevolence. The only difference, roughly, is that the former allows for and mandates preference for those near and dear to one, whereas the latter rules that out, at least at ground-floor level. But partiality toward near and dear is quite compatible with substantial concern for all human beings, whether known to one or not, and (like Virginia Held) I have in what follows argued that the morality of caring can and should take in a concern not just for those one intimately knows or may come to know, but for those one cannot ever really become acquainted with and whom one may learn about only as members of some group or nation one has heard of.

Along the way, however, we shall also have to examine the concept of love. We have a high opinion of love—of love for others and even, under certain aspects, of self-love; and I think we need to spend some time discussing (our) ideals of love if we are to attain a proper understanding of the difference between loving particular people and a more generalized or humanitarian concern for human beings as such. It will turn out that love is *morally* distinctive in ways that have not been previously considered, and that fact then needs to be taken into account by the general, though partialistic, ethic of caring this book is ultimately committed to.

However, agent-basing is sufficiently rare or unfamiliar as an approach to ethics that the present book, especially in its earlier chapters, seeks to answer objections to such an approach that will undoubtedly occur to the reader. I hope to persuade you thereby that basing morality ultimately in a motive like caring or (universal) benevolence or even love makes a good deal of sense, and, having done so, I want to go on to examine the main areas of ethics that lie outside the morality of individual action.

Thus, having applied notions like caring, benevolence, and love to questions of individual morality (the morality governing an individual's actions), I shall argue that an ethic of caring can be extended to take in issues of social justice and of just legislation. Far from siding with those who have said that caring and compassion stand opposed to, or are at the very least distinct from, considerations of justice, I shall attempt to show how an ethic of caring or benevolence can actually yield *its own distinctive conception of justice*. Then, in the second part of the book, I shall go on to develop an agent-based theory of practical reason, which can be used to launch an agent-based theory of human good and the good life. This is a great deal to take on, but I have found that the more I examine and explore the possibilities of this way of approaching ethics, the more resources it proves itself to have and the more promising, for all systematic purposes, it seems. Let me try, then, to persuade you of all this.

May 2000   M.S.
College Park, Maryland

ACKNOWLEDGMENTS

This book has been a long time in the making. The idea of agent-basing, which may be its most distinctive feature, occurred to me around 1980, when I was living and teaching in Ireland. But after spending a good deal of time working on the promise and precedents of agent-basing, I thought of some criticisms of the whole approach that led me to drop the project for three or four years. I only returned to it when, some years later and having returned to the United States, I saw what seemed to me to be a fairly decisive way to answer the earlier doubts (chiefly, the charge of "autism" against agent-based views which I discuss in chapter 1). However, it wasn't till the early 1990s that I saw the promise of connecting agent-based virtue ethics with the moral sentimentalism of Hutcheson, Hume, James Martineau, and Nel Noddings. Till about two years ago, the book existed (if at all) only in the form of connected but separable essays, but it has finally coalesced after a period of hectic activity.

The book has accumulated many debts in the process of coming into being. I would like to thank Peter French, the editor of *Midwest Studies in Philosophy*, for permission to make use of material from my papers "Agent-Based Virtue Ethics" (vol. 20) and "Love and Justice" (vol. 22) in chapters 1 and 5, respectively. I am similarly indebted to the editors of *Social Philosophy and Policy* for allowing me to use material from articles entitled "The Justice of Caring" (vol. 15, no. 1) and "The Virtue in Self-Interest" (vol. 14, no. 1) in chapters 4 and 6, respectively. Finally, I want to thank Wolfgang Spohn and Kluwer Publishing for allowing me to use material from my "Motives, Rules, and Rationality," forthcoming in a conference volume entitled *Rationality, Rules, and Structure*, in chapter 7 of the present book.

I am also very grateful to Peter Ohlin for his encouragement of the present project and his assistance during the publication process and to readers for Oxford University Press (and another press) for many useful comments. For help on single chapters or articles on which chapters have been based, I am especially indebted to Marcia Baron, Richard Fyfe, Jorge Garcia, Patricia Greenspan, Virginia Held, Brad Hooker, Rosalind Hursthouse, Judy Lichtenberg, Nancy Matchett, Chris Morris, Nel Noddings, Susan Moller Okin, Ellen Frankel Paul, Philip Pettit, Christine Swanton, and Peter van Inwagen. Most of all, I want to thank Scott Gelfand, Thomas Hurka, and Sam Kerstein for their trenchant remarks on large portions (or the whole) of the manuscript.

CONTENTS

PART II: PRACTICAL
RATIONALITY AND HUMAN GOOD

PART I

Morality and Justice

ONE

AGENT-BASED VIRTUE ETHICS

1. Virtue Ethics

We are in the midst of a tremendous revival of interest in virtue ethics, but till quite recently almost everything that has appeared in this vein has been of Aristotelian inspiration. The present book attempts to take virtue ethics in a somewhat different direction, one both more theoretical and at the same time more radical and "pure" than most familiar virtue ethics. It offers a systematically *agent-based* account of virtue ethics, and to get clear about what this involves—and how such an approach may or may not be promising—I think we need to draw some distinctions. To begin with, something should be said, briefly, about what virtue ethics is (there exist differences of opinion about how virtue ethics is to be defined, but I think we needn't belabor them here).

Recent interest in and calls for a revival of virtue ethics are in fact somewhat ambiguous. Some ethicists have simply wanted to see one or another preferred set of moral principles supplemented or complemented by an account of virtuous traits and actions. Others have sought a genuinely *free-standing* ethics of virtue, and the idea of virtue ethics is today widely understood as involving an ethical approach independent of other major traditions. But what, then, distinguishes virtue ethics from other ways of doing ethics?

As in so many other places in philosophy, exact definitions are difficult to come by, but the main contrast, as I have already sug-

gested, is with forms of ethics based in moral laws, rules, and principles. In virtue ethics, the focus is on the virtuous individual and
on those inner traits, dispositions, and motives that qualify her as
being virtuous. (Some forms of virtue ethics do allow for general
moral rules or even laws, but these are typically treated as derivative
or secondary factors.) Many modern philosophers think of the moral
life as a matter of relating properly to moral rules, but in the virtue
ethics of the ancient world and in those few instances of virtue ethics
one finds in modern or recent philosophy, the understanding of the
moral or ethical life primarily requires us to understand what it is
to be a virtuous individual and/or what it is to have one or another
particular virtue, conceived as an inner trait or disposition of the
individual. So the first thing we can say about virtue ethics in an
attempt to distinguish it from other approaches is that it is *agent-
focused*.

But another important feature needs to be mentioned. An ethics
of rules will typically characterize acts as morally right or wrong,
morally permissible or obligatory, depending on how they accord
with appropriate rules. Such moral epithets are called "deontic"
(from the Greek word for necessity), and they contrast with another
class of ethical epithets where there is less immediate or ultimate
connection with rules, namely, "aretaic" (from the Greek word for
excellence or virtue) ethical terms like "morally good," "admirable," "virtuous." Virtue ethics makes primary use of aretaic terms
in its ethical characterizations, and it either treats deontic epithets as
derivative from the aretaic or dispenses with them altogether. Thus
an ethics of virtue thinks primarily in terms of what is noble or
ignoble, admirable or deplorable, good or bad, rather than in terms
of what is obligatory, permissible, or wrong, and together with the
focus on the (inner character of the) agent, this comes close enough,
I think, to marking off what is distinctive of and common to all
forms of virtue ethics: both the ancient virtue ethics of Plato, Aristotle, the Stoics, and the Epicureans and the modern virtue ethics,
for example, of the nineteenth-century British ethicist James Martineau. (Once we have these two features of virtue ethics clearly in
view, we can also see that neither of them characterizes consequentialism, with its traditional focus on *obligatory actions* rather than
on goodness of character.)

However, the agent-based virtue ethics I shall be pursuing in what
follows is more radical and in some sense purer than other, more

familiar forms of virtue ethics, and the primary task of the present chapter will be to characterize what is distinctive about such an approach and (to begin) to say something in defense of it. An agent-based approach to virtue ethics treats the moral or ethical status of acts as entirely derivative from independent and fundamental aretaic (as opposed to deontic) ethical characterizations of motives, character traits, or individiuals. And such agent-basing is arguably not to be found in Aristotle, at least on one standard interpretation.

Certainly, Aristotle seems to focus more on the evaluation of agents and character traits than on the evaluation of actions. Moreover, for Aristotle an act is noble or fine if it is one that a noble or virtuous individual would perform, and he does say that the virtuous individual is the measure of virtue in action. But Aristotle also allows that nonvirtuous individuals can perform good or virtuous acts under the direction of others, and, in addition, he characterizes the virtuous individual as someone who *sees* or *perceives* what is good or fine or right to do in any given situation.

Such language clearly implies that the virtuous individual does what is noble or virtuous because it is the noble—for example, courageous—thing to do, rather than its being the case that what is noble—or courageous—to do has this status simply because the virtuous individual actually will choose or has chosen it. Even if right or fine actions cannot be defined in terms of rules, what makes them right or fine, for Aristotle, is not that they have been chosen in a certain way by a certain sort of individual. So their status as right or fine or noble is treated as in some measure independent of agent-evaluations, and that would appear to lead us away from agent-basing as defined just above.

In that case, if the virtuous individual is the measure of what is fine or right, that may simply mean that she is in the *best possible position to know/perceive* what is fine or right; similarly, if acts are right if a virtuous individual would perform them, that still leaves open the possibility that the virtuous individual would perform them *because* they are right. But the suspicion may nonetheless linger that Aristotle intends an explanation in just the opposite direction and holds, instead, that acts are right *because* virtuous individuals would perform them. In that case, Aristotle might have an agent-based—not merely an agent-focused—view of ethics.

But if we choose to understand the nobility or rightness of actions simply as what a virtuous agent would choose, then it becomes at the very least problematic how a virtuous agent can also perceive the rightness or nobility of an action and decide on that very basis to perform it. Moreover, if the rightness of actions is constituted by hypothetical facts about the virtuous, we cannot, on pain of circularity, say that virtuousness consists (in part) in a disposition to see and do what is right or noble; and presumably, therefore, we shall want some *other* account of what virtuousness consists in.

One way to do this would be to treat the virtues or virtuousness in (grounding) relation to *eudaimonia*, and some recent virtue ethicists understand Aristotle precisely along these lines. Thus in her influential article, ''Virtue Theory and Abortion,'' Rosalind Hursthouse interprets (and defends) Aristotle as deriving all evaluations of actions from independent judgments about what a virtuous person would characteristically choose and about what counts as a virtue, but basing these latter, in turn, in judgments about, a conception of, *eudaimonia*. But if (as is commonly believed) Aristotle understands/ explains *eudaimonia* largely in terms of virtuous activity, then it becomes difficult to see how Aristotelianism can be consistently grounded in the way indicated by Hursthouse, and in any event such an interpretation does not treat Aristotelian ethics as agent-based. It treats the evaluation of actions as derivative from independent aretaic character evaluations and to that extent the view can be described as an *agent-prior* one, but since the character evaluations are not regarded as fundamental and are supposed to be grounded in a theory or view of *eudaimonia*, the theory is not agent-based in the above terms.[1] (I assume here that *eudaimonia* and the ideas of

---

1. *Philosophy and Public Affairs* 20, 1991, pp. 223–46. Note that although the view defended in the present book ties act-evaluation to the actual motives of the agent, the above definition of agent-basing allows for the possibility of ultimately grounding act-assessments in claims about *hypothetical* virtuous agents. I am not aware of anyone who wants to characterize Aristotle (or any other historical figure) as such a hypothetical agent-baser, but recently Scott Gelfand has explicitly been working on hypothetical forms of agent-basing.

In any event, standard ideal observer (and response dependence) theories are *not* (hypothetically) agent-based or even agent-prior, for although they may define rightness in terms of the attitudes of a hypothetical observer possessing what are ordinarily taken to be virtues—e.g., lack of bias or distinterestedness—the theory doesn't or needn't *say* that these traits are virtues nor attempt to spell out what all the virtues are independently of its specification of the right. Indeed, such views leave it open that an ideal observer should condemn her own disinterestedness, and so they clearly do not commit themselves to any account of good inner traits or motives as the basis for their accounts of right action.

well-being and a good life are not themselves aretaic, even though some ethical views treat them as closely connected to or based in aretaic notions).

Thus there are (at least) two ways of construing the structure of Aristotelian virtue ethics, one of which (Hursthouse's) treats his view as agent-prior and the other of which (my own, though I am hardly the first to interpret Aristotle this way) sees Aristotle as offering a (merely) agent-focused and rather intuitionistic conception of ethics. The doubts mentioned briefly just above are what incline me in the latter direction, toward an interpretation according to which the rightness and nobility of action are not constituted by any relation, hypothetical or actual, to virtuous agents, and virtuous agents perceive (and act on) such rightness without making use of rules or principles. Such a view allows us to define or understand virtue and virtuous agents in relation to right or noble actions and (noncircularly) to understand or explain *eudaimonia* in terms of virtue and virtuous/noble actions.

Whatever the relative merits of the above two differing interpretations, however, there appears to be no reason to think of Aristotle as proposing an agent-based form of virtue ethics: that is, one that treats the moral or ethical status of actions as entirely *derivative* from independent and *fundamental* ethical/aretaic facts (or claims) about the motives, dispositions, or inner life of moral individuals. Views of the latter kind obviously represent a radical form of virtue ethics, and indeed agent-based views are in a familiar sense more *purely* virtue ethical than other forms of virtue ethics. Many philosophers distinguish ethical theories by which of the main ethical concepts— the good, the right, and virtue—they make explanatorily primary, and only agent-based forms of virtue ethics *do* treat virtue (claims/ facts about what is admirable or morally good in people) as explanatorily primary.

Perhaps, then, it is rather surprising and even anomalous that it turns out to be somewhat difficult to find clear-cut historical examples of agent-basing. The most uncontroversial example of agent-basing I know of is that of the nineteenth-century British ethicist James Martineau, and we shall have a good deal to say about Martineau in what follows. But Plato, for example, is in the above terms a less pure instance of virtue ethics. Plato does insist, certainly, that we evaluate actions by reference to the health and virtue of the soul, but he seems also to think that (appreciation of) the Form of the Good represents a level of evaluation prior to the evaluation of souls, with souls counting as virtuous when properly appreciating and being guided by the value inherent in the Form of the Good.

To that extent, Plato's view is agent-*prior*, but not agent-*based*. So we in fact have a three-way distinction and contrast here among Aristotle, Plato, and Martineau: with Aristotle (interpreted as an intuitionist) committed to an agent-focused, but neither an agent-prior nor an agent-based, virtue ethics; with Plato and Hursthouse('s Aristotle) advocating an agent-focused and agent-prior, but not an agent-based, view; and with Martineau defending a pure virtue ethics that is agent-focused, agent-prior, *and* agent-based. (Clearly, being agent-based entails, but is not entailed by, being agent-prior and being agent-prior entails, but is not entailed by, being agent-focused.)

But even if the above points about Plato and Aristotle are granted, it might be wondered why I regard Martineau as the best historical example of agent-basing, of "pure" virtue ethics. Aren't there in fact numerous uncontroversial and clear-cut instances of agent-basing throughout the history of ethics? I am not sure. One might claim, for example, that Hume was an agent-baser, citing (among other things, though perhaps most notably) the passage in the *Treatise of Human Nature* (book 3, part 2, opening of section 1) where Hume says that "all virtuous actions derive their merit only from virtuous motives." Yet taken by itself, this passage at most establishes Hume's credentials as a defender of agent-priority; and since Hume also seems to hold that the virtuousness of motives depends to some extent on their utility, on their having good consequences for people, I think it would be difficult to claim Hume as an agent-baser as well. (A similar point can also be made about Leslie Stephen's *The Science of Ethics*.)[2]

Perhaps a more promising historical lode of agent-basing may be found in the Christian ethics of agapic love. Augustine, Malebranche, and many other Christian thinkers have regarded love for God as grounding love for one's fellow creatures and all moral virtue as well, and since love is an inner state, Christian morality (of this kind) may well be thought to exemplify agent-basing.[3] And it

---

2. Leslie Stephen, *The Science of Ethics* (London: Smith Elder, 1882), pp. 155, 158, but especially 206.

3. See St. Augustine, *Ten Homilies on the First Epistle of Saint John*, Seventh Homily, section 8, in John Burnaby, ed., *Augustine: Later Works* (Philadelphia: West-

may well do so. But that conclusion is, nonetheless, far from unproblematic or obvious. Much depends on how one understands God's love for us and the relation between that love and human love toward God and other (human) creatures. If loving all other human beings is admirable or obligatory simply because all (agapic) love, whether our own or God's, is clearly morally good and praiseworthy, then we probably have an instance of agent-basing. But if we say (and there are hints and more than hints of this in Augustine, Malebranche, and other Christian ethicists of agape) that love is obligatory for and praiseworthy in us *because* we owe God obedience or submission as our Creator and/or Redeemer and God *wants* us to love one another, then we seem to be presupposing an independent deontological rule or standard, and the view we are committed to is not (purely or primarily) agent-based. (Similarly, if we think of a loving God as constrained by certain considerations of justice—as Malebranche seems to do—then our ethics is once again not really agent-based.) Finally (and just to muddy the waters a bit further), if we say that we should love and be good to one another because we have a duty of *gratitude* toward God, then the ethics of love may have ceded its primacy to an ethics of gratitude, but the latter may well be conceivable in agent-based terms.

So it is difficult to find uncontroversial examples of agent-basing in the history of ethics, and other figures that may be thought to represent historical instances of agent-basing—for example, Abelard, Schopenhauer, Kant, Hutcheson, Nietzsche, Spinoza, and certain Chinese and Indian thinkers—offer varying forms of resistance to being interpreted in this fashion. Still, the sheer number of thinkers who come close to, or exemplify important aspects of, agent-basing is impressive and should offer a certain amount of encouragement to those who wish to pursue "pure," agent-based virtue ethics in a more self-conscious and clear-cut manner.[4] But before I

---

minster Press, 1955), and Nicolas Malebranche's *Treatise on Ethics* (Boston: Kluwer, 1993).

4. In his little book *Ethics*, 2d ed. (Englewoods Cliffs, N.J.: Prentice Hall, 1973), pp. 63f., William Frankena distinguishes what I am calling agent-based approaches from other forms of virtue ethics. He calls such approaches "trait-deontological theories" and treats them as having some promise. But his characterization of virtue ethics more generally seems to run together agent-focused and agent-prior views (cf. what he says on page 16 about Aristotle).

say more about particular ways of developing agent-based virtue theories, there are some very worrying objections to the whole idea of agent-basing that must first be addressed.

2. Objections to Agent-Basing

Most of the literature of recent virtue ethics has been more or less explicitly antitheoretical, and because the agent-based (and moral sentimentalism-inspired) approach I shall take is so very theoretical, I would like to begin by defending theory against antitheory. Notable recent antitheorists like Annette Baier and Bernard Williams have been very critical of ethical theory's quest for hierarchically ordered, exceptionless, and universally applicable moral principles. They have said that the theorist's preference for impartiality and simplicity has led moral theories to posit an underlying unity to all moral thought and conceive all moral disputes as resolvable by decision procedures that see all moral complexities as reducible to and measurable in terms of some single commensurating moral consideration or factor.[5]

But it is far from clear that everything that deserves the name of moral theory has all these tendencies. Many think of Aristotle as a moral theorist par excellence, but he denies the possibility of exceptionless universal principles and has no place in his philosophy for the idea of a single kind of moral consideration in terms of which all moral issues can be resolved. Nor is Aristotle's view impartialist, if by that one means a view that requires one to treat all people equally and without partiality or preference. One might, then, conclude that Aristotle is no moral theorist, but my own preference is to allow a wider understanding of the notion.[6] Nor is it even clear that Kantian ethics and consequentialism exemplify all or most of the theoretical tendencies decried by the antitheorists. In any event, in what follows I hope to show you that we need theory in ethics and thus that theoretical virtues like simplicity and unifying power have some weight in deciding what kind of ethical view to adopt.

---

5. See Annette Baier's *Postures of the Mind* (Minneapolis: University of Minnesota Press, 1985); and Bernard Williams's *Ethics and the Limits of Philosophy* (Cambridge, Mass.: Harvard University Press, 1985).

6. Such a preference is well defended in Robert Louden's *Morality and Moral Theory* (New York: Oxford University Press, 1992).

To be sure, intuitive considerations also have considerable weight, and it is my view that consequentialism and certain other theories have unwelcome and anti-intuitive implications that hobble them as an approach to morality. But I think the real issue for ethics is *what kind of ethical theory to adopt, not whether we need theory in ethics*. The idea that our moral understanding of things is too rich and complex to be reduced to universal principles or to require, in the name of some inappropriate scientific ideal, any kind of simplifying unification in terms of a single factor or small set of such factors is not per se objectionable. Indeed, it has a certain attractiveness. But I want to now show you, as briefly as I know how, that our ordinary intuitive moral thought is not just complex, but subject to paradox and internal incoherence, and this is a far less acceptable situation than what the antitheorists imagine to be the case. In fact, it is what makes moral theory both necessary and desirable.

Consider the problem of moral luck as discussed by Thomas Nagel.[7] A person driving along a lonely country road and paying too much attention to the scenery might swerve into the oncoming traffic lane, incur no accident, and blame herself very little if at all for her inattention or negligence. And our own attitude, thinking of such a case on its own, would normally be quite similar. However, if we imagine the same scenario except that a car in fact is coming in the opposite direction, with the result that an accident occurs and the other driver or a passenger in her own car is killed, the negligent driver will very much blame herself. And our own inclination, say, as observers would be very similar. Yet the difference between the two cases is, from the standpoint of the agent, a matter of luck or accident, and our common-sense moral intuitions find it implausible and morally repugnant to believe that differences in blameworthiness and other serious moral differences between people should be a matter of luck or accident, beyond anyone's control or advance knowledge. So the moral judgments we make and intuitions we have about cases of negligence are in fact inconsistent (as a set), hardly an acceptable state of affairs for the moral philosopher.

Let me mention another area in which our ordinary moral intuitions fail to cohere with one another. Our common moral thinking treats it as sometimes obligatory to do good things for others and

7. See the paper "Moral Luck" in Thomas Nagel, *Mortal Questions* (Cambridge: Cambridge University Press, 1979).

almost always obligatory to refrain from harming them. But there is no similar moral obligation in regard to benefiting oneself or refraining from doing damage to one's prospects or even one's health. This difference is captured by saying that common-sense morality is self-other asymmetric in regard to our obligations. But why shouldn't we have moral obligations to advance and not to damage our own prospects, our own happiness? Common sense (check this in yourself!) has an answer ready for this question, and it is that it makes no sense to suppose there is an obligation to do things we are already inclined to do and can naturally be expected to do. Since we naturally and expectably do care for our own interests, there can't be—there is no moral need for—an obligation to do so.

But aside from the issue whether people really can be expected to take care of their own interests in a rational way (think of all the self-destructive, lazy, or health-risking people you know), the just-given explanation actually is incoherent or incongruent with other intuitive moral assumptions. For example, we are naturally very concerned to help those who are near and dear to us and typically lack this degree of practical concern for strangers or people we don't know. Yet according to common sense we have obligations to our near and dear that we *don't* have toward others. And that is the very opposite of what one should expect given the above rationale for the absence of an obligation to pursue and advance our own well-being. Common-sense thinking turns out to be subject to other paradoxes or incongruities of this sort, and that means there is something wrong with common sense. Our intuitions turn out to clash among themselves, and if we are to attain to full coherence in our ethical thinking, we are forced to reject at least some intuitions. But which ones? Well, to decide *that* issue, we need to look for a way of understanding ethics that allows us to avoid incoherence/paradox, and that task requires us to be philosophically and morally *inventive*.

Similar problems have notably occurred in other areas of philosophy. When naive set theory turned out to be self-contradictory, different theorists began proposing different ways of grounding arithmetic in set theory, and the validity and success of those different approaches were measured in terms of theoretical considerations like simplicity, scope, and explanatory power. Likewise, when it turned out that our intuitive assumptions about what statements scientifically confirm what others were inconsistent, the desire for a coherent understanding of scientific confirmation led philosophers of science to propose different ways of formally understanding confirmation, and, again, the success or promise of their proposals was judged partly in terms of how much ordinary thinking they preserved, but also partly in terms of theoretical desiderata like simplicity, scope, etc.

Why should it be any different in ethics? Given that intuitions clash, ingenuity is needed to come up with something that avoids paradox, and if moral intuitions cannot settle everything, then theoretical considerations, philosophical considerations, seem relevant to our task, given the analogy with what happens in other areas of philosophy and *the desire to come up with some kind of coherent ethical view of things*.[8] Bernard Williams has criticized ethical theorizing for simplifying and unifying what seems rich and complex. We have, he thinks, not too many ideas, but too few.[9] And to be sure a moral theory *can* oversimplify ethical phenomena, leave too many things we believe or feel out of account. But Williams misses the point that at least in some respects our ethical thought has too many ideas, rather than too few; for if our intuitive thought contains contradictions or paradoxes, something has to be eliminated in order to attain the kind of ethical understanding we are looking for. He overstates the case, then, against moral theory. A theory that blurs intuitive ethical distinctions and phenomena has a strike against it, but we do need some sort of theory in ethics and have to abandon some intuitions if we are to gain the sort of paradox-free understanding in that domain that has been and is being sought in set theory, confirmation theory, and a host of other areas in philosophy. Let us now turn to some objections to agent-based theorizing in particular.

One thing that seems wrong in principle with any agent-based (or even agent-prior) approach to moral evaluation is that it appears to obliterate the common distinction between doing the right thing and doing the right thing for the right reasons. Sidgwick's well-

---

8. Someone might say: no theory is needed if we consider our task simply to be that of *preserving as many intuitions as possible while avoiding paradox*. But this would be a mistake, for clearly some intuitions are more important to us than others and have greater forcefulness or scope; it is not numbers, but weighted numbers that are important to us, and in fact theory is inevitable when one tries to devise ways of assigning such weightings, of figuring out how to weigh, say, scope vs. strength in determining the importance of intuitions (for preservation).

9. See *Ethics and the Limits of Philosophy*, pp. 116f.

known example of the prosecutor who does his duty by trying to convict a defendant, but who is motivated by malice rather than by a sense of public duty seems to illustrate the distinction in question,[10] and it may well seem that agent-based virtue ethics would have difficulty here because of the way it understands rightness in terms of good motivations and wrongness in terms of the having of bad (or insufficiently good) motives. If actions are wrong when they result from morally bad motives, doesn't that mean that the prosecutor acts wrongly in prosecuting someone out of malice (assuming that malice is morally criticizable)? And isn't that a rather unfortunate consequence of the agent-based approach?

I am not sure. Sidgwick himself seems to grant a certain plausibility to the idea that the prosecutor acts wrongly if he prosecutes from malice. What *is* implausible, rather, is the claim that the prosecutor has no duty to prosecute (or recuse himself and let someone else who is less biased prosecute). And that doesn't follow from the agent-based assumption that he acts wrongly if he prosecutes from malice.

But how can such a duty (or obligation) be understood in agent-based terms? Well, consider the possibility that *if he doesn't prosecute or let someone else prosecute*, the prosecutor's motivation will *also* be bad. Those who talk about the malicious prosecutor case often fail to mention the motives that might lead him *not* to prosecute. With malice present or even in the absence of malice, if the prosecutor doesn't either prosecute or recuse himself and allow someone *else* to prosecute, one very likely explanation will be that he lacks real or strong concern for doing his job and playing the contributing social role that that involves. Imagine that, horrified by his own malice, he ends up not prosecuting and unwilling even to think about letting someone else do so. This action too will come from an inner state that is morally criticizable, namely, one involving (among other things) insufficient concern for the public (or general human) good or for being useful to society.

So the idea that motives or inner traits are the basis for evaluating actions that they underlie or that express them doesn't have partic-

10. See Henry Sidgwick, *The Methods of Ethics*, 7th ed. (Indianapolis: Hackett Publishing, 1981), p. 202.

ularly implausible results. And it allows us something like the distinction between doing the right thing and doing it for the right reason. In particular, it allows us to say that the prosecutor has a duty (or obligation) to prosecute or else recuse himself in favor of another prosecutor, because if he doesn't, we shall in the normal course (barring his having a heart-attack, nervous breakdown, religious conversion, or the like) be able to attribute to him defective or deficient motivation of a kind that makes his action wrong. Yet we can also say that if he prosecutes, he acts (will act) wrongly, even if another person, with different motivation, would have acted rightly in doing so. This allows us then to distinguish between doing one's duty for the right reasons and thus acting rightly, on the one hand, and doing one's duty for the wrong reasons and thus acting wrongly. And this is very close to the distinction between right action and acting rightly for the right reasons, except for the fact that it supposes that when the reasons aren't right, the action itself is actually *wrong*. But we have already seen that this idea in itself is not particularly implausible, and so it turns out that the above-mentioned complaint against agent-basing turns on a faulty assumption about the inability of such views to make fine-grained distinctions of the sort we have just succeeded in making.

However, there is a group of further objections to the whole idea of agent-based ethics (or at least to the kind of agent-basing I shall be advocating here) that may more fundamentally represent what seems objectionable and even bizarre about such theories of morality. If the evaluation of actions ultimately derives from that of (the inner states of) their agents, then it would appear to follow that if one is the right sort of person or possesses the right sort of inner states, it doesn't morally matter what one actually *does*, so that the admirable person, or at least her actions, are subject to no genuine moral requirements or constraints. (Compare St. Augustine's "Love and do what you will.")[11] In this light, agent-basing seems a highly autistic and antinomian approach to ethics, one that appears to undermine the familiar, intuitive notion that the moral life involves—among other things—*living up to* certain *standards* of behavior or action. Furthermore, agent-basing also seems to contravene the

---

11. See St. Augustine's *Ten Homilies on the First Epistle of St. John*, p. 316.

maxim that 'ought' implies 'can', for if badly motivated people have obligations but everything such people can do counts as wrong, they have obligations that they are unable to fulfill.

However, none of these damning conclusions in fact follows from the character of the agent-basing defended here (or from that of certain agent-prior views about which it is possible to raise similar objections). A view can be relevantly agent-based and still not treat actions as right or admirable simply because they are done by a virtuous individual or by someone with a good or admirable inner state. Nor does such an agent-based theory have to say, with respect to each and every action a virtuous individual is capable of performing, that if she were to perform that action, it would automatically count as a good or admirable thing for her to have done.

Thus consider a very simple view according to which (roughly) benevolence is the only good motive and acts are right, admirable, or good to the extent they exhibit or express benevolent motivation on the part of the (actual) agent. (We can also assume actions are wrong or bad if they exhibit the opposite of benevolence or deficiently benevolent motivation in the agent). To the extent this view treats benevolence as fundamentally and inherently admirable or morally good, it is agent-based. But such a view doesn't entail that the virtuous individual with admirable inner states can simply choose any actions she pleases among those lying within her power, without the admirability or goodness of her behavior being in any way compromised or diminished. For assuming only some reasonable form of free-will compatibilism, a benevolent person is typically *capable* of choosing many actions that *fail to express or exhibit* her (inner state of) benevolence. Thus, if one is totally benevolent and sees an individual needing one's help, one presumably will help and, in doing so, exhibit inner benevolence. But it would also have been within one's power to refuse to help, and if one had refused, one's actions *wouldn't have exhibited benevolence and would therefore presumably have been less admirable than they would or could have been otherwise, according to the simplified agent-based view just mentioned.*

So it is not true to say that the kind of agent-basing discussed and defended in this book entails that what one does doesn't matter morally or that it doesn't matter given that one has a good enough inner character or motive. The person who exhibits benevolence in her actions performs actions that, in agent-based terms, can count as morally superior to other actions she might or could have performed, namely, actions (or refrainings from action) that would *not* have demonstrated benevolence. Acts therefore don't count as admirable or virtuous for agent-based theories of the sort just roughly introduced *merely because* they are or would be done by someone who is in fact admirable or possessed of admirable inner states; they have to exhibit, express, or reflect such states or be such that they *would* exhibit, etc., such states if they occurred, in order to count as admirable or virtuous. And we may conclude, then, that it is simply not true that agent-based theories inevitably treat human actions as subject to no moral standards.

Furthermore, the idea of agent-basing is also entirely consistent with the maxim that 'ought' implies 'can'. Presumably, one cannot change one's motives or character at will. But a thoroughly malevolent individual who sees a person he can hurt may still have it within his power to refrain from hurting that person, even if we can be sure he won't in fact exercise that power. And the act of refraining would fail to express or reflect his malevolence and would therefore not count as wrong. Given (the kind of) agent-basing (we are considering), such an individual has an obligation not to act in ways that express inferior motives, but if the above is correct, he has it in his power to fulfill that obligation. Thus agent-basing is consistent with 'ought' implies 'can' and allows genuine moral standards to govern our actions, but the standards it advocates operate and bind, so to speak, *from within*.

However, even this metaphor must be taken with caution, because it seems to imply that for (certain) agent-based views the "direction of fit" between world and moral agent is all one way, with the world simply having to fit the agent. It seems to imply, that is, that on such views the moral life is a matter of securing good motivation and acting on it, independently of ascertaining facts about what is needed out in the world around one. If such were the case, then agent-basing would entail a kind of autism or isolation from the world that would make one wonder how any such ethics could possibly be adequate. But agent-basing doesn't in fact yield isolation from or the irrelevance of facts about the world, and one sees this if one considers how the kinds of motivation such theories specify as fundamentally admirable invariably want and need to take the surrounding world into account. If one is really benevolent or wants to be socially useful, one doesn't just throw good things around or give them to the first person one sees. Benevolence, for example, isn't benevolence in the fullest sense unless one cares about who exactly is needy and to what extent they are needy, and such care, in turn, essentially involves wanting and making efforts to know relevant facts, so that one's benevolence can really be useful. Thus someone acting on that motive must be open to, seek contact with, and be influenced by the world around her—her decisions will not be made in splendid isolation from what most of us would take to be the morally relevant realities, and for an agent-based view, therefore, the moral value of a motive like benevolence isn't free-floating, but depends, rather, on the *kind* of internal state it is and, in particular, on the *aims and hopes it has, and the efforts it makes, vis-à-vis the world*. The worries mentioned above, then, really have no foundation, and everything we have just said about benevolence also applies to the foundational motivations of other agent-based views.

However, I think I need to mention one further potential worry before we launch into our account of particular agent-based virtue-ethical views. For it might be thought that if one regards certain motives as fundamentally admirable and seeks to explain the right-ness and wrongness of actions ultimately in terms of motives, one is treating the claims about motives as certain and immune to cor-rection, and such overconfidence offends the spirit of rational ethical inquiry and theorizing. Such a thought, however, would be mistaken. If judgments about the ethical status of motives ground claims about right and wrong action, then *the claims about right and wrong action that a given agent-based view yields can be used to test the validity or reasonableness of its grounding assumptions*. Thus if an agent-based view has implications for the evaluation of actions that we find intuitively unacceptable, if many of the things it tells us are right seem, for example, terribly wrong, then that agent-based view becomes at least somewhat questionable, and we are given reason to question what it says about the fundamental admirability of cer-tain motives.

Most ethical theories make some sort of ground-floor ethical as-sumptions, intuitively or initially plausible assumptions used to ex-plain or derive other ethical judgments/facts but not themselves based on any further ethical assumptions. Hedonism (the view that all and only pleasure is intrinsically good for people) is treated as just such a ground-floor explanatory assumption in many forms of utilitarianism, but these forms of utilitarianism and the hedonism they assume are both at least open to question if they yield particular moral judgments we find intuitively (or theoretically) unacceptable or absurd. And something exactly analogous also holds for agent-based moral conceptions. As in science, the use of initially plausible or intuitive grounding ethical assumptions doesn't require us to treat such assumptions as sacrosanct and is entirely in keeping with intellectual open-mindedness.[12]

Of course, since the kind of agent-basing we shall be focusing on implies that our knowledge of the goodness, rightness, and wrongness of particular actions depends ultimately on our knowledge of the motivation behind them, and since knowledge of people's motives is frequently difficult to acquire, such agent-based morality must assume that it is also frequently difficult to evaluate actions. However unwanted such a conclusion may be, it may nonetheless be realistic. Presumably, we would all like to be able readily to tell right actions from wrong actions, but most experience and a great deal of theory tell us that this is often, and perhaps even usually, not an easy thing to do. To that extent, the implications of agent-basing for moral epistemology are not particularly implausible, even if they are somewhat unwelcome.

3. Morality as Inner Strength

Having now, I trust, quelled the charges of autism, antinomianism, and theoretical overconfidence or close-mindedness that it is initially tempting to launch against agent-based approaches, I would like us to consider some interesting and even promising examples of agent-based ethical theories. Looking back over the history of ethics, it strikes me that there are basically two possible ways in which one can naturally develop the idea of agent-basing: one of them I call

12. Is there any reason to think that the judgments about the good upon which utilitarianism ultimately bases itself are less controversial than judgments about the moral admirability of motives? Considering the reasons given by Rawlsians to try to avoid making use of judgments about the good, probably not. Agent-basing may be less familiar than other approaches, but if, as I believe, moral judgments about motives can be made on a strong intuitive basis, then, since ethical judgment has to start somewhere, we have reason to explore the potential of agent-based ethics.

"cool," the other "warm" (or sentimentalist). We saw earlier that Plato's agent-prior view relates the morality of individual actions to the health and virtue of the soul, but in the *Republic* (book 4) Plato also uses the images of a strong and of a beautiful soul to convey what he takes to be the touchstone of all good human action. And I believe that ideas about health and, especially, strength can (without further, grounding reference to the Form of the Good) serve as the aretaic foundations for one possible kind of agent-based virtue ethics. Since, in addition, it is natural to wonder how any sort of altruism, any sort of *humane concern for other people*, can be derived from notions like health and strength, agent-based approaches of this first kind can be conveniently classified as "cool."

By contrast, James Martineau's agent-based conception of morality treats compassion as the highest of secular motives, and some of the philosophers who have come closest to advocating agent-based views—Hume, Hutcheson, and nowadays Jorge Garcia and Linda Zagzebski—have placed a special emphasis on compassion or, to use a somewhat more general term, benevolence as a motive.[13] I believe these notions can provide the focus for a second kind of agent-based view (actually, as it turns out, a pair of views) that deserves our attention, and since such views build altruistic human concern explicitly into their aretaic foundations, it is natural to speak of them as "warm." Because such views are also more (directly) influenced by British moral sentimentalism than by any other historical movement in ethics, we can equivalently speak of "sentimentalist" agent-basing as well.

Since Plato's discussion of health and strength is older than any discussion of benevolence I know of, I would like first to discuss agent-basing as anchored in the idea of strength. But metaphors/ images of health and strength also play an important role for Stoicism, for Spinoza, and for Nietzsche, though none of the latter offers a perfectly clear-cut example of an agent-based or even agent-prior account of ethics. Still, these views cluster around the same notions

---

13. See James Martineau, *Types of Ethical Theory*, 2 vols. (Oxford: Clarendon Press 1885, rprt. 1891); Hume, *A Treatise of Human Nature*, 1739; Francis Hutcheson, *An Inquiry into the Original of Our Ideas of Beauty and Virtue*, 4th ed., 1738; Jorge Garcia, "The Primacy of the Virtuous," *Philosophia* 20, 1990, pp. 69–91; and Linda Zagzebski, *Virtues of the Mind: An Inquiry into the Nature of Virtue and the Ethical Foundations of Knowledge* (Cambridge: Cambridge University Press, 1996).

that fascinate and influence Plato, and I believe they can naturally be extrapolated to a modern-day version of the virtue-ethical approach of the *Republic* and, in particular, to a genuinely agent-based "cool" theory that regards inner strength, in various of its forms, as the sole foundation for an understanding of the morality of human action.

For Plato, good action is to be understood in terms of the seemingly consequentialistic idea of creating and/or sustaining the strength (or health, etc.) of the soul, but to me it seems more promising to explore the idea of actions that *express* or *reflect* inner strength, and so *morality as inner strength*, as it seems natural to call it, should proceed on that basis. And remember too that the attempt to anchor everything in the Form of the Good led us to deny agent-based status to Plato's view. An agent-based morality that appeals to the notion of inner strength must therefore treat strength (in various forms) as an ultimately admirable way of existing and being motivated as a person and must show us how to frame a plausible morality of human actions on that basis.

Now the idea that there is something intuitively admirable about being strong inside, something requiring no appeal to or defense from *other ideas*, can perhaps be made more plausible by being more specific about the kind(s) of inner disposition and motivation I have in mind in speaking of inner strength. Consider, for example, the courage it takes to face unpleasant facts about oneself or the universe. Self-deception about whether one has cancer may make the end of one's life less miserable and even make things easier for those taking care of one, but still it seems far more admirable to face such facts. And intuitively such courage is not admired for the good it does people, for its consequences, but rather because we find courage, and the inner or personal strength it embodies, inherently admirable and in need of no further defense or justification. Here, then, is one form of inner strength that might plausibly be said to be justified at a ground-floor level, that is, in agent-based terms.

What *doesn't* seem plausible, however, is the idea that any contemporaneously relevant and inclusive morality of human action could be based *solely* in ideas about inner strength. What does inner strength have to do with being kind to people, with not deceiving them, with not harming them? And if it doesn't relate to these sorts of things, it clearly cannot function as a general groundwork for morality.

The same problem, the same question, comes up in connection with Plato's defense of morality in the *Republic*. That dialogue begins with the problem of explaining why anyone should be moral or just in the conventional sense of not deceiving, stealing, and the like. But Plato ends up defining justice in terms of the health or strength of the soul and never adequately explains why such a soul would refrain from what are ordinarily regarded as unjust or immoral actions. Even the appeal to the Form of the Good seems just a form of handwaving in connection with these difficulties, because even though Plato holds that healthy, harmonious souls must be guided by the Good, we aren't told enough about the Good or health or harmony to know why they would direct us away from lying, stealing, and the like. Doesn't a similar problem arise for an agent-based theory appealing fundamentally to the notion of inner strength? It certainly appears to, but perhaps the appearance can be dispelled by pointing out connections between strength and other-regarding morality that have largely gone unnoticed.

In *Beyond Good and Evil* and elsewhere, Nietzsche points out the possibility of being moved to give things to other people out of a self-sufficient sense of having more than enough, a superabundance of things. Nietzsche claims that this kind of "noble" giving is ethically superior to giving based on pity or a sense of obligation, but what is most important for present purposes is that Nietzsche has pointed out a way in which altruism can be justified in terms of the ideal of inner strength. (This is ironic, because Nietzsche is a self-proclaimed egoist, but he actually seems to be aiming at a view that is "beyond" the dichotomy of egoism and altruism). Any person who begrudges things to others no matter how much he has seems needy, too dependent on the things he keeps for himself, and pathetically *weak*, whereas the person who generously gives from a sense of superabundance seems both self-sufficient and strong within.

This kind of inner strength seems intuitively and inherently admirable. Yet such generosity is pretty clearly not egoistic. To give to others out of a sense of one's own superabundant well-being is not to try to *promote* that well-being, and so Nietzsche has given us an example of genuine altruism based in the ideal of strength. I believe we could find other examples of altruism based on (other forms of) inner strength, but even so, there is a general problem with this whole approach that has led me to think there are probably more promising ways to develop an agent-based virtue ethics.

The problem, in a nutshell, is that morality as strength treats sentiments or motives like benevolence, compassion, kindness, and the like as only *derivatively* admirable and morally good. And this seems highly implausible to the modern moral consciousness. To be sure, compassion cannot always have its way; it sometimes must yield to justice or the public good, and a compassion or generosity that never pays any heed to the agent's own needs seems masochistic, ethically unattractive, lacking in self-respect. But still, even if compassion has to be limited or qualified by other values, it counts with us as a *very important basic moral value*. And it seems to distort the aretaic value we place on compassion, benevolence, kindness, and caring for others to regard them as needing justification in terms of the (cool) ideal of inner strength or indeed any other different value. Such a criticism clearly touches the Kantian account of benevolence, which tries to derive its moral value from facts or postulates about our rationality and autonomy; and indeed many philosophers have criticized Kant for treating the value of benevolence as merely derivative and holding, in addition, that benevolence that is not guided by respect for the moral law lacks moral worth altogether. But the first of these criticisms can also be made of morality as strength, and so I would propose at this point to introduce and discuss a form of agent-based virtue ethics that is immune to this problem precisely because it bases all morality on the aretaic value, the moral admirability, of benevolence.[14] However, it turns out that there are two different forms or ideals of benevolence on which one might plausibly wish to base a warm (or sentimentalist) agent-based theory. It is time we discussed them.

4. Morality as Universal Benevolence

Martineau's *Types of Ethical Theory* represents perhaps the clearest example of agent-basing one can find in the entire history of ethics, and I believe that the advantages of a virtue ethics based on compassion or benevolence can best be brought to light by considering

---

14. The traditional Stoic defense of concern for others brings in the notion of *oikeiosis* (roughly, familiarization or appropriation), rather than relying mainly or exclusively on ideals of health and strength. Such an approach (whether or not it can be pursued in agent-based fashion) has a certain amount in common with the warm agent-basing that will be the focus of the rest of this book.

in turn the structure of Martineau's theory and the criticisms that Henry Sidgwick made of that theory.

Martineau gives a ranking of human motives from lowest to highest and, assuming as he does that all moral decisions involve a conflict between two such motives, holds that right action is action from the higher of the two motives, wrong action action from the lower of the two. Martineau's hierarchy of motives ascends (roughly) as follows: vindictiveness; love of sensual pleasure; love of gain; resentment/fear/antipathy; ambition/love of power; compassion; and, at the apex, reverence for the Deity.

Sidgwick objects to the rigidity of this hierarchy, pointing out that circumstances and consequences may affect the preferability of acting from one or another of the motives Martineau has ranked.[15] Thus contrary to Martineau, there are times when it is better for reasons of justice to act from resentment rather than compassion, and the love of sensual pleasure might sometimes prevail over a love of power or gain (especially if the latter were already being given ample play). Sidgwick concludes that conflicts between lower motives can only be resolved by appeal to the highest ranked motive or, alternatively, to some supremely regulative general motive like justice, prudence, or universal benevolence—none of which is contained among the more particular motives of Martineau's hierarchy. That is, all conflicts of Martineau's lower motives should be settled by reference to reverence for the Deity or by reference to some regulative or "master" motive like benevolence. (This would not be necessary if we could devise a more plausible and less priggish hierarchy than Martineau's. But no one has yet suggested a way of doing that).

Sidgwick then goes on to make one further (mistaken) assumption. He assumes that for a motive to be regulative, it must be regulative in relation to the ultimate *ends* or *goals* of that motive. And this entails that if we confine ourselves to secular motives, take seriously the fact that compassion is the highest secular motive in Martineau's ranking, and as a result choose universal benevolence (i.e., universally directed or *impartial* benevolence) as supremely regulative, actions and motives will be judged in terms of the goal of universal benevolence, namely, human or

---

15. *The Methods of Ethics*, ch. 12.

sentient happiness. Somehow, we have ended up not with a more orderly or unified form of agent-based view, but with *act-utilitarianism*. And this has happened because Sidgwick ignores the possibility of an agent-based view that judges actions from either of two conflicting motives in terms of how well the two motives exemplify or approximate the motive of universal benevolence *rather than* in terms of whether those actions achieve or are likely to achieve certain goals that universal/impartial benevolence aims at.

Thus suppose someone knows that he can help a friend in need, but that he could instead have fun swimming. The good he can do for himself by swimming is a great deal less than what he can do for his friend, but he also knows that if he swims, certain strangers will somehow indirectly benefit and the benefit will be greater than anything he can provide for his needy friend. However, the man doesn't at all care about the strangers, and though he does care about his friend, he ends up taking a swim. In that case, both "actualist" and "expectabilist" versions of act-utilitarianism will regard his action as the morally best available to him in the circumstances. It actually has better consequences for human happiness than any alternative would have had, and its expectable utility is greater than the alternative of helping his friend, since the man *knows* he will do more good, directly and indirectly, by swimming. But there is a difference between *expecting* or *knowing* that an act will have good consequences and being *motivated* to produce those consequences, and if we judge actions in agent-based fashion by how closely their motives exemplify or approximate to universal benevolence, then it is morally *less* good for him to go swimming for the selfish reason he does than to have sought to help his needy friend, and this is precisely the opposite of what standard forms of act-utilitarianism have to say about this situation.

Thus in order to rule out agent-based views making use of the notion of compassion or benevolence, it is not enough to undermine complicated views like Martineau's, for we have seen that there can be an agent-based *analogue* (or *"interiorization"*) of utilitarianism that morally judges everything, in unified or monistic fashion, by reference to universal benevolence as a *motive that seeks* certain ends instead of by reference to the actual or probable *occurrence* of those ends. And this distinctive *morality as univer-*

sal benevolence contrasts with utilitarianism in some striking further ways we have not yet mentioned.

Utilitarians and consequentialists evaluate motives and intentions in the same way as actions, namely, in terms of their consequences. (I am here ignoring rule-utilitarianism because for the usual, familiar reasons I believe it to be less plausible, less theoretically coherent, than act- or direct-utilitarianism.) Thus consider someone whose motives would ordinarily be thought not to be morally good, a person who gives money for the building of a hospital, but who is motivated only by a desire to see her name on a building or a desire to get a reputation for generosity as a means to launching a political career. Utilitarians and consequentialists will typically say that her particular motivation, her motivation in those circumstances, is morally good, whereas morality as universal benevolence, because it evaluates motives in terms of how well they approximate to universal benevolence, will be able, more commonsensically, to treat such motivation as less than morally good (even if not very *bad* either). Of course, when we learn of what such a person is doing and, let us assume, of her selfish motivation, we may well be happy and think it a good thing that she has the egotistical motives she has on the occasion in question, given their good consequences (and one's own benevolence). But we can intuitively *distinguish* between motives that, relative to circumstances, we are glad to see and it is good to have occur and motives we genuinely admire as morally good, and consequentialism standardly leads to a denial and collapse of this plausible distinction by morally evaluating motives solely in terms of their consequences. By contrast, morality as universal benevolence, precisely because it insists that the *moral* evaluation of motives depends on their inherent character as motives rather than on their consequences, allows for the distinction and comes much closer to an intuitive conception of what makes motives morally better or worse.

As an agent-based analogue of utilitarianism, morality as universal benevolence is, however, open to many of the criticisms that have recently been directed at utilitarianism, for example, the frequently heard claim that utilitarianism is too demanding. But this problem can perhaps be dealt with on analogy with the way utilitarianism and consequentialism attempt to deal with the criticism of overdemandingness: namely, either by arguing against it outright or, as I have suggested elsewhere,[16] by accommodating it through an adjustment of its principle(s) of right action. A satisficing version of (utilitarian) consequentialism can say that right action requires only that one do enough good, and it can then offer some agent-neutral, impartialistic conception of what it is, in various situations, to do enough good for humankind considered as a whole. And a satisficing version of morality as universal benevolence can (in a manner already indicated in the way we stated that view earlier) say that acts are right if they come from motivation that is *close enough* to universal benevolence—rather than insisting that acts reflecting anything less than that morally highest motive cannot count as morally acceptable. Someone who devoted most of her time, say, to the rights of consumers or to peace in Northern Ireland might then count as acting and living rightly, even if she were not impartially concerned with human welfare and sometimes preferred simply to enjoy herself. So there are versions of morality as universal benevolence that allow us to meet the criticism of over-demandingness, even if we think that criticism does have force against versions of the view that require us not to express anything less than the morally best motives or moral dispositions, when we act.

Some forms of utilitarianism are also, however, criticized for having an overly narrow conception of human well-being and in particular for treating all well-being as a matter of the balance of pleasure over pain. This criticism doesn't hold for (certain) pluralistic forms of consequentialism, and neither, interestingly enough, does it apply to morality as universal benevolence. The latter is not committed to any particular conception of human well-being and is quite happy to allow us to admire a person's concern and compassion for human beings without attributing to that person or ourselves having a settled view of what human well-being consists in. (If someone has a *perverse* sense of what is good for people—for example, thinks that pain is in itself good for you and acts accordingly—then the benignness of their motivation is questionable, and they are presumably self-deceived as well.)[17]

16. See, e.g., my *Common-Sense Morality and Consequentialism* (London: Routledge, 1985), esp. ch. 3.

17. But can we admire someone's benevolence or compassion toward other people if we don't think that it is (impartially speaking) *a good thing* for human beings

Finally, utilitarianism has been criticized for its inability to account for certain aspects of deontology, and these criticisms presumably also extend to morality as universal benevolence (although, as I shall argue later, not necessarily to every form of warm or sentimentalist agent-basing). Strict deontology tells us it is wrong to kill one innocent person in order to prevent a number of other innocent people from being killed or dying. However, since benevolence involves not only the desire to do what is good or best overall for the people one is concerned about, *but also the desire that no one of those people should be hurt or suffer*, morality as universal benevolence can explain why we might be horrified at killing one to save many, even if in the end it holds that that is what we morally ought to do. I conclude, then, that although both consequentialism and morality as universal benevolence are open to a good many familiar criticisms, they have ways of responding to the criticisms. Moreover, they have systematic advantages over many other approaches to morality because of their relative systematicity or unified structure. But, as I suggested earlier, morality as universal benevolence seems to have intuitive advantages over its more familiar utilitarian/consequentialist analogues. Though it is a view that to the best of my knowledge has not previously been explicitly stated or defended, it is in many ways more commonsensical and plausible than utilitarianism and consequentialism, and at the same time its reliance on the ideas of benevolence and universality ought to render it attractive to defenders of the latter views and make them ask themselves whether it wouldn't be better to accept an agent-based "interiorized" version of their own doctrines. If consequentialism and utilitarianism have present-day viability and appeal, agent-based morality as universal benevolence does too.[18]

---

to be happy or well-off, and doesn't that mean that judgments of admirability, rather than providing an agent-based foundation for morality, themselves rest on claims about what constitutes an objectively good state of the universe? In fact, I don't believe there is any reason to think that human admiration requires this much metaphysics. Rather, concern for human well-being can seem admirable to us in the light of our knowledge of what human beings *are* (their capacities and vulnerabilities vis-à-vis faring better or worse in their lives) without issues about what is a good or bad situation from the standpoint of the universe (or, for that matter, issues about the intrinsic moral worth of human beings) coming into the picture.

18. Hutcheson, in *An Inquiry*, takes universal benevolence to be inherently the

However, we have not yet exhausted the promising possibilities of agent-basing, and at this point I would like us to consider one final way of utilizing ideas relating to benevolence within an agent-based virtue ethics. Some educationists and philosophers have recently been exploring and developing the idea of an ethic or morality of *caring*, and in the next section I shall push or disambiguate this idea in the direction of a new kind of agent-based view.

5. Morality as Caring and Further Aspects of Agent-Basing

It is possible to ground an agent-based ethical theory in an ideal of *partial* benevolence, of caring *more* for some people than for others. We find at least the potential for such a view in St. Augustine's *Ten Homilies* and in his *De Moribus Ecclesiae Catholicae* (15.25), where it is said that all virtue is based in love for God (though, as I mentioned earlier, Augustine sometimes appears to import non-agent-based elements into his arguments). But it is also possible to develop a purely secular agent-based view that puts a premium on caring for or benevolence toward some people more than others, and it is this possibility that I want to consider in what follows.

In her ground-breaking *In a Different Voice*, Carol Gilligan argued that men tend to conceive morality in terms of rights, justice, and autonomy, whereas women more frequently think of the moral in terms of caring, responsibility, and interrelation with others.[19] And at about the same time Gilligan's book appeared, Nel Noddings sought to articulate and defend in its own right a "feminine" mo-

---

morally best of motives, but evaluates actions in terms of how well they further they goals of such benevolence. This view lies midway between morality as universal benevolence and utilitarianism, morally assessing motives in the manner of the former, but actions in the manner of the latter, i.e., consequentialistically. As a result, it is open to the usual objections that are made of hybrid moral views (like rule-utilitarianism).

19. Carol Gilligan, *In a Different Voice: Psychological Theory and Women's Development* (Cambridge, Mass.: Harvard University Press, 1982). Although Gilligan's methodology and findings have been called into question, it is still important to consider the ethical issues of "justice" vs. "caring" that her book brings to our attention.

rality centered specifically around the idea of caring.[20] Since caring is a motivational attitude, the whole idea of a morality of caring suggests the primacy of motivation within any such view and thus seems to move us in the direction of agent-basing. But in fact Noddings's specific articulation and defense of caring involve a mixture of agent-based and other considerations, and we need to disentangle some of these before we can be in a position to show that the ethic of caring is *most plausibly defended in agent-based terms.*

In her book, *Caring: A Feminine Approach to Ethics and Moral Education,* Noddings seems to want to relate everything in morality to caring about particular individuals, rather than bringing in independent principles of justice or truth-telling or what-have-you, and this is characteristic of agent-basing. However, in addition to emphasizing the moral goodness (and obligatoriness) of acting from care (toward people we know or are involved with), she also says that we should try to *promote* caring in the world, and this seems to bring a consequentialistic and indeed perfectionistic element into her treatment of morality. But Noddings never says that the promotion of caring is an independent or fundamental moral value, and if it is not, then there is in fact a way of *deriving* it from an agent-based partialistic ethic of caring.

Consider the reasons one might have for trying to get (certain) people to care more about (certain other) people. Couldn't one's reason be that by getting them to care more, one could eventually bring about more good for humanity generally or for the people one cares about? If one really wants to help (certain) people, working to get them to care for one another's welfare might have a multiplier effect, allowing one at least indirectly to help more people overall than if one always simply promoted welfare directly. A caring person might thus see the promotion of caring as the best way to promote what she as a caring person is concerned about, and in that measure, the concern for and promotion of virtuous caring on the part of others would be an instance of caring itself conceived as a fundamental form of moral excellence and would thus be accommodable within an agent-based theory of the moral value of caring.

20. Nel Noddings, *Caring: A Feminine Approach to Ethics and Moral Education* (Berkeley: University of California Press, 1984).

Perfectionism and good results as such would not have to come into the matter.

In another area, however, Noddings does veer sharply from agent-basing. She claims (and many others have agreed with her) that caring for particular individuals (more than others) is obligatory and virtuous because it is *constitutively necessary to important human goods* that are realizable only in close relationships. (This is different from saying that caring is admirable because of its good *consequences*.) Such an explanation takes us definitely away from agent-basing, but I wonder how cogent it is. If parental love, say, is obligatory and virtuous *because* it is essential to the good(s) of family life, why isn't a child just as obligated to take love or other things from her parents and accounted morally virtuous or admirable for doing so? The difference here seems to depend on a *fundamental difference in admirability* between caring for and being cared for, and that sits well with an agent-based morality that deems caring to be morally virtuous as such and apart form its constitutive role in certain goods.

Similarly, the devotion of a tutor to a retarded child can be very admirable, even if it might be *better* if their relationship were not needed. The moral admirability or virtuousness of such caring seems not to be grounded in the desirability of a relationship, but to stand in need of no further justification; and so, once again, it would seem that a virtue-ethical morality of caring is best conceived and formulated in specifically agent-based terms.[21] The caring individual needs to be responsive to the particularities, nuances, and complexities of a larger interpersonal and social context, but that doesn't have to mean that values attaching to that context determine the moral value or admirability of caring. The context may rather set (some of) the tasks that an independently valuable attitude of caring will want to take up and accomplish.

---

21. Noddings (*Caring*, pp. 68ff.) makes the moral value of caring depend in part on whether the person cared for receives the benefit of knowing he or she is cared for, and this too takes us away from agent basing. But critics have questioned her assumption here, because it seems invidious to make the moral value of caring depend on accidental or uncontrollable circumstances. (See, e.g., Debra Shogan, *Care and Moral Motivation* [Toronto: OISE Press, 1988], p. 57.) I propose we drop the assumption from any account of the ethic of caring.

Still, a systematic agent-based account of morality that puts a moral premium on caring for specific or special individuals needs to say more than Noddings herself says about self-concern and about appropriate attitudes and actions toward strangers and people we don't know. No reasonable ethics should decry or begrudge self-concern and self-assertiveness in moral agents, and as feminists and others have recently noted, it would be ironic and morally counter-productive for any new ethics to focus exclusively on aspects of feminine moral thought and activity that have typically restricted and been used to restrict the freedom and self-fulfillment of women. An ethic of care or concern exclusively or even primarily for favored *others* seems, then, to be morally retrograde, but there is no reason why a feminine or feminist ethic of caring shouldn't allow and even advocate self-concern (and self-assertiveness).

There is also the problem of appropriate concern for and treat-ment of strangers and people we don't know. But a partialistic mo-rality that advocates greater concern for near and dear can still deplore *indifference* to others;[22] and if the moral floor of nonindif-ference, of humane caring, is not set too low, an agent-based mo-rality as caring will, I believe, be able to treat the usual questions of justice and human rights in a plausible, but highly distinctive way. A great deal more needs to be said about the structure or character of such a philosophically defensible morality of caring, but for the moment, at least, warm agent-based virtue ethics has two funda-mentally different options it has to consider: one, an impartialistic morality of universal benevolence, the other, a partialistic ethic of caring.

As agent-based, both approaches evaluate actions in relation to (the agent's) motivation, but at this point a further distinction needs to be made regarding the kind of (warm) motivation agent-based views can base their accounts of right action on. Martineau, for example, evaluates actions in relation to the agent's situationally specific occurrent motives. If compassion welling up within one leads one to help another person at some cost to one's own comfort or pleasure, then one's action is right because it resulted from the

22. Cf. Virginia Held's *Feminist Morality* (Chicago: University of Chicago Press, 1993), p. 223; and my "Agent-Based Virtue Ethics," *Midwest Studies in Philosophy* 20, 1995, pp. 97, 101.

morally better of the two particular motives that operated on that occasion. But Martineau's view only works under rather simplifying and seemingly unrealistic assumptions about the moral life—in particular, that morality always involves a choice between only two specific or particular motives. And, apart from Martineau's idiosyncratic view, it also seems implausible to hold that one invariably acts rightly if one is influenced to act by some motive that counts (in general) as a good one. Someone who cares about the well-being of one particular person and acts for that person's benefit acts, in some individualistic or narrow sense, from a good motive. But if such action involves neglecting the well-being of other people he knows or doesn't know, then it may demonstrate an overall bad character and may count as wrongdoing. So any agent-based virtue ethic that evaluates actions in relation to particular or single occurrent good motives is open to the objection that good motives (toward some) are insufficient to insure that one is acting morally (on the whole).[23]

However, such an objection precisely cannot be made of an agent-based theory that judges actions in relation to *an agent's total or overall motivation*, and I believe such a more holistic approach represents the best way to develop agent-basing. Thus, someone who neglects the vital interests of many people in order to help a friend or relation in some trivial way can be said to act wrongly because, even if she has a particular good motive, her action reflects overall motivation that we would deplore (we would say that she has too much concern for near and dear and/or too little for human beings generally). And by the same token, if an action reflects good enough overall motivation, then an agent-based virtue ethics will want to insist that it *is* morally acceptable.[24]

23. For an example of this objection, see Marcia Baron, ''Kantian Ethics'' in M. Baron et al., *Three Methods of Ethics: A Debate* (Oxford: Blackwell, 1997), p. 61.

24. It is worth pointing out here that someone's overall or total motivation isn't to be thought of simply as the sum of his particular or occurrent motives (during some period of time). An individual who always does nice things for his family, but who on one occasion kills a stranger to whom he has taken a strong dislike, may almost always act on good situation-specific occurrent motives. But that doesn't mean that his overall motivation is morally good or acceptable. Overall motivation (as conceived here) is a matter of someone's general disposition, and a person disposed to kill (some) people he takes a dislike to lacks a real humanitarian concern for people, however much or often he seeks to help people he likes. Humanitarianism

Of course, this means that if someone with fully benevolent or caring motivation is foiled in her aims and ends up hurting, or failing to help, the people she (properly) is seeking to help, her actions don't count as morally wrong; and can a morality really take so little heed of consequences as to allow such actions to pass uncriticized? But in an important sense agent-based moralities *do* take consequences in account because they insist on or recommend an overall state of motivation that worries about and tries to produce good consequences. Someone genuinely concerned with the well-being of another person wants good consequences for that other (for their own sake and independently of any ulterior motive). It is nonetheless true, though, that agent-based moralities may judge someone in a morally favorable or at least not unfavorable light when her active concern for others or a particular other goes awry, and this may seem too lenient because someone who tries to help people may do so unthinkingly and carelessly, and this, surely, would be a realistic basis for moral criticism.

But as I indicated earlier, someone who has the fullest concern for the well-being of another won't be slapdash or heedless in this way. This is not an empirical claim, but arguably points to a criterion, a constitutive element, of genuine concern; and if someone does make every effort to find out relevant facts and is careful in acting, then I think she cannot be criticized for acting immorally, however badly things turn out. (Contrast Zagzebski, *Virtues of the Mind*, part 2, section 2.) On the other hand, if the bad results are due to her lack of intelligence or other cognitive defects she is incapable of learning about, we can make epistemic criticisms of her performance, but these needn't be thought of as moral. (If one has cognitive defects one is capable of learning about, but one doesn't care enough to find out about them, then, once again, the genuineness of one's benevolence can be called into question.)[25]

---

constitutively involves a (general) disposition or tendency to *resist* giving in to aggressive or destructive impulses toward others (or lack such impulses altogether), and if someone's overall motivation or character fails to include such a tendency, we consider it morally undesirable or bad (though not necessarily the worst we can imagine).

25. This example suggests a way for agent-based ethics to deal with the general topic of negligence. Someone who acts negligently may exhibit a lack of real concern for others at the time he acts. But it is also possible for present negligence solely to reflect an *earlier* lack of concern, and when that happens, agent-basing will criticize an agent for what he did or failed to do earlier (e.g., for failing to make an effort to

Moreover, none of this seems out of keeping with our ordinary thinking about morality. When Kant in the *Groundwork* says that we shouldn't fault the actions of someone whose best efforts are undone or misdirected by step-motherly (sic) nature, he speaks to a deep current in ordinary, intuitive moral thought, and though there are some cases, to be mentioned in later chapters, where the failure to attain good results seem difficult to separate from moral criticism, I think for the moment that the agent-based assumption that the moral acceptability or rightness of action is insured by having good overall or total motivation is not particularly implausible.

Note, however, that as I understand the notion, an agent's overall motivation at a given time may include a tendency to act "out of character" in some circumstances, that is, roughly, a tendency in some circumstances to do things that one wouldn't do in most circumstances. Thus when someone acts out of character, what she does can nonetheless be assessed, in agent-based fashion, in terms of the totality of her motives/dispositions. Now, given what was said above, it may not be odd to suppose that good total character or motivation is a *sufficient* condition of not acting wrongly, but once one recognizes the possibility of "uncharacteristic" actions, one may well wonder whether it is *necessary* to evaluate actions in relation to total motivation. For most of us have some inclination to think that isolated and uncharacteristic good deeds are always possible. But this is not, in fact, so obvious.

We usually admire it if a man devotes a great deal of time and energy to helping an old woman, but if the woman is an Aryan and the man is Hitler or Goebbels, then we will tend not to admire those deeds (again, check this on yourself!), and that seems to be because of what we know about the man's overall character or motivation. By contrast, the case of Sydney Carton in *A Tale of Two Cities* (who does "a far, far better thing" than he has done before) may strike us differently precisely because Dickens leads us to imagine a miraculous last-minute change in his overall character. If what I am saying here is correct, then those acts that are really admirably good

---

change certain harmful habits), rather than for any present action. (Kantian ethics tends to take a rather similar view of negligence.)

By the way, it is worth noting that someone who has "good intentions" but never even tries to help others can be criticized as lacking in (true or real) benevolence, so nothing in the present view contradicts the idea that the road to hell is paved with (among other things) good intentions.

and praiseworthy will be those that show their doers as not only meeting minimal standards of human decency but as going beyond what we normally expect of people. The example of the Good Samaritan has this character because we assume that the Samaritan who helps the Jewish man who fell among thieves and was left for dead by the side of the road shows himself willing to make great efforts and sacrifices not only on behalf of people of his own tribe or ethnicity but on behalf of *any human being*; and such a person presumably does have a good overall character.[26]

On my agent-based approach, therefore, cases like that of the Good Samaritan are the paradigm of a morally praiseworthy and genuinely admirable (as opposed to just permissible) deed, and though we have hardly exhausted the topic, I will at this point proceed under the assumption that agent-based views, whether impartial or partial, wish to evaluate action in relation to the agent's total or overall motivation. And the motivation in question will be warm rather than cool, because that seems to be the only plausible way in which a general humane concern for human beings, a general humanitarianism, can function as an integral and ground-floor element of moral thought and moral value (something that it fails to do, though in differing ways, both in Aristotle's and in Kant's ethics).

But notice this. In making the assumption that a warm or sentimentalist approach is the most plausible form of agent-basing, I am

---

26. If we assume—contrary to the implication of the original parable—that the Samaritan is willing to help a Jew but *not* one of his own people, then his actions, to the extent we feel we can understand them at all, will seem to exemplify a kind of rebellion against or contempt toward his own people, more than positive humaneness, and this will tend to undercut or stymie our admiration for what he is doing. That very fact illustrates the way in which our admiration for particular deeds seeks to relate those deeds to overall character rather than to narrowly conceived promptings or impulses and thus supports the approach taken here. This topic needs further exploration, but let me just mention another consideration that favors holistic assessments of particular actions.

The civility that characterized the antebellum South may not strike us as particularly admirable if we bear in mind how unjust that society was. So, quite possibly, certain (individual or social) traits may not count as virtues if they are not accompanied by certain other (more important) virtues, and connections of dependency between putative virtues move us in the direction of holistic assessment. Such holistic assessment of admirability and virtue doesn't commit one to the unity of the virtues, but it leaves us closer to that idea than if we held that uncharacteristic acts can be assessed in isolation. For more on some of these issues, see my *Goods and Virtues* (Oxford: Clarendon Press, 1983, rprt. 1990), ch. 3.

ruling out or putting aside not only cool agent-basing, but mixed or pluralistic views that treat (various forms of) concern for (other) sentient beings as only one ground-floor element in a total theory of morality. Certain sorts of motivation and/or inner traits not directly or exclusively concerned with human or sentient well-being may be regarded as fundamentally admirable—for example, curiosity, humility generally (or in the face of nature's power and beauty), (intellectual) honesty, frankness, and sheer intelligence— and an agent-based approach might try to base all of morality in fundamental assumptions about the moral goodness or badness (and comparative importance) of a range of traits or motives not exclusively focused on sentient well-being. This is, in fact, what James Martineau was trying to do, but that historical example and the implausibility of other variations on this idea that I have also considered have discouraged me from pushing agent-based virtue ethics in this direction. (There is also the problem that many admirable traits that don't seem directly concerned with sentient well-being are not easily or self-evidently seen as *morally* admirable). So in what follows, I shall pursue the kind of agent-based approach to virtue ethics I *do* find promising—and we shall therefore confine our attention to developing warm or sentimentalist views of morality that focus on (concern for) human or sentient well-being.

However, there are some important questions we haven't yet addressed. We haven't said anything about the role of conscientiousness within warm agent-basing or about whether the moral principles advocated by agent-based theories are appropriately action-guiding. Neither have we considered whether warm agent-based approaches can serve usefully in the solution of practical moral difficulties. These topics raise some deep issues for and about agent-based/ sentimentalist ethical views and will require the whole of the next chapter.

MORALITY AND THE PRACTICAL

1. Is Agent-Basing Practical?

A warm agent-based virtue ethics that puts a fundamental emphasis on a person's motives and, more particularly, on a person's overall morally relevant motivation will say, for example, that an act is morally acceptable if and only if it comes from good or virtuous motivation involving benevolence or caring (about the well-being of others) or at least doesn't come from bad or inferior motivation involving malice or indifference to humanity. The emphasis on motivation will then be fundamental if the theory claims that certain forms of overall motivation are, intuitively, morally good and approvable in themselves and apart from their consequences or the possibility of grounding them in certain rules or principles. Every ethical theory has to start somewhere, and an agent-based morality will want to say that the moral goodness of (universal) benevolence or of caring about people is intuitively obvious and in need of no further moral grounding.

However, such agent-based views face a difficulty that must now be mentioned. If someone encounters a perplexing moral problem, it somehow seems irrelevant and even objectionable for her to examine *her own motives rather than facts about people and the world* in order to solve it. Yet is not this what agent-basing allows for and even prescribes? For example, does not morality as (universal or partialistic) benevolence tell us that whether it is morally good, right, or acceptable, say, to oppose the taking of heroic measures to keep an aged dying parent alive depends on the motives of the person in question, and is this at all helpful for someone who *does not know* whether to advocate or oppose heroic measures for a dying or suffering parent? Looking inward at or for motives presumably will not help to solve that person's problem, and so, where we most need moral guidance, it would seem that agent-basing not only is irrelevant but makes it impossible to find a solution to one's moral difficulties. (Similar criticism can also be made of agent-prior views more generally).

Some defenders of virtue ethics are willing to grant that virtue ethics—whether agent-based or otherwise—cannot be applied to practical moral issues, but would claim none the less that virtue ethics can give us the correct theory or view of morality.[1] However, it would make things easier for virtue ethics if we could show that (agent-based) virtue ethics *can* be applied, and I believe we can accomplish this by making further use of what was said earlier about the way that an internal state like benevolence focuses on, and concerns itself with gathering facts about, the world. If one morally judges a certain course of action or decision by reference to, say, the benevolence of the motives of its agent, one is judging in relation to an inner factor that itself makes reference to and takes account of facts about people in the world. One's inward gaze effectively "doubles back" on the world and allows one, as we shall see in more detail in a moment, to take facts about the world into account in one's attempt to determine what is morally acceptable or best to do. But neither, on the other hand, is this doubling-back unnecessarily duplicative or wasteful of moral effort, if we assume that motive is fundamentally at least relevant to the *moral* character of any action. For if we judge the actions of ourselves or others simply by their effects in the world, we end up unable to distinguish accidentally or ironically useful actions (or slips on banana peels) from actions that we actually morally admire and that are morally good and praiseworthy.

Consider, then, someone who hears that her aged mother has suddenly been taken to the hospital and who flies from a distant city

---

1. See, e.g., Edmund Pincoffs, *Quandaries and Virtues* (Lawrence, Kansas: University of Kansas Press, 1986).

to be with her. Given morality as benevolence in some form or other and assuming she is her mother's sole living relative, how should she resolve the issue of what morally she ought to do with or for her parent when she gets to the hospital? Should she or should she not, for example, advocate heroic measures to save her mother? Surely, morality as (one or another form of) benevolence doesn't give her an answer to this question, but what is worth noting is that, given the woman's ignorance, as we are assuming, of her mother's particular condition and prospects, there is no reason for most moral theories to offer an answer to that question at this point. But morality as benevolence *does* offer her an answer to the question what morally she should do when she gets to the hospital. It tells her she morally ought (or would be wrong not) to find out more about her mother's condition and prospects, as regards quality and duration of life and certainly as regards future suffering and incapacity. And it can tell her this by reference to her actual motives, because if she does not find out more and decides what to do or to advocate about her mother solely on the basis of present relative ignorance, she will demonstrate a callousness (toward her mother) that is very far from benevolent. To decide to pull the plug or to allow heroic measures without finding out more about her mother would demonstrate indifference or callousness toward her, and on that basis, morality as benevolence can make the moral judgment that she ought to find out more before making any decision. (Morality as inner strength could be shown to yield a similar conclusion.)

Then, once the facts have emerged and assuming they are fairly clear-cut and point to horrendously painful and debilitating prospects for her mother, the woman's decision is once again plausibly derivable from morality as benevolence. At that point, it would be callous of her to insist on heroic measures and benevolent or kind not to do so and the proper moral decision can thus be reached by agent-based considerations.

But surely, someone might say, the woman herself does not think in such terms. She is worried about whether her mother would have a painful or pleasant future existence, for example, not about whether she herself would be acting callously if she sought to prolong the mother's existence. Are you sure? Could she not morally justify her decision not to allow heroic measures *either* by reference simply to likely future sufferings if the mother were kept alive or by saying: it would be (have been) callous of me to try to keep her alive, given her prospects. Surely there is nothing unusual or inappropriate about the latter as an expression of moral problem-solving.

But in fact, a problem arises at this point because, even if morality as benevolence can be used to answer practical moral questions, there is no reason why someone whose motives are ideal from the standpoint of such a theory *has to think in specifically moral terms*. If someone is universally benevolent, they will act to promote universal good, looking for ways in which people, or sentient beings, can be made happier on the whole. But that doesn't necessarily require them to believe a moral theory like utilitarianism or some form of morality as benevolence. Nor need they ask themselves what they ought to do or what is right for them to do. They may simply ask themselves what will help people the most, and if they do merely that, they may still count as admirably benevolent in the highest degree.

But if benevolence means caring (intrinsically) about the welfare of others and doesn't require the benevolent person to be addressing specifically moral questions using specifically moral theories or principles (this is part of what Hume meant when he characterized benevolence as a "natural" motive),[2] then one may ask why a benevolent person ever *would* consult a moral theory or principle or worry about the moral goodness or rightness of his or her own actions or motives—rather than simply try to help others. A benevolent person may have become convinced (by others?) that utilitarianism or some agent-based morality of benevolence is the correct theory of right and wrong, but there seems to be absolutely no reason why such a person should be distracted by considerations of morality from the desire and effort to help others.[3]

In that case a philosopher or anyone else who believes in some agent-based morality of benevolence or caring may be *able* to use that theory to solve a practical moral problem, that is, say (what the agent-based view would say about) what is right or wrong to do in

2. See *Treatise* book 3, part 3, section 1. In what follows, I shall not *rely* on the distinction between natural and other motives, but I believe it would be possible to make sense of it.

3. Compare Stephen Darwall, *The British Moralists and the Internal 'Ought': 1640–1740* (Cambridge: Cambridge University Press, 1995), esp. chs. 8 and 9. The present chapter owes a considerable debt to Darwall's trenchant discussion of Francis Hutcheson and of British moral sentimentalism more generally.

a certain situation. But a deeply benevolent adherent of such a view would still have no reason to consider such an explicitly moral issue, and the same holds true for adherents of utilitarianism as well. If they are sufficiently benevolent, they won't be interested in whether what they are doing counts as obligatory or wrong. So in the end, both utilitarianism and agent-based views *can* be applied, but there may well be no reason for a suitably benevolent person to (want to) do so.

Of course, act-utilitarianism treats it as entirely contingent whether it is morally good to be benevolent, and thus it allows the possibility that we should be worried about issues of right and wrong *rather than* purely benevolent. But if morality as (one or another form of) benevolence is correct and benevolence is always and non-contingently the morally best of motives, then the *real problems of the moral life* don't involve determining and acting on what is right, but determining as best one can what has good results for people and acting accordingly. On such a view, the most moral thinking doesn't involve thinking about morality, and the morally good person isn't guided by a theory or (agent-based) moral principle or even a sense of rightness as much as by a good heart that seeks to do good for and by people.

So the life, the moral life, of the ideally benevolent good person will contain practical concerns, but those concerns will directly engage with issues of human or sentient well-being rather than with questions of moral right and wrong (or obligation). And that means that for an agent-based account of morality a split—amounting to what Michael Stocker has called a schizophrenia—will exist for ideally benevolent good people. Facts or assumptions about what makes their motives and actions morally good or right will not figure within (the intentionality of) those motives, or be what is ultimately important from the standpoint of those motives, since the motives and actions of such people will aim at something outside themselves and lack any intrinsic concern for their own nature.

Now certainly this goes against one very strong vision of the moral life, the Kantian, according to which the morally good person guides herself, or is guided, by moral ideals or rules and this is an essential and desirable feature of morality. Virtue ethicists have questioned whether moral virtue always requires such moral action-guidance and have argued further that it is sometimes morally better to be guided by feeling than to be guided by morality or conscience.[4] But the idea that an ideal moral individual might have *no* interest in moral questions goes beyond these previous assumptions and seems to *court* the accusation of schizophrenia. However, I believe that a split between moral theory/principles and what moral people think about is not as inappropriate or implausible as some have thought, and I would like briefly to discuss two examples from the previous history of virtue ethics in order to explain why.

Bernard Williams's famous example of the man who, faced with a choice between saving his drowning wife and saving a drowning stranger, decides that he is morally permitted (or obligated) to save his wife was intended to show that it is sometimes better to act from feeling than to act from a moral principle (such a husband has "one thought too many"). In addition, however, Williams is so convinced that moral principles are action-guiding and (in that sense) practical, that he concludes from his example that the situation he has described is beyond or outside of morality, and that means that it is *not* morally permissible or obligatory for the husband to save his wife.[5]

But do we really need to take his example to this extreme? Wouldn't it be more plausible to say that the man *is* morally permitted or obligated to save/prefer his wife, but that there is no reason why he should have to think about or be guided by morality or moral

---

4. However, the issue here is complicated, because of a distinction some recent Kantians have drawn between "primary" and "secondary" motives. According to Marcia Baron (in *Kantian Ethics Almost Without Apology* [Ithaca, N.Y.: Cornell University Press 1995], ch. 4) and speaking very roughly, duty is a primary motive if one acts with and because of the occurrent thought that a certain act is one's duty; it is a secondary motive if one has the general desire to do one's duty and that desire exerts a kind of background influence in any situation in which one has to decide how to act. Baron holds that an action motivated primarily by benevolence or affection and only secondarily by duty can have moral worth, but this clearly then does permit a kind of split between good motives and moral principles, allows someone to act morally well at a given time without at that time considering the moral quality of her actions. Moreover, I don't know of any Kantian who thinks a primary motive of conscientiousness can ever detract from the moral excellence or goodness of an action (though Baron, *Kantian Ethics*, p. 123, comes fairly close), but that is precisely the view I wish to defend here.

5. See Bernard Williams, "Persons, Character, and Morality," in *Moral Luck* (Cambridge: Cambridge University Press, 1981), pp. 17f.

thinking in that kind of emergency? Something like this seems true, for example, about self-defense. In commonsense terms, it is plausible to suppose that people are morally permitted to kill in self-defense (when killing is the only way they can defend themselves), but no one thinks that a person confronted with a man with a meat cleaver should take time to consider whether she is permitted to kill her assailant. What the right of self-defense and the idea of justifiable homicide seem to entail, rather, is a permission to defend oneself without having to think about morality, and given the moral character of these very ideas, it follows that there are moral issues and moral permissions that an agent doesn't have to and really has no reason to think about. The moral permission/right to kill in self-defense is not a practical, acting-guiding permission/right, but rather a standard by which morally non-self-conscious action can be judged morally acceptable. And so in this one area of ordinary morality we have an explicitly moral standard that is not primarily an action-guide, not primarily practical.[6]

A similar point can be made about a man's permission to favor his drowning spouse. It seems plausible to suppose that that permission applies precisely to someone who doesn't and isn't likely to think about whether he is permitted to save his wife. What

---

6. Notice that if the moral *permission* to kill in self-defense is not primarily addressed to moral agents, then the (principle stating that there is an) *obligation* not to kill except in self-defense (or for certain other specified reasons) has at least one non-action-guiding qualification built into it and is thus itself not strictly or univocally action-guiding, or practical. Note too, however, that even the permission to kill in self-defense can indirectly guide action by telling us, for example, that (in certain circumstances) it might be all right and even advisable to purchase a gun. But in philosophical parlance to say that a principle is action-guiding is to say that it guides one to do things that *it itself mentions*, so the fact that the permission to kill in self-defense can lead some to *purchase a gun* doesn't in itself render that permission practical in the primary sense of the term.

However, the principle that it is permissible to kill in self-defense can also be addressed to a pacifist who has to decide whether to defend himself, and in this usage it does function in a primary practical fashion. Still, in most cases the principle is invoked to justify behavior or actions that it is assumed aren't (haven't been, won't be) guided by that very principle. And since most people aren't pacifists, the raison d'etre for the permission to kill in self-defense has standardly been a concern to deal fairly with cases where a person kills in response to a perceived threat and without considering the moral status of her action. For more on this topic, see my *Commonsense Morality and Consequentialism* (London: Routledge, 1985), ch. 4.

he or anyone else in his circumstances is permitted to do is *not* think about whether he is morally permitted to save his wife and *not* hesitate to save his wife.[7] So this example of Williams's and the moral permission of self-defense show us two moral principles/ standards that *make sense only if in fact there is some sort of split between valid moral principles and what guides action*. In these cases at least, the schizophrenia Stocker invokes seems harmless and, in fact, essential to making sense of our moral understanding of things.

Interestingly enough, Stocker's own famous example of the man who conscientiously visits his hospitalized friend also tends to undermine the force of the accusation of schizophrenia.[8] Stocker holds that there is automatically something wrong with a split between one's (supposedly justified) moral principles and what motivates one's actions, but his example of the man who visits his friend from a sense of duty rather than out of friendly feeling actually favors accepting such a split. Stocker says that it is morally better or more virtuous to act from feeling than to act from a sense of duty (when visiting a sick friend), but what about this very claim? The claim is a fairly general one and itself amounts to a moral principle or standard, yet for the very reasons Stocker has mentioned, it would be inappropriate and undesirable for the claim to function as a practical action-guide. The person who acts from a sense that it is morally better to act from feeling than to act conscientiously *fails to act from feeling and is for that very reason criticizable in Stocker's own terms*. And so a split between valid morality and what guides or motivates us is absolutely presupposed by and is needed to support and make sense of Stocker's claim that it is better to act from feeling than from duty.

Thus Stocker himself mentions a moral principle or standard that both seems plausible and yet is inappropriate for the guiding of action, and his own arguments therefore tend to support the

7. I think Kant too can hold that this is permissible, but Kant would still presumably disagree with Williams's claim that there is something wrong with the person who thinks about his moral permissions in this sort of circumstance. It is facts of this latter sort (if facts they are) that I believe lead us toward positively *advocating* or *recommending* a split between moral principles and what guides action.

8. See Michael Stocker, "The Schizophrenia of Modern Ethical Theories," *Journal of Philosophy* 73, 1986, pp. 453–66.

idea that some parts of morality are not practical, but rather constitute standards by which actions are judged from the outside or after the fact. Far from being something automatically to be feared, schizophrenia is endemic to and helps to make sense of some very important parts of morality. And in that case one may wonder why the split between morality and action-guidance couldn't or shouldn't be conceived in more general terms. If there is nothing per se wrong with schizophrenia, is there any obvious reason to cavil at the idea of a morally good person *never* acting from a sense of duty?

Of course, utilitarianism too allows for this possibility, since it judges moral goodness and rightness by results and people might do more good acting from immediate concern for others than they would do by acting conscientiously. And Stocker certainly takes utilitarianism to task for allowing the contingent possibility of such a split. However, the split I have argued for is not merely contingent. An agent-based morality of benevolence will want to say that concern for the well-being of others is the best of motives quite apart from its results, and its idea that there is no reason for the morally good person to be concerned about specifically moral issues is for that reason not based on contingent assumptions about what attitudes cause or are likely to cause what consequences. In effect, a morality of benevolence sees both attention to moral principles/theories and intrinsic conscientious concern for the moral character of one's actions as by their very nature *getting in the way of one's concern for others* (and, indeed, in the way of personal relations more generally). To that extent, someone who is worried about the moral character of his or her actions will count as less *directly* involved with others and less (purely) benevolent than someone who is simply occupied or absorbed in helping those others.

So the split between moral principles/theories and morally ideal motivation is inevitable for an agent-based morality of (one or another form of) benevolence in a way it is not for utilitarianism. And the above discussion should in any event indicate that utilitarianism cannot simply be dismissed on account of its potential schizophrenia any more than agent-based views can be. Much of morality requires such a split and the ideal of someone who is so absorbed in helping others that s/he doesn't think about whether what s/he is doing is right or wrong is attractive enough, I believe, to call the Kantian model of morality into question—perhaps even attractive enough to persuade us that a split between motivation and theory is desirable.[9]

But what about people who are less than ideal, people who are selfish or greedy or insouciant of others' welfare? How are they to move toward the moral ideal, become better people, if they are not reminded of the wrongness of (too much) selfishness, etc.; and doesn't this tend to reinstate the Kantian model or ideal of the moral life in which thought about right and wrong, and conscientiousness, have a central and desirable role to play? I think not.

I would never want to claim that thinking about right and wrong and that conscientiousness can never play a causal role in getting people to become better people (in agent-based terms), and later in this chapter, I want to describe ways in which conscientiousness is compatible with being morally good (understood, once again, in agent-based terms). But the assumption that conscientious thought about right and wrong (and obligation) is essential to improving people's motives (making them morally better) seems mistaken. If someone is, say, greedy, one can hope to make them less so, not necessarily by reminding them of the badness of greed or the wrongness of certain things they have done, but by making them more aware of the effects of (their) greed on other people. If we assume that human beings have a basic capacity for empathy and sympathy with others (an assumption the moral sentimentalists tended to make and one which I shall be discussing and citing supporting literature for later on, in Chapter 4), then making someone vividly aware of the effects of certain kinds of actions (or attitudes) on people's welfare can change the way that person *feels* about those actions (or attitudes) and make a difference, for good, to her act-effecting motives. So I don't think explicit moralizing is necessarily the best or

9. In speaking here of an ideal of someone absorbed in helping others, I am not thinking of people who are interested in helping only certain other individuals (like their friends and family), but rather of someone whose overall pattern of motivation involves an admirable level of concern for other people generally. Whether that morally ideal pattern should involve equal concern for all human beings (as with morality as universal benevolence) or whether it should involve partiality toward near and dear combined with a substantial level of humanitarian concern for everyone else (as with a plausible version of the ethic of caring), I am for the moment leaving open, but whatever that ideal overall pattern is, it will *insure right action without the agent's having to think about specifically moral issues* (cf. the discussion of Chapter 1).

most effective way to make people better in agent-based (or, for that matter, consequentialist) terms; and there is no reason to doubt the existence of a nonmoralistic, nonconscientious path to moral improvement that fits in well with the sentimentalist agent-based claim that morally ideal individuals are not preoccupied with right and wrong, etc. (I am indebted here to discussion with Sam Kerstein).

But let me say a bit more at this point about why a split between motivation and theory may be held to be desirable. Consider what recent defenders of a "feminine" ethic of caring have said about the difference between male and female moral thinking (we don't have to believe the distinction in question really correlates with gender in order to grant it philosophical significance). Men, it is said, think in terms of rights, justice, and autonomy, women in terms of caring, responsibility for others, and connection with others. Clearly, a focus on caring in and of itself stresses our connection with other people, and defenders of an ethic of caring argue that some of our relationships exist and have moral importance for us independently of our own choice. By contrast, so-called masculine thinking about morality effectively emphasizes a kind of disconnection or separateness from others. For example, contract theory tends to conceive the individual as starting off with certain rights against (interference by) others and as autonomously bringing about moral connection with (and obligation to) others through his or her own choice. Similarly, in Kantian ethics, moral obligations to others are secondary to and derivative from our self-legislating autonomy as individuals.

Now the idea of opposition between moral views emphasizing separateness and moral views emphasizing connection was mentioned in the first edition of Gilligan's *In a Different Voice*; but it has assumed (even) greater importance as a theme in the most recent edition of the book.[10] The idea of such opposition can in any event, I think, help us better understand the choices implicit in recent and traditional moral philosophy. I also believe that the dichotomy between separateness and connection can serve to explain why a morality based in benevolence or caring should favor a distinction between the concepts mentioned in moral theories or principles and the concepts that move an ideal moral agent. If an ethic of caring

10. See Carol Gilligan, *In a Different Voice: Psychological Theory and Women's Development* (Cambridge, Mass.: Harvard University Press, 1993), p. xxvi.

or benevolence is going to criticize the supposedly masculine moral emphasis on rights and autonomy for the separateness they presuppose in or impose on our morality, then an ethic of caring or benevolence also has reason to question the stress on action-guiding principles and on conscientiousness that one also typically finds in masculine moral philosophies. For, as I suggested earlier and as defenders of caring have also pointed out, to the extent we make use of moral rules or claims to guide our actions toward others or have an intrinsic conscientious concern with the moral character of our actions, our connection with other people is less immediate, less personal, than it is if we simply concern ourselves with their welfare.[11]

Thus an ethic that thinks morality should be based in connection rather than separateness has every reason to question whether life should be led according to rules or principles and to question whether the morally good person needs to draw explicitly moral conclusions or make explicit moral claims or be conscientious in order to act well. If obligations based on caring treat us as connected with others and if it is desirable to think of morality in that fashion, then the general principle we have thereby justified, the principle, roughly, that it is wrong to act from indifference and right to act from caring or benevolence, will not be one we want people to act from. For if they do, they will be less connected with others than if they are directly concerned with other people's welfare. So for someone who thinks the moral life should be understood in terms of the value of connection, there are reasons of consistency, or at

11. In *Caring: A Feminine Approach to Ethics and Moral Education* (pp. 5, 13, and 25f.), Nel Noddings makes the point about principles getting in the way of personal connection. And Francis Hutcheson (in *An Inquiry into the Original of Our Ideas of Beauty and Virtue*, 4th ed., 1738) is critical of concern for the moral character of one's own actions, claiming that such concern is selfish rather than morally good. (See Darwall's discussion, *British Moralists*, p. 232, where it is also pointed out that what Hutcheson is saying here "turns on its head" the Kantian view that material motives like benevolence are invariably instances of self-love and that only formally conscientious conduct can be morally good.) Stocker ("Schizophrenia") also claims that the use of principles interferes in an unfortunate way with personal connection. But if he thinks that, then Stocker should either reject all moral principles or *accept* a split between justified principles and agential motives. In any event, it should be clear that the view being defended here has in various ways been anticipated by others.

least congruence, to espouse a morality of caring or benevolence while at the same time holding that such a morality and its principles will ideally not guide the behavior of fully moral individuals (nor have to guide individuals who are becoming more moral). The split between theory/principles and the motives of ideally good actions thus derives from the same emphasis on connection that leads one to prefer an ethic of caring or benevolence to masculine views that value ideals like autonomy and the rights of the individual against others and that thereby see morality as based in separateness.

If what I am saying is correct, then the Kantian and contractarian moralities are also internally consistent: emphasizing separateness both in their views about how our obligations arise and in their views about the action-guiding role of those obligations. And the idea that these two aspects of separateness (and the two opposing aspects of connection) go together is also evidenced by the history of act utilitarianism. Act utilitarianism is the one major modern moral theory that doesn't insist upon obedience to rules/principles and conscientiousness, and it also treats our obligations to others as not voluntarily contracted or due to our autonomy, but rather as due to our sometimes involuntary or unchosen causal connections, to the fact that we often (simply) find ourselves in a position to affect the well-being of (ourselves and) other people.

The example of utilitarianism (along with that of moral sentimentalism) shows that some previous male thinking emphasizes connection more than separateness, but the example also corroborates the idea that there is a strong correlation between emphasis on separateness as a basis for obligation and emphasis on conscientiousness and rule following. So if an agent-based ethic of benevolence or caring emphasizes and values connection (unlike morality as strength, which clearly stresses separateness), then there are reasons why it should question or downplay the importance of conscientiousness.[12] And if some moral philosophers are suspicious of an ethic of benevolence or caring because it doesn't have an important or honored place for conscientiousness, that may reflect their own *general* preference for separateness as a basis for moral philosophy.

---

12. I am indebted to Nancy Matchett for discussion of some of these ideas.

2. The Value of Conscientiousness

However, even if the morally best person according to an agent-based morality of benevolence or caring is someone who isn't conscientious but rather is involved in helping others, such a morality needs to be able to say something about those who *are* conscientious. Conscientious concern to do what is right or to do one's duty is, after all, a motive, and a morality of motives needs to say something about how that motive is to be assessed. If it is not the morally best of motives because the morally best person wouldn't be concerned with duty as such, what should we think about those who do have that motive and act in accordance with it?

In general, an agent-based morality of benevolence or caring will say that patterns of motivation are good to the extent they resemble or come close to (a certain overall pattern of) benevolence or caring, but it is difficult, for example, to say how close conscientiousness comes to benevolence precisely because it isn't specifically concerned with human well-being in the way benevolence is. Total malice involves an attitude toward human well-being that seems the very opposite of benevolence, and if benevolence is regarded as the best of motives, then malice will perhaps be considered the worst; and certainly indifference to others, another attitude toward human well-being, is closer to benevolence than malice is. Similarly, if we think of a particular form of benevolence, universal benevolence, as best, then a benevolence that takes in most people as objects of its concern is better than one that is indifferent to the well-being of all but a few people, and so on and so forth. But conscientiousness or dutifulness doesn't as such appear to be an attitude toward people's well-being, and for that reason, it is difficult to fit it into a scheme that compares motives, like malice, indifference, and benevolence, in terms of the different attitudes they take toward such well-being.

However, even apart from agent-based and utilitarian moralities, duty for duty's sake is sometimes problematic or at least controversial.[13] It is not altogether unintuitive to suppose, for example, that

13. For interesting criticisms of (pure) conscientiousness that bear some resemblance to those offered here, see J. N. Findlay, *Values and Intentions* (London: George Allen and Unwin, 1961), pp. 213f.; and John Rawls, *A Theory of Justice* (Cambridge, Mass.: Harvard University Press, 1971), pp. 477f. On the more general

the conscientiousness of a Nazi prison camp guard who executes Jews and gypsies because he thinks it is his duty to do so lacks some of the moral value of most ordinary conscientiousness because of the way it *goes against* humanitarian concern for others. Still, the prison guard may be benevolent under some aspects or to a certain degree, and his decision to execute certain prisoners might even occur after a struggle with humanitarian feelings or instincts that (as he might think) had tempted him to save those prisoners or at least not harm them himself. Thus such a person may be a mixture of conscientiousness and weaker or stronger benevolence, and it is important that we figure out how to assess such a mixed or mingled state of motives.

However, in order eventually to be able to do so, I think we first have to consider conscientiousness as an ideal type. We need to figure out what to say about someone who always does his duty for its own sake and who *altogether lacks intrinsic desires or motives concerning the well-being of others*. Such an exclusively or purely conscientious person may help people out of a sense of duty, but if he does so, no other motives impel him in that direction: for example, he is not happy to be able to help people rather than (because of duty) have to harm them. (By contrast, our prison camp guard might sometimes be relieved not to have to hurt certain people or to be morally permitted to help them). The person we are describing is thus indifferent to the well-being of other people as such, and anyone moved by the kinds of examples Stocker and Williams have described to us will likely agree that such a person('s motivation) is highly criticizable.[14]

Still, there is a difference between sheer indifference to others and an indifference to others that accompanies or might accompany a conscientious concern with doing one's duty (or acting rightly). As Derek Parfit has reminded us, we nowadays don't think of egoism as a kind of *moral* theory or viewpoint, and by the same token a person doesn't count as conscientious or concerned with doing her duty, if she doesn't (think she sometimes has to) act against her own self-interest. Conscientiousness thus involves the existence of some

themes of the present chapter, compare and contrast Jonathan Bennett's "The Conscience of Huckleberry Finn," *Philosophy* 49, 1974, *passim*.

14. Baron (*Kantian Ethics*, p. 123) also seems to agree with this.

sort of limit on a person's selfishness or self-centeredness, and this certainly also holds for the pure or exclusive conscientiousness of someone who lacks all independent or intrinsic concern for other people's well-being. (By "independent concern" and "intrinsic concern," I mean concern not strictly derivative from one's concern with what one takes to be the dictates of duty.) Such a person lacks the concern for others we think so highly of in someone who is benevolent or really cares about others, but he at least puts something (the moral law if not, except derivatively, the welfare of others) ahead of his own self-interest and to that extent possesses a trait we (also) think well of in the benevolent individual. Ideal benevolence involves (intrinsic) concern for others and limits to (intrinsic) self-concern or self-absorption, and both factors are thought of as having moral value.[15]

So an exclusively dutiful person has something morally good about them in a way that someone who is both self-absorbed and indifferent to others does not. And what I propose at this point (and what seems very much in the spirit of warm agent-basing) is to evaluate the exclusively conscientious individual *on the basis of* her nonderivative motives concerning human well-being. Such a person can be considered morally equivalent, in other words, to someone who is emotionally indifferent to others but who is also not self-absorbed, and there is something morally good about such a person's overall motivation, though on the whole their character and motivation are not good and are indeed morally bad.

Now this doesn't mean that everything done by the exclusively conscientious person is bad or wrong, for not everything done by such a person reflects or expresses their morally bad motivation. Such a person will get out of bed in the morning and that act won't presumably reflect their indifference to or insufficient concern for

---

15. These factors may not be entirely separable from one another: even if a limit to intrinsic self-absorption doesn't involve intrinsic concern for others, the latter may actually entail the former. But it is not important to press this point. Also, the assumption that it is good or better if one puts something ahead of self-concern seems to entail that it is better if someone puts the preservation of mud puddles ahead of his own well-being than if he is simply and totally concerned with his own well-being. This may be controversial, but we do have some inclination to say of such a person: "well, at least there is something that is more important to him than himself," and I want to take this literally.

others, and neither, too, will those conscientious actions they perform which (are intended to) help others. But when a purely conscientious person does harmful things to others from a sense of duty,
their actions presumably *do* reflect an insufficient concern for others,
and since such an overall motivational state is a bad one, those
actions are regarded as wrong from the standpoint of "warm" agent-
based views.[16] The fact of their conscientiousness doesn't redeem
the actions, according to such theories, but that is exactly what we
should want to say if (to revert to our previous example) we believe
that the conscientiousness of a prison camp guard who has some
feeling for humanity but harms Jews and gypsies nonetheless doesn't
redeem what *he* does.

So far we have focused on individuals whose basic motivation is
either totally conscientious *or* totally focused on human well-being,
but that discussion can presumably be of use to us in dealing with
more realistic cases where actions are overdetermined or causally
influenced by both conscientiousness *and* motives like benevolence.
We need, that is, to consider people who (like most of us) combine
some degree of intrinsic concern to do what is morally right with
some degree of intrinsic concern about the well-being of other peo-

---

16. These purely conscientious actions don't reflect the agent's lack of intrinsic
concern for others, because s/he would do the same thing if s/he had such concern
but allowed it to yield to considerations of duty. What the actions in question here
reflect, therefore, is the fact that the person *either* lacks intrinsic concern for others
or lets such concern yield to conscientiousness. But since each disjunct entails that
the individual isn't intrinsically concerned (strongly) enough with the well-being of
others, and thus that their overall motivation is bad, the acts in question count in
agent-based terms as wrong.

Notice too that if a malicious person has to choose among helping, hurting, and
ignoring someone in dire need, a decision to ignore would reflect, not their malice
toward others, but the fact that they have no desire to help people (that they are
indifferent or worse), and since (any overall motivational state that included) this
motivational state is morally bad and undesirable, the decision to ignore is wrong in
agent-based terms. As Hutcheson (*An Inquiry*) was well aware, considerations like
these allow us to assign varying degrees of moral badness or goodness to actions—
everything will depend on how much of the badness or goodness of the person's
overall motivation is expressed or reflected in any given action. When the malicious
person has a chance to torture, her act of torture will express or reflect more badness
than when she has to choose either helping or ignoring and chooses the latter. For
she would do the latter even if she weren't malicious (and were merely indifferent
to others), but this is not true of the act of torture.

ple: people who possess a desire to help people that is not derived from sheer conscientiousness, but also have a concern to act rightly that is not simply ancillary to their desire to help people. From an agent-based standpoint, such more complex motivation will (other things being equal) be superior to that of the exclusively conscientious individual, but inferior to that of the person for whom the concern to help others and that alone is basic. But *how much* superior and *how much* inferior will depend on the relative strength of the independent motives of benevolence (or caring) and conscientiousness and, more particularly, on certain counterfactual questions.

Let us imagine, for example, that in a particular case someone helps another person partly out of benevolent fellow feeling, but partly also because she thinks it is right to do so. Here, the two motives work cooperatively, so to speak, but it might also be true that one of them usually wins out over the other *when they clash*. Take our Nazi camp guard. There might be occasions when his sympathy and benevolence and his sense of duty worked together to bring about some action, but we might still want to say that his conscientiousness was stronger than his humane sentiments if the former always predominated over the latter in situations where the two were at odds—for example, where duty tells him to execute some Jews whom he feels reluctant, on humane or sympathetic grounds, to kill. On the other hand, if we imagine a different Nazi camp guard who for reasons of humane sympathy frees Jews and connives at their escape all the while thinking that he is acting wrongly and feeling guilty for doing so (shades of Huckleberry Finn's feelings about not turning in the slave Jim), we have the opposite case of someone whose humane feeling is or tends to be stronger than his conscientiousness—even if on some occasions, again, the two motives will work together to bring about some action.

But if the latter person's benevolence always wins out over his sense of duty when they clash, can we really assume that he possesses any sort of intrinsic conscientiousness? I think we can, because there may be circumstances where human well-being is not at issue, but where the person feels very strongly that he ought to do what is right. If he has promised a dying friend that he will water her petunias after she dies, then his conscience may tell him to do so, even if he knows that that will make no overall difference to anyone's happiness or well-being; and such a sense of duty seems real enough, even if it always loses out to benevolence when they conflict and is in that sense lexically posterior to it.

Still, the total character of a person with *such* conscientiousness isn't very far from that of the purely benevolent individual. Both always resolve issues concerning human well-being in favor of such well-being, and this similarity should, I think, make us regard the person whose intrinsic conscientiousness is, in causal terms, lexically posterior to her benevolence as pretty much in the same league, morally, as someone who is purely benevolent. If the purely benevolent individual is a moral ideal, then I think an agent-based morality will naturally regard the person just described as at least morally good. Such a morality doesn't evaluate people directly in terms of their conscientiousness, but rather in terms of how strongly they exemplify or fail to exemplify certain motives concerned with human (or sentient) well-being, and someone in whom benevolence wins out not only over contrary motives like selfishness and indifference but also over the sense of duty *shows very strong and pervasive benevolence.*[17] Such a person is, again in agent-based sentimentalist terms, a far cry from someone who is exclusively conscientious or whose conscientiousness usually wins out over benevolence, and the latter individuals count in agent-based terms as having overall a bad or unacceptable character, precisely because of how weakly or nonexistently intrinsic benevolence features in their motivational dispositions.

Of course, if one believes that anyone who acts against conscience (like the prison camp guard who frees Jews or, on some standard interpretations, Huckleberry Finn) cannot really be morally praiseworthy, one will reject the above account of the moral life. But by the same token, if certain examples of counter-conscientious benevolence move one to approval and even admiration, then the larger picture we have drawn will also, I think, make sense. For what I have argued is admirable is not just any form of counter-conscientiousness, but the rejection of duty on the basis of benevolent motives, and this presupposes that a particular person's sense of duty runs counter to benevolence. In such cases, the person's

---

17. The examples we are discussing also raise interesting questions about how one is to understand weakness of will, but I won't pursue such issues here.

moral code is severely defective (from the standpoint of a morality that centers around one or another form of benevolence), and so it seems a morally good thing about them that their humane sentiments work against and make up for such a defective sense of morality.[18]

Having sketched a view of the relationship between conscientiousness and overall moral character, let me now say a bit more about the relation of conscientiousness to the moral evaluation of *actions*. When benevolence and conscientiousness conflict and the agent acts from benevolence, his actions reflect that benevolence because he wouldn't have done what he did (and acted against conscience) if he hadn't been benevolent. So we can say that the Nazi guard who helps Jews and feels guilty about it afterward acts well or praiseworthily, because his actions express or reflect an overall benevolent good character. If he helps even Jews and goes against his own sense of duty in doing so, then it is plausible to think of him as a kind of (morally deluded) Good Samaritan, someone with strong and nonparochial, humanitarian concern for people, and what he does reflects that humanitarianism in a very clear way. On the other hand, the prison camp guard who conscientiously, but reluctantly executes Jews acts in a way that expresses and exhibits his less than powerful benevolence and thus, given what we have been saying, acts wrongly.

However, there are also cases where an act is causally influenced by both conscientiousness and benevolence, and in line with what we have so far been saying, our evaluation of such cases ultimately depends on which (if either) of the influencing motives plays a more important role in bringing about the action. Thus the Nazi prison camp guard who saves Jews may in some other circumstance have an opportunity to be benevolent that accords with his conscience, and when he in that instance acts from both benevolence and duty, I think we can say that his actions reflect his benevolence more than his conscientiousness (and that he is motivated more by benevolence than by conscientiousness), if we believe (on the basis, at least partly, of the example of his treatment of Jews) that he would be

18. The benevolence of the prison camp guard who frees Jews seems diminished by the fact that it hesitates in the face of a contrary conscientiousness, yet somehow also enhanced by the fact that it overcomes such a powerful contrary force. Comparing the moral value of such benevolence with that of the purely benevolent individual who doesn't think about morality may not be an easy task.

much more likely to do what he is doing if he weren't conscientious than if he weren't benevolent. By contrast, when the prison camp guard who reluctantly executes Jews acts in a way that is motivated by both benevolence and conscience, we may be in a position to say his actions reflect, and are motivated by, conscience more than benevolence and, if we are agent-basers, we will attribute less moral merit to his doubly motivated actions than we will want to attribute to the doubly motivated actions of the guard who (on another occasion) counter-conscientiously saves Jews.

3. Moral Conflict

However, there is one final objection to agent-based morality that needs to be discussed at this point. We have just seen how conscientiousness can be evaluated from the standpoint of an agent-based morality of (one or another form of) benevolence. In the process, we have considered cases in which conscientiousness and benevolence clash and seen how the present approach wishes to judge cases involving such disharmony. But we haven't yet focused on the sort of disharmony that involves a conflict between selfishness, or the desire to make an exception of oneself, and morally good desires. It is important for agent-based views to be able to explain how morality and temptation (or selfish impulse) can clash and be successfully resolved within the individual; and one might well ask whether such an explanation is possible on a theory that places so little emphasis on moral principles and conscientiousness. It is all very well and good for someone whose motives and dispositions are all wonderful not to (have to) think about moral rules, but what about a divided self, someone subject to antimoral temptations (impulses)? How can we make sense of the ability to overcome these unless we put a primary or at least a major emphasis on moral rules? For isn't it adherence to moral principles/rules and/or conscientious concern to do what is right that prevent people from doing what is wrong in situations where they are tempted and divided? How else can this happen (when it happens)?[19]

19. Both Stephen Darwall (*British Moralists*, pp. 280f.) and Marcia Baron (*Kantian Ethics*, p. 127) make this kind of objection to sentimentalist approaches of the sort I am advocating here.

If sentimentalist agent-based virtue ethics sees the moral life as primarily or fundamentally a matter of motives that are independent of conscientiousness, it needs to be able to answer this objection. It must offer some sort of plausible explanation of moral conflict and its resolution in terms of such motives or else risk the accusation that it is inadequate to one of the most important aspects of the moral life. And I want to show you now that the agent-based account of the moral life is not impoverished in this way: moral conflict and its more or less successful resolution *can* be understood independently of imputations of conscientiousness (though there is also something to be said about conscientious resolutions of moral conflicts). And to show you how, let me make use of an already familiar example.

While I am visiting my sick mother in the hospital, I may have to do a number of things on her behalf: consult with doctors, find out about second opinions, keep her affairs at home in order, investigate legal issues about her will, etc. All of these can take time and energy and be very wearing, and at a certain point it would be understandable if I, or anyone else, were tempted to skimp on these activities in a way that would allow me to have more free time to see friends or have a really good meal or have one evening, finally, to myself. Where moral activity is strenuous in this way, counter-moral temptations or impulses are very likely to arise, and we must now consider what an agent-based account of morality that, for example, treats benevolence or kindness toward those near and dear to one as part of ideal overall motivation can say about how I or anyone else might resist the temptation to give a mother short shrift.

Certainly, if one *is* tempted, sorely tempted, to give one's mother short shrift, then one counts as less praiseworthily motivated than if one isn't tempted. But even someone who has such an impulse may have inner resources for resisting it, and in the first instance those resources will include *what is good* about the agent's motivation. One afternoon, as one is about to take a long subway ride to the office of a doctor who one may need to engage to give a second opinion about some aspect of one's mother's condition, one may say to oneself "to heck with this; I think I will just go out and see a good movie." But one may still not succumb to this temptation if one is, in addition to having various self-interested temptations or impulses, a kind or caring person. For if one is a kind person, then that kindness is very likely *to reassert itself* after one has expressed to oneself the desire to throw everything over for a movie. If one is tempted to see the movie, one is also likely to remember or soon realize what it will mean if one doesn't seek the second opinion— it will mean that one is taking preventable and serious risks with one's mother's whole future; and if a person is really kind(ly disposed toward his or her mother), knowledge of these implications will very likely *reengage that very kindness*.

In effect, temptation represents a threat to the (moral) goals of kindness (or caring or benevolence) in cases like the one we are considering, and when a strong motive's goals are threatened, that is very likely to alert and send an alarm to the person whose motive is thus threatened. Temptation/impulse/pressure/fatigue may make us momentarily forget our kindness, may tip us toward a moral capsizing, but if we are also possessed of genuine kindness, the tipping boat will also have a built-in tendency to right itself, regain its balance, a tendency activated by realizing the dire consequences of acting on the felt temptation. And the thought specifically of right and wrong may not come into the matter from the agent's perspective.

So I think an agent-based model of morality can make it understandable that someone should be tempted by a momentary (or not so momentary) desire that goes against the tendency of his morally approvable kindness and yet also pull himself out of that temptation by virtue (excuse me!) of that same moral tendency. A strong kindness will tend to oppose, to resist, to fight, to recoil from an impulse or desire that goes against that kindness (by the way, the same can be said in the opposite direction, and if someone who is always taking care of others also has strong enough desire to do something for himself, the latter desire will eventually assert itself against the "temptations" of self-abnegation).

Now it may not be clear in advance whether someone's inner kindness is sufficiently strong to right the boat in the face of various selfish impulses. But the point is that motives like kindness are not just occurrent feelings, but have their own tendencies and capacities and involve a wide range of counterfactual dispositions. And a sufficient inner kindness will tend to reassert itself against various impulses and therefore allow a space in which a moral agent can and will resist temptation(s), though, of course, and by the same token, if the inner motivational resources are sufficiently *weak* (the range of counterfactual dispositions sufficiently narrow or patchy), the temptation may well be succumbed to.[20] But this entire explanation has been given within an agent-based setting, and so I think we can see now that a morality that grounds everything in some sort of motive/desire or pattern of such is fully capable of understanding the moral dispositions and capacities not only of unified moral agents but of divided selves as well. We don't have to suppose that an agent is guided by moral principles or is explicitly conscientious in order to understand how moral temptations can be resisted, and in calling these temptations moral, I am referring not to the explicit content of the tempted agent's thought, but to the fact that they involve what we think (and the agent too would agree) are morally better or worse impulses. A morally ideal person need not think about morality, but neither need a morally tempted person who resolves a conflict in a morally approvable manner.

Of course, explicit moral thinking and/or conscientiousness sometimes (often) do play a role in resolving moral conflicts, for example, conflicts between the goals of good motives and those of selfish motives. But I think we should evaluate such cases in accordance with the approach defended above, and that means, for one thing, that if a moral conflict is resolved primarily through conscientiousness and without much influence on the part of benevolent fellow-feeling, the conflict resolution and resultant behavior are not themselves morally good or praiseworthy (they don't show a morally good overall state of motivation, though they are not necessarily wrong either). On the other hand, and as we saw earlier, there is *something* good (to be said) about any form of conscientiousness, even that of the exclusively conscientious individual, because such a person is at least not (predominantly) self-centered and egotistical. So when someone, anyone, chooses duty over selfishness, their choice and action reflect an overall state of character about which something good can be said (''at least he's not self-centered''), and, in line with agent-basing, that means that there is also something good (to be said) about what they choose to do. Conscientiousness may on occasion reflect a lack of overall good character and even an overall bad character, but the present agent-based view does save

20. Nothing here supposes that, if the agent whose benevolence isn't strong will predictably not resist temptation, then such an agent lacks the freedom to resist temptation. I believe we should accept some form of freewill compatibilism.

the ordinary intuition that there is always something good to be said about conscientiousness and about conscientious resolutions of inner conflict that result in someone's overcoming the temptation to be selfish or self-centered.

Note, however, that our entire discussion till now has not explicitly addressed the issue of whether it is *rational* to be moral (act morally). Later on, in chapter 7, I shall be proposing an agent-based theory of practical rationality that will allow us to address this question. But first there are a number of central problems concerning the *content* of individual and social morality that need to be considered.

THREE

THE STRUCTURE OF CARING

The warm agent-based style of virtue ethics doesn't regard morality as action-guiding or practical in the traditional or usual sense,[1] but we are still seriously considering two variants on such an approach—impartialistic morality as universal benevolence and a partialistic ethic of caring—and we ultimately have to decide between them. We won't be in a position to do this until we have articulated both views in the best manner possible. But I think it is easier to do this with morality as universal benevolence. I think what was said in Chapter 1 about this form of agent-basing gives us a fairly good picture of the nature and implications of such a view, but I have found it much more difficult to spell out something equally specific for an agent-based ethic of caring. Noddings and others have certainly had a great deal to say about caring, but I believe (and this will emerge in what follows) that their work leaves

---

1. Aristotle's ethics has long been held to emphasize "natural" motives more than conscientiousness and thus to stand in marked contrast with Kantianism. But some interesting recent work of Christine Korsgaard's calls that interpretation into question and asks us, for example, to see Aristotle's emphasis on acting "for the sake of the noble" as actually rather similar to what Kant says about acting from a sense of duty. (See her "From Duty and for the Sake of the Noble: Kant and Aristotle on Morally Good Action" in *Aristotle, Kant, and the Stoics: Rethinking Happiness and Duty*, ed. S. Engstrom and J. Whiting, Cambridge, 1998, pp. 203–36). If Korsgaard is on the right track here, then warm agent-basing differs from Aristotelian virtue ethics in a further important way (not mentioned in Ch. 1 of this work).

a great many philosophical issues and questions unaccounted for. A general or systematic ethic of caring (and I hope to answer those caring ethicists who decry any attempt to systematize their view) faces a number of philosophical or theoretical choices, and I propose to consider these and attempt to articulate the overall structure of a plausible ethic of caring in the present chapter.

But an ethic of caring for individuals doesn't automatically tell us about how society should run, and in the chapter that follows this, I hope to explain how an individual ethic of caring can be extrapolated, in agent-based terms, to an account of social morality and of social justice in particular. Then, having dealt with caring in a fairly systematic philosophical way, it will be time to return to impartialistic agent-basing and consider how morality as universal benevolence can likewise be embodied in an account of social morality and justice. That will put us in a position, finally, to choose between our two basic styles of (warm) agent-basing, and at that point I hope to be able to explain to you why I prefer a systematic ethic of caring to any impartialistic approach to morality.

1. Caring and Love

In a talk before the Society for Women in Philosophy given in 1988, Nel Noddings argued that our obligations to people we don't know cannot be accommodated through the notion of caring, because caring requires an ongoing relationship.[2] This has led many philosophers and others to conclude that the ethic of caring cannot function as a total approach to morality and has to be supplemented by the sorts of considerations of rights and justice that are the hallmark of traditional "masculine" moral thinking. However, some ethicists have resisted this concession and defended a more inclusive or embracing conception of caring that treats concern for distant others as *one kind* of caring. In other words, we can distinguish between Nodding's particular conception of caring and what the concept or notion of caring itself allows, and relative to the latter, it makes perfectly intelligible sense to distinguish two kinds of caring: what we might call intimate caring versus what we can call humanitarian car-

2. A version of this talk was published in *Hypatia* 5, 1990.

ing.[3] And I propose that we think of a morality of caring as taking in both these kinds of caring—and perhaps gradations in between. In other words, a good human being can be thought of as being concerned about (the welfare of) people s/he knows intimately, and also, to a lesser extent but still substantially, concerned about (the welfare of) human beings generally, and the most important question we—or anyone else—must ask, in trying to articulate a plausible overall personal morality of caring, is how these two modes of caring can be brought together or integrated within such a morality.

But since, in fact, there are gradations of caring or concern about others (our concern for co-workers is typically less than what we feel for near and dear, but greater than what we feel toward human beings we don't know), it might be suggested that a partialistic morality of caring should drop the caring categories just mentioned in favor of a more quantitative approach. If we are supposed to be more concerned about some people than about others, maybe we should try to quantify the differences. Perhaps we should subscribe to a kind of "inverse-care law" that requires less, but still substantial, concern for people the further they are from one in personal or social-psychological terms and then, in order to apply the law, work out a theory of how steep the curve of lessening concern ought to be. If we do, then we will have to ask, for example, whether we should care ten times as much or whether we should care a hundred times as much about the well-being of a spouse than about that of a stranger; and we will also have to ask where fellow workers, childhood friends, our cousins, etc. all fit into these multiplication tables. And even though such quantification seems very contrary to the spirit in which the idea of a feminine ethic of caring was originally advocated, it *might* be claimed that we have to pay this price if we seek a morality of caring that covers all our relations with other human beings.[4]

3. On this point see Held, *Feminist Morality*, p. 223; and my "Agent-Based Virtue Ethics," *Midwest Studies in Philosophy* 20, 1995, pp. 97, 101. In her most recent thinking, Noddings too has been exploring forms of caring not tied to people we know or have met.

4. I won't here consider whether caring also ought to include concern for sentient beings generally or possibly, even, for the environment. It is difficult enough to work out a caring morality vis-à-vis (other) human beings, but I assume that if we can do

In fact, however, I don't think we have to pay this price because the above inverse-care approach doesn't actually fit the phenomena of moral caring, and there is a less quantitative approach that (I believe) *can* do them justice. The inverse-care law may well be true, inasmuch as it does seem morally appropriate to care more for people the closer they are to one. But as we shall see later, the attempt to quantify that principle and say just how many times more we are to care for spouses than for cousins or strangers yields a moral view which is out of keeping with what it is to care for or about a spouse or friend. And there is another, less quantitative, kind of approach to caring that can do much better.

The view I want to propose emphasizes *balance* as between intimate caring (our concern for near and dear) and humanitarian caring (our concern for people in general). But the term "balance" is sometimes used very vaguely at least by philosophers, and what I have in mind is a quite specific, though hardly technical notion (one that, as far as I can tell, has been philosophically rather underused). I shall be discussing this notion of balance in some detail, but, of course, in speaking of balance between the two categories of caring, I am ignoring distinctions within or intermediate between those categories. One can and should care more about some friends or relations than about others, and co-workers are neither "people in general" nor among our intimates; but I believe all these issues will be a matter of fine-tuning once we have spelled out an ideal of balance between intimate and humane caring. And focusing on these two categories (rather than on some set of three or five categories one might have come up with) has a kind of naturalness and inevitability to it, because (as we shall see) what we want to say about (the morality of) general concern for human beings derives in some measure from what we want to say about the love we feel toward close friends, family, and spouses (or significant others).[5]

If a parent has two children and loves them, the concern s/he feels for the one and the concern s/he feels for the other do not naturally amalgamate into some overall larger concern for their ag-

that, we will be in a position to decide what we need to say about our relations with the nonhuman world.

5. I here also ignore self-concern, which I shall eventually want to treat as a category additional to intimate caring and humanitarian caring.

gregate well-being. Instead, those concerns in some sense remain separate from one another, and by that I (at the very least) mean that a loving parent will not always seek to do what is good or best *on the whole* for his or her two (or three or however many) children. Let me illustrate this.

Imagine that a parent—say, a father—has two children in their twenties, one independent and successful, the other dependent and handicapped. If he loves them (equally), he will invariably make efforts on behalf of both and pay attention to both. If, for example, there really isn't much that he can do for the handicapped child, he will tend nonetheless to expend both time and money in an effort to promote that child's welfare—in effect, he will "show the flag" of concern even where his efforts can deliver very little. But this is not solely or even chiefly because that is the worse-off child, so that (Rawlsian) considerations of justice impel him to do the most he can to raise the level of the worst-off objects/subjects of his proper concern. For that would mean, for one thing, that he should neglect or skimp on time, money, attention, and efforts for the more advantaged child, and love wouldn't permit such a thing. By this I don't mean that love is to be thought of as embodied in a moral principle that needs to be consulted regarding what is permissible or good for one to do—but rather, and more simply, that if he really loves the better-off child, the father will ipso facto (i.e., as a matter of sheer psychology) wish to devote time and money and, more generally, make efforts on that child's behalf—independently of the fact that the other child is handicapped and much worse off.

Thus consider the different possibility that the father might be in a position to do a great deal for the worse-off child and that the better-off one can manage fairly well (and without resentment) on her own. Imagine, further, that efforts on behalf of the former will always achieve more good than he would have been able to accomplish by instead helping or paying attention to the better-off child. In such a situation, both Rawlsian and utilitarian/consequentialist considerations of justice favor always helping the worse-off child, and the case can certainly be made that, from an impersonal or objective standpoint, it would be (a) better (thing) if the handicapped child always received the father's attention. Still, given what it is to love (children equally), a loving father *won't* in fact (always) do what promotes the greater overall or aggregate good of his children, but, rather, will show substantial concern for each child.[6] Or, to put things slightly differently, a loving father with two children will *strike some sort of balance* between the concern or love he has for the one and that which he has for the other, and that means he will at least some of the time help and/or pay attention to a much-better-off child, even though that time could be spent doing more good for the other and producing more total or aggregate good as well.

Once again, however, I am not here supposing that such a parent is guided by explicit moral principles or rules that dictate such behavior. Anyone who needs to make use of some overarching principle or rule in order to act in a "balanced" way toward his children can be suspected of an unloving, or at least a less than equally loving, attitude toward those children; and I am suggesting, by way of contrast, that equal concern for children by its very (unself-conscious) nature tends to lead a person to allot efforts and attention in a somewhat balanced way. But more needs to be said now about what balance amounts to, and perhaps the first thing that can and should be said, is that it is not the same thing as equality (or even near-equality).

When there is some sort (or measure or degree) of balance between two concerns, neither concern can be said to *dwarf* the other and the relation between them can't be viewed as *disproportionate* or *lopsided*. Or, to put it somewhat differently, when a person has just two basic concerns, for x and for y, then to say that those concerns are in some sort of balance is ordinarily to say that the person isn't *mostly* concerned with x and isn't *mostly* concerned with y. It is easy enough, moreover, to extend these clarifying phrases to situations in which *more than two* concerns (or interests, etc.) are said to be in (some sort of) balance, but, in any event, it should be clear that none of these familiar notions entails equality or even near-

---

6. In a sense of "unfair" that every child understands, it will be unfair if the parent doesn't show substantial concern for each child. But I believe—and later on in this chapter and subsequently will offer (further) reasons for thinking—that this fairness (or at least, and more generally, the kind of deontology in which it plays a role) is not ultimate based in a moral rule or norm, but depends, rather, on our understanding of what love is and on our intuitive sense of the moral value of love and other kinds of partialistic feeling and concern. The child who complains of unfairness or bad treatment is in a sense complaining about how much she is, or isn't, loved.

equality between the things that are said to be in some sort of balance. The idea of balance I am invoking is fairly specific, but it (desirably, I think) leaves more leeway and is more flexible than any standard notion of equality. And the idea of (there being some sort or degree of) balance will soon turn out to be of particular use to us in clarifying the overall structure of a plausible ethic of caring.

2. Balanced Caring

We have just seen that love and loving concern for particular known individuals tend to allocate themselves in a nonaggregative and, more specifically, a balanced way. But there are other kinds of concern that *do* operate aggregatively. For example, a person may wish the people of Bangladesh well and even make charitable contributions toward their well-being, without knowing, much less loving, any particular individual in that country. And such a humane or humanitarian attitude of caring tends to yield or embody utilitarian-like aggregative thinking of the sort love rules out. Given such an attitude, the moral concern one feels for an unknown Bangladeshi (whose name one has perhaps happened to hear) is fungible, so to speak, within the larger humanitarian concern one feels for the Bangladeshi people or Bangladesh as a whole, and indeed that larger concern seems appropriately subsumable, in turn, under the even larger concern that a moral humanitarian has for (unknown) people generally. When concerns are thus fungible within some larger concern(s), considerations of overall utility or good apply to them, and this means that when one acts in a humanitarian fashion, one doesn't, as with love, feel the need to help any given individual or group (whose name, again, one may happen to have heard) at some *cost* to considerations of overall or objective good.

Thus when one is actuated by humanitarian considerations, one's smaller concerns, rather than remaining separate, coalesce or melt together. Where there are tragedies, say, in Bosnia and Bangladesh, the pure humanitarian will want her charitable donations to do as much good as possible, and that means it doesn't matter to her particularly if it turns out that, according to such an overall reckoning, all her money (or efforts) should go to Bosnia rather than to Bangladesh. Of course, if one has been to or knows people in a given country, that may alter the situation in just the way that knowing particular individuals makes or can make a difference to how one is concerned about them. One may then care, and care a great deal, about whether one's efforts or charitable contributions go to one group (or person) rather than to some other. But as an ideal type, humane or humanistic concern is importantly different from the loving concern we feel toward friends, family, and significant others, and this distinction needs to be built into any ethic of caring that makes room, as it seems plausible to do, for both humane and intimate caring.

Balance governs how we (are to) treat people within the sphere of intimate caring; and some sort of aggregation governs our treatment of them within the sphere of humanitarian caring. But this still leaves us with the problem of how these two forms of caring relate to one another: of how they are to be integrated within a morally good or decent person or within an account of morality that tells us when people are decent or act rightly. I want now to argue that such people will *balance* those larger concerns in something like the way that we have seen occurs when a person loves two individuals; and this view of the overall structure of a morally good person's involvement with (other) people I call *balanced caring*.

According to this conception of morality, there will be some degree of balance between the concern she has for people she is intimate with and the concern she has for people generally, but the balance or nonlopsidedness as between these concerns has to be understood *in sensu composito* rather than *in sensu diviso*. That is, the balance is not between the concern the moral individual has for any given intimate and the concern she has for any unknown other person, but rather between the concern she has for her intimates *considered as a class* and the concern she has for all (other) human beings *considered as a class*. So I am claiming, in effect, that the overall structure of a morally good or decent person's concern for others (and I shall talk about self-concern at some length later in this chapter) involves two kinds or instances of balancing. Her concern for people she loves or is intimate with will express itself in a balanced fashion—as with the father we described above;[7] but there

---

7. Love typically involves much more than concern with someone's welfare (e.g., a desire to be with the person and to be loved in return), but I think the concern with welfare is the essential and required *moral* element in the intimate caring that we think is morally incumbent on us vis-à-vis near and dear. Note, too, that although

will also be some measure or degree of balance between the concern she feels for the whole group of people she loves and her concern for the class of human beings generally, what we can call her humanitarianism, and this latter, larger balance will be perhaps the most distinctive feature of her overall moral dispositions.[8] Still, I propose that the latter balance be understood as much as we can on analogy with the balance vis-à-vis individuals one loves that we discussed earlier.

The father who loves both of his children very much will devote his energies and attention to them in a nondisproportionate or non-lopsided way; and something similar can be said about someone whose humanitarianism is in some sort of rough balance with her concern for (the class of) those near and dear to her, her intimates. Such a person will devote a good deal of time, money, and effort

we may be able, according to agent-basing, to morally criticize someone who cannot bring himself to love, say, his own child, that person can at least avoid performing (wrong) actions that reflect a lack of concern for the child's well-being (relative, say, to another of his children whom he does love). Agent-basing can uphold the principle that "ought" implies "can" for actions, without doing so for feelings/motives, but the account of social morality offered in chapters 4 and 5 gives absolutely no foothold to the idea of punishing people for feelings/motives they cannot help having or to the idea that they deserve blame or some other bad thing happening to them because of their criticizable feelings/motives.

8. The idea of balance as between intimate and humane caring is more than a little reminiscent of Kant's bipartite account of our imperfect duties in the *Doctrine of Virtue*. Kant says that we have an duty to adopt the happiness of others and our own self-development as ends, and although he doesn't explicitly recommend balance between these ends, that idea is rather consonant with what he *does* say. Imperfect duties are duties we don't always have to be fulfilling (when we sleep we fulfill the perfect duty not to kill, but not the injunction to promote others' happiness). But this doesn't mean that someone can't be criticized for a particular action in light of those duties. Our duty to promote others' happiness allows us a certain latitude as to whom, when, and how much to help, but if we can help someone in bad straits at no cost to ourselves or anyone else and we refuse to do so, then we show ourselves not to have the good of others *in general* (as opposed to the good of *certain* people) as an end and are criticizable as such. An agent-based view that requires (balanced) humane concern for people generally will also allow us to criticize such (in)action.

Marcia Baron makes this point with respect to Kant's views in "Kantian Ethics" in Baron et al., *Three Methods of Ethics* (Oxford: Blackwell, 1997), pp. 17f. And Hutcheson (*An Inquiry into the Original of Our Ideas of Beauty and Virtue*, 1738) also says that particular actions can show one to lack a given (general) motive. However, for an entirely opposed view of these matters, see Julia Driver, "Monkeying with Motives: Agent-Basing Virtue Ethics," *Utilitas* 7, 1995, pp. 281–88.

to relieving human suffering and, more generally, to promoting the well-being of other human beings generally. But that will not lead her to neglect those she loves because she will also be devoting a good deal of time, etc., to *them*. (This is deliberately not *precise*, but in this area I think it is desirable to allow some leeway in this fashion.)

In that case it is likely that a morally good or decent individual will sometimes, indeed often, be doing things for those she loves or cares most about, when she could be doing *more* good for humanity as a whole. She will spend money on her daughter's college education or on family vacations every summer, when she could instead have saved several lives by giving that money to Oxfam or some other charitable organization.[9] But this is analogous with what we saw balance yield in the case of the loving father, for such a father will devote a good deal of time and money to a less needy child even if efforts and expenditures directed toward his other child would always produce greater benefits.

According to Peter Singer and many (other) contemporary utilitarians, we are morally obligated to reduce ourselves and our families to a condition of poverty or near-poverty, given that we can relieve more and more serious human suffering by doing so than we can prevent by keeping the money for ourselves.[10] But balanced caring lacks this implication and to that extent it is less demanding than most familiar forms of consequentialism. However, if caring for intimates is to be balanced against humanitarianism, then hu-

9. In unpublished work, Ramon Das has pointed out that the kind of balance I am talking about may sometimes permit one not to help people whose plight is immediately present to one and whom one can easily save from death or disaster. The people whom one can save through Oxfam are typically far away. But if we imagine a case where a person with a family to support works at home, but lives near a river where (she knows) poor children are always drowning, then (assuming, inter alia that she cannot get people to organize safety measures) balanced caring will presumably tell her to spend a good deal of time saving lives; however, it will also permit her to spend a good deal of time working at home, even if that same time could be spent *saving additional lives*. The present case can plausibly be treated the same as Oxfam, unless known proximity or sheer obtrusive immediacy somehow make a difference from the standpoint of caring. This last possibility will be discussed a bit further in Chapter 4.

10. See Peter Singer, "Famine, Affluence, and Morality," *Philosophy and Public Affairs* 1, 1972, 229–43.

manitarianism will have considerable weight against, or in relation to, our concern for intimates, and so an ethic of balanced caring doesn't tell us that we can keep (almost) all our money for ourselves and mostly devote ourselves to our own projects and commitments, in a manner that is familiar from the work of Bernard Williams. If one's integrity, one's deepest identity, is privatistic or narrow enough, then a morality of balanced caring will not find it acceptable. It will see the integrity of a given individual as involving a concern, say, for his own family (and we will be able eventually to make the same point about self-concern) that is disproportionate to his concern for other human beings generally, and such a morality will then say that such an individual ought to (is wrong not to) devote more time and money and energy to others than his current integrity, than (to use Korsgaard's phrase) his current practical identity, calls for.

So an ethic of balanced caring falls somewhere between the extreme demandingness of a Singerian or consequentialist morality and the extreme lack of demandingness we find in Williams's theory of moral integrity. It permits us to devote more time, energy, and money to our own families (and, as we shall see, ourselves) than Singer wants to allow. However, it also tells us that it is morally wrong to spend as much time as almost all of us do helping those we most naturally want to help, namely, those near and dear to us. Rather, we must devote a quite substantial amount of our money, efforts, time, concern toward humanity generally; and for almost all of us, this would represent a real sacrifice (beyond any we are now making).[11]

11. For Williams's views, see, e.g., his "A Critique of Utilitarianism" in J. Smart and B. Williams, *Utilitarianism: For and Against* (Cambridge: Cambridge University Press, 1973). It would be interesting to see whether a morality of balanced caring is more or less demanding than moralities that require us to make efforts which, if everyone else made comparable efforts, would yield the best results for humanity as a whole. (See, e.g., Derek Parfit, *Reasons and Persons* [Oxford: Oxford University Press, 1984]; and Liam Murphy, "The Demands of Beneficence," *Philosophy and Public Affairs* 22, 1993, pp. 267–92.)

Incidentally, Frances Kamm has objected to the ideal of balanced caring on the grounds that if someone in one's family, say, one's mother or father, desperately needs one's constant attention, it would be wrong and it is at least not obligatory to devote oneself substantially to large public causes and thereby to some extent neglect one's parent. But this seems far from obvious. The intense needs of one or more

3. Balanced Caring versus Aggregative Partialism

None of the above speaks directly to the issue of whether or why we should accept an ethic of balanced caring. We have been drawing out the implications of this conception of morality, but nothing we have said yet (clearly) indicates its superiority to the kind of quantitative partialistic approach we mentioned earlier (much less to impartial views of morality), and it is time for us to speak to this issue.

If one makes a quantitative use of the above inverse-care law, one is committed to an ideal of *aggregative* partiality or partialism that doesn't in fact suit the (whole idea of an) ethic of caring. For I assume that a caring ethic wants to make room for love, and the implications of aggregative partialism, as we shall see in a moment, are repugnant from or to the standpoint of love. Just as someone who loves a given person, a child, will not aggregate that love with his love, say, for another child, but will insist on showing love to both, a person who loves some group of people—that is, loves every person in a given group or class—will be unwilling to neglect that group for the sake of other considerations or values. And I believe that (at least in the present-day world) that is precisely what aggregative partialism calls on us to do.

If we are told, for example, that we are to be ten times more concerned with a spouse than with someone in a distant land whom we don't know, then we are being told that a spouse counts the same as ten unknown others, and this only makes sense if we are (at least other things being equal) to prefer the interests, as we perceive them, of our spouse to those, say, of nine other individuals. But by the

members of one's family hardly absolve one (if that is the right word) from concern for one's country or humanity generally, and during the heyday of the civil rights movement, a person with a desperately sick parent wouldn't, it seems, have been justified in turning away from such a public cause for the duration of the parent's illness. Such larger causes continue to exert great moral pressure on us even when we are practically involved with the needs of near and dear (Sartre, after all, treats the choice between joining the Free French and caring for a helpless aged mother as a moral *dilemma*), and the view, therefore, that when there are pressing larger social-political issues, a person should not be exclusively involved in family problems—a view that our account of balanced caring indeed commits us to—doesn't seem to me to be as implausible as Kamm has (in an unpublished symposium) suggested.

same token, such aggregative assumptions seem to imply that we should neglect our spouse if doing so will help us to save more than ten lives, and this will be especially and overwhelmingly true if this neglect leaves our spouse still alive and with a minimally decent life. Given the numbers of lives one is (nowadays) in a position to save if only one is willing to deprive one's family of certain positive benefits or luxuries, an aggregatively applied inverse-care law leads in the same direction and to many of the same (unpalatable) conclusions that follow from Singer's or consequentialism's impartial approach.[12]

And there is nothing sacrosanct about the numbers assigned above: other numbers (within reason) would yield a similar conclusion. Given the idea that our concern for unknown others and our concern for those near and dear to us are quantitatively fungible or aggregatable relative to certain initial, partialistic weightings, we will not be permitted to show (much) concern for those near and dear to us, given certain sorts of familiar assumptions about what we can do to benefit (the rest of) humanity generally. And such a conclusion is intolerable from love's own standpoint. If we really love certain people, we are going to be unwilling to stop showing that love, and our concern for their well-being, because of the enormously greater good we can/could do by devoting ourselves and our money entirely to people whom we don't (yet) know. But rather than assume this means that there is something wrong with love—that love is, for example, morally insensitive or inhumane—I would like the reader to look into her own heart and then, perhaps, consider whether, given the importance and value we place on love, we don't have to reconsider Singer's or the consequentialist's conclusions about our obligations to others. I think (and the reader must decide for herself whether she agrees) that the love we feel for those near and dear to us is unwilling simply or utterly to yield to considerations having to do with sheer numbers of needy others. But if love is therefore not fungible within some larger (partial) benevolent reckoning, we must give up on aggregative partialism because it is untrue to

12. A view very close to aggregative partialism has been defended, e.g., by C. D. Broad in "Self and Other," in *Broad's Critical Essays in Moral Philosophy*, ed. D. Cheney (London: George Allen and Unwin, 1971).

what we think or feel love involves, and that in turn gives considerable sustenance to an ideal of balanced caring. For balanced caring doesn't allow love to be submerged within or swamped by other, larger considerations, and an explicit morality of such caring will then want to insist that widespread human need or suffering can at most only weigh against, or counterbalance, the importance that love has for us.[13] So if we truly admire the love we feel for some people rather than others—and we shall have to return to this question when, in a later chapter, we again examine impartial conceptions of morality—, there is reason to move partialistic agent-basing away from a quantitative aggregative approach and in the direction of balanced caring.[14]

13. For the purposes of the present discussion, I have been assuming that humanitarian caring is somewhat at odds with intimate caring, or love, because although a good person cares more about the welfare of someone near and dear to her, the reader of this book will generally be in a position to do *more good* for people she doesn't know. Earlier utilitarians like Mill and Sidgwick held that most readers of their books were in a position to do more good close to home than far away (or to strangers), but contemporary writers like Peter Singer have clearly convinced us otherwise (at least with regard to present readers and present circumstances). However, where one's own near and dear are threatened with death by disease, malnutrition, or violence, this assumption may not hold, and in such cases humanitarian concern may yield impulses in the same direction as one's intimate caring. In other words, I am assuming that one's near and dear are also objects of a person's concern for human beings as such or generally, and in some (indeed, many) cases, therefore, intimate and humane caring may not tug in opposite directions and may thus both dictate the neglect of people one doesn't know. Short of science-fiction scenarios, people in the Third World may actually find themselves in this position. But the moral problem for First Worlders is that they are constantly having to choose between intimate and humane caring, and it is this problem that I, like so many others, have tried to offer an answer to above. However, we can and should supplement that answer by claiming, further, that by and large where balance between intimate and humanitarian caring is *not* an issue and one and the same course of action does the greatest good for near and dear and also for larger humanity, a good person who knows this will be motivated to prefer such action to its alternatives.

14. In *On Sharing Fate* ([Philadelphia: Temple University Press, 1987], pp. 41ff.), Norman Care discusses something like the idea of balanced caring and argues (to my mind unconvincingly) that it implicitly makes the individual (and her narrow circle) more important than the rest of humanity and so is unstable (or collapses back into a fairly egocentric or selfish view of morality). But I don't know what he would say about the account of balance presented here.

4. Self-Concern

We still, however, need to say how self-concern, concern about one's own well-being, fits into an ethic of balanced caring, and, not surprisingly, I want to suggest that it fits in via a relation of balance. I think, in other words, that we should treat self-concern as a third kind or category of caring comparable to intimate caring and to humane or humanitarian caring, so that we can think of the moral individual as exemplifying a three-way balance among these kinds of caring. (However, "self-caring" sounds too weird to be useful as a designation for this third kind of caring.)

Such a view implies that we have moral obligations to ourselves and to our own happiness, that it is wrong always to sacrifice oneself and one's well-being for (the good of beloved or unknown, etc.) others; and there is something attractive, but also very controversial, about such first-person moralism. Many would prefer to say that it is (merely) unwise or irrational or timid to defer to others' interests, but hardly wrong, morally wrong, to do so. And indeed, thinking in a more traditional, Christian or Victorian fashion, many people are inclined to think that selflessness and self-denial are morally *superior* to any tendency to assert one's rights or interests as against others.

Thus, if self-assertiveness is regarded as a moral virtue, the idea of a three-way balance among self-concern, intimate caring, and humane caring makes sense. But if one thinks highly of selflessness, then self-concern will have to fit differently into a morality of caring, and I want now to explore a bit how this latter might be accomplished, borrowing some ideas from Scott Gelfand.[15] Gelfand points out that our intuitive permission to be more self-concerned than concerned about any other person may be just that, a permission. In traditional terms, we aren't *required* to have or act on such greater self-concern, and so he proposes that we think of the balancing relation between self-concern and concern about certain classes of others as a sufficient condition of morally permissible action, rather than a necessary condition.

Connecting these considerations with the proposal I have been

---

15. See his as yet unpublished dissertation "Morality and Justice as Restricted Benevolence" (University of Maryland).

sketching, one can insert self-concern into the picture in the following fashion. Concern with intimates as a class and excluding the agent must be balanced against concern for (the rest of) humanity. This much is required. But then it is merely permissible that self-concern be in balance with each of these other concerns. That is, someone whose actions express or reflect some sort of balance among self-concern, intimate caring, and humane caring acts rightly or permissibly, but s/he may also act permissibly and will indeed act supererogatorily if her actions reflect a *lesser* degree of self-concern than that just mentioned.

So balance between humane and intimate caring is morally necessary or obligatory, and, similarly, not having *too much* self-concern vis-à-vis the other two categories is also obligatory. One's self-concern cannot be so strong that it is for that reason out of balance with the other two concerns, so there is a morally required or obligatory limit on how much self-concern is permissible or acceptable in a person's life. But there is no such limit on how *little* self-concern one may permissibly have. Thus according to the view under consideration, there are two ways self-concern can be out of balance with the other two class-concerns, but only one of these makes for impermissibility (for one's being open to moral criticism), and the other in fact makes for supererogation. And all this would leave the relation between humane and intimate caring as described earlier intact, since as between these two concerns, balance is both morally permissible and morally obligatory or required.

Alternatively, we may want to treat self-assertiveness on behalf of one's own interests not only as permissible, but as a positive virtue that we are morally required to balance against both intimate and humane caring for others. This would make the overall structure of an ethic of caring somewhat simpler than what was proposed just above, but it isn't clear to me which of these ways of treating self-concern (and selflessness) is the more plausible.[16] Having said as much, let us now enter into the long-delayed topic of deontology.

16. Whatever type of balance involving self-concern turns out to be morally most appropriate, it is worth noting how difficult it often is to disentangle self-concern from intimate and/or humane caring, as, for example, when the help one has given one's children or some international peace organization also represents a happy achievement of one's own life. But such entanglements clearly make it easier to balance, rather than more difficult. The reader of *From Morality to Virtue* (New York:

5. Sentimentalist Deontology

Any agent-based virtue ethics needs to take a stand about deontology, and in Chapter 1 I stated that morality as universal benevolence, because it is a kind of internal analogue of act- or direct-utilitarianism, seems incapable of justifying standard deontological views, for example, the claim that it is wrong to kill one innocent person when that is the only way to save a greater number of innocent persons (and other things are presumed equal). Deontology has a strong hold on our moral intuitions, and it probably counts against any view if it is incapable of allowing for or justifying deontology. But all views have severe problems, so that the fact, if it is one, that utilitarianism cannot account for deontology needn't rule it out as an approach to moral or moral theory. And this is all the more obvious in light of the difficulty that views *committed* to deontology have in justifying deontological claims via their own theoretical assumptions—I am here thinking especially of Kantian ethics. But what I want to argue in what follows is that an agent-based morality of (balanced) caring can allow for and even help us to understand the moral underpinnings of deontology (the same may be true for morality as universal benevolence, but it is better, easier, to focus the argument on partialistic caring).

Now it may seem that an agent-based ethic of caring will sometimes require us to sacrifice, even to kill, some (innocent) individuals in order to save a greater numbers of other (innocent) individuals. How, for example, can caring about the well-being of one's family *preclude* the permissibility and advisability of killing one family member (or a stranger) to save the rest (in the kinds of dire circumstances that are the stuff of Greek tragedy)? But in what follows I would like briefly to sketch some reasons for thinking that a morality of caring (and perhaps both morality as universal benevolence and aggregative partialism as well) does allow for a substantial kind of deontology.

I believe that a person who loves or cares about another person will be reluctant and often unwilling to kill or hurt them for the sake

Oxford University Press, 1992) will see here that I am still wrestling with, though (given the *other* theoretical considerations that are in play in the present book) less committed about, the issues of self-other symmetry that were the principal focus of the earlier book.

of saving a somewhat larger number of others whom they love or care about. But the typical adherent of deontology will presumably want to reply that that reluctance and/or unwillingness comes from an independent commitment to certain moral rules or principles, rather than arising with or out of motives, emotions, or sentiments. If that were so, then deontology as such would be unavailable to any agent-based view that wished to *remain* agent-based, but I think the matter is far less clear than the above reply assumes, and this may become clearer if we look at some *different* motives/emotions/sentiments: in particular, if we look at hatred and other motives *opposed* to love and caring.

Imagine an uncle who for some reason hates his three nephews. All three want to go to medical school, and (given that their parents are dead and other relatives unavailable) all three are living with a friendly neighbor, but hoping to get the money for medical school from their uncle (whom they don't know hates them). The uncle has reason to believe that the neighbor is willing to help the boys through medical school but won't save money to that end if he believes that the uncle is willing to do so. So the uncle figures that if he helps the oldest of the boys, the neighbor will spend his extra money elsewhere and won't have anything for the other two when, at spaced intervals, they are ready for medical school. If, then, the uncle doesn't help the first nephew, the other two will be helped, but if he does help him, he can prevent the other two from being helped. However, there is something galling to him about this last option; the idea of doing something that will make his first nephew *grateful* to him simply sticks in his craw, and so it is hatred that leads him to deny the first nephew help and thus do something that on the whole is less bad for those he hates.

But if a negative emotion can understandably lead someone to produce results that are overall less bad, then why shouldn't positive feelings like caring and love lead someone to do what produces results that are on the whole less good? And the point of bringing in a negative emotion like hatred is that someone who acts from hatred is far less open to the suspicion that they are basing their actions on independent moral considerations or rules than is someone who acts from love. When someone who loves another person refuses to kill that person in order to save others she loves, it can be suspected that that refusal is less a matter of love and more a matter of the fact that someone who loves will also wish to fulfill her independently given (ruled-based) moral obligations toward those she loves. (Such a view is to be found, e.g., in Rawls's *A Theory of Justice*.)[17] But there is presumably no such thing as the morality or deontology of hatred (no such thing as an ''antideon-tology'' based, as it were, on antipathy). So when the uncle acts as I am assuming he does, what he does comes from and is understandable in terms of his motives/feelings.

Something similar also naturally arises in connection with (less intense) negative attitudes toward groups (rather than specific known individuals). Consider an Englishman who really dislikes the French and who finds himself in a position where he can prevent others from helping a number of French people by himself helping a single Frenchman. Couldn't such a person naturally say/think: ''I'm not going to help any frog, no matter what others may stupidly want to do''? But if negative emotions both toward particular individuals and toward groups can (independently of grounding moral rules) give rise to a refusal to bring about overall worst results, what good reason do we have to deny the opposite possibility to positive attitudes toward groups and individuals of the kind an ethics of caring praises?[18]

But isn't the uncle irrational to think and act as he does, and aren't such examples, therefore, inappropriate analogues to cases in which love and caring are deontologically contoured or restricted? Not necessarily. Presumably, the argument here doesn't rest on the simple assumption that the uncle is irrational to hate in the first place (or that all hatred is irrational), but depends, rather, on the idea that the uncle acts irrationally *given* his hatred and, in particular, on the claim that in acting as he does the uncle goes against and thwarts *his own desires*.

However, this assumption is far from plausible, and in fact it contradicts our (original) description of the uncle example. We de-

---

17. Cambridge, Mass.: Harvard University Press, 1971, pp. 485–90.

18. Thomas Hurka has pointed out to me that cases like Sophie's Choice also support the idea that deontological attitudes can be based in emotion rather than in rules. Sophie is reluctant to choose one of her children for the death camps, even if that is the only way she can insure that they won't both be killed. And she would understandably have been even more reluctant to ''cooperate'' if she had actually had to *kill* one of her children to prevent both from being killed. But this reluctance or more seems to have more to do with her feelings about her children than with any rule or moral considerations.

scribed the uncle as not wanting/desiring to help his oldest nephew even if that is the only way he can hurt the other two nephews and do maximum damage to those he hates, and any (purely hypothetical) decision on his part to help the oldest nephew would fulfill fewer of his actual desires than what he in fact does. If we say that the uncle is thwarting some of his own desires, we do so because we (in a question-begging fashion) assume that anyone who hates a group of people (and is subject to no competing practical considerations) will always prefer to do what is worst on the whole for that group. But since the uncle of our example doesn't (in the case at hand) have that particular preference, he is not (at least on balance) thwarting his own desires and cannot be accounted irrational on that basis. Of course, one could say that his nonmaximizing attitude is as such irrational, but then it would be difficult to avoid the very questionable and (presumably) unwelcome conclusion that deontology too is irrational, and the analogy with positive attitudes like love and caring concern would in any event be sustained rather than undercut by such an argument.

In that case, I think we have been given reason to think that nonmaximizing "deontological" attitudes don't have to presuppose moral rules or standards and represent one way at least in which sentiments like caring and love can naturally develop or flow. I say "one way" because nothing we have said precludes the possibility of hating and contemning, or of caring and loving, in a maximizing "nondeontological" way. Even if the uncle described finds it too galling to help one nephew as a means to hurting the other two, another possible hating uncle might swallow his own gall and, in a desire to maximize ill-effect, bring himself to help the first nephew. And by the same token, I don't think anything I have said puts us in a position to claim that a loving or caring person couldn't conceivably kill one to save two.

But it would hardly be surprising if *some* sorts of love and caring turned out to be morally unacceptable, and an agent-based, sentimentalist account of deontology can hold that anyone willing to kill in order to save (a few) extra lives has morally bad or unacceptable overall motivation (like a person who loves some human beings but has *no* concern about others). Such a claim seems intuitively plausible—it would certainly seem so to most nonphilosophers asked to consider it; and an agent-based view can treat that claim as a ground floor ethical judgment (though one, of course, that could gain or lose in plausibility depending on what else an overall agent-based theory, or its competitiors, might have to say). In that case, we also have agent-based reasons to say that it is wrong to act on (i.e., do what reflects) a willingness to kill in order to save extra lives, and this is deontology (or a part of deontology, though analogous arguments would hold for other relevant parts of deontology).

Now we saw earlier that the uncle who is unwilling to help the first nephew isn't basing his attitude on any moral rule or standard, and so, clearly, whether one is moved by antipathy in that direction or has an opposed, "consequentialist" attitude that makes one willing to help the one nephew in order to thwart the other two *is not a matter of whether one adopts or rejects a certain moral rule or standard.* Given our argument above, then, we can likewise say that whether one has a "deontological" unwillingness to kill in order to save others or a "consequentialist" willingness to do so needn't be a matter of whether one accepts or rejects a certain rule, etc. In that case, we can also say that moral assessments of such attitudes as better or worse, bad, unacceptable, or good needn't involve an (implicit) evaluation or acceptance of any prior rule, etc.

At this point, however, a skeptic might still have doubts about these claims and feel that rules have somehow (been) sneaked into the present view despite the appearance of agent-basing. It might be said, for example, that I have been developing a mere variant on Rossian-type rule-oriented intuitionism, one that brings in (fundamental) act-governing rules not directly, but via motives to conform to such rules. Even if the motives I have discussed don't *have* to be conceived as motives to conform to one or another rule or principle, it can be strongly suspected that that is what they really are, and if so, then what is offered here is traditional deontology with superfluous window dressing. Talk about motives, rather than grounding the deontology in agent-based fashion, obscures the focus on rules that invariably lies at the heart of any (such) deontology.

This is an important objection to consider, though in the end I think it is mistaken. But seeing the nature of the mistake will in the end highlight the distinctive character of, and lend further support to, the agent-based, sentimentalist approach to deontology advocated in these pages.

The deontology of killing is actually atypical of deontology. It involves a distinction (roughly) between killing and letting die (or killing people as a by-product versus killing people intentionally or as a means to an end), but it doesn't or needn't involve the kind of (relative or partial) indifference to well-being that is typical of the (rule-oriented) deontology of lying, promise-breaking, and deception. The latter clearly also distinguishes, for example, between lying and allowing lies, and presumably it requires that one not lie even if doing so is the only way to prevent (a few) others from lying. But in addition such deontology involves the idea that there is something wrong with lying or promise-breaking even if it has no bad results, that sometimes one shouldn't lie or deceive or break a promise even if no one is thereby harmed.

Something like this *could also* be said about killing, because it make a certain sense to say that one shouldn't kill even if no one is thereby harmed. In most cases, killing automatically involves harming someone, damaging their interests, doing something negative as far as their well-being is concerned (one can't say making them worse-off than they were before because after their death they presumably aren't around to be worse off than they were before). But if someone is suffering, it may be clear that death may help them, not harm or hurt them (though I hope I may be excused from getting into the complex metaphysical-cum-ethical issues that this topic can sometimes involve); and in that case, the caring person may well be willing to kill. However, many of those who speak of the sanctity of life believe that there is some sort of rule that forbids (or by which God forbids) killing, taking life, even when that is helpful to the interests of the person killed. If one says this, then as with lying, deception, and promise-breaking, one is treating not killing, not taking life, as obligatory somewhat independently of the way it causally affects human well-being; one is treating killing the way Ross treats promise-breaking, as having its own special moral weight.

Such a deontology of killing really is rule-oriented, and Rossian-type deontology vis-à-vis lying and nonfidelity to promises also has this character—it tells us (that there is substantial moral reason) not to lie or deceive even if that is helpful to the person lied to or deceived. (Similar things may be said about deontological strictures about stealing, but I want to simplify the discussion). So there are actually two possible levels (or degrees?) of deontology about killing, lying, and the like, one level that distinguishes killing, etc., from letting die or letting deception occur, etc., and another "deeper" level where the connection to well-being is more tenuous and where the stricture against killing, etc., is supposed to hold (to some extent) even if well-being is enhanced for those affected by one's actions or inactions.

The latter represents what I call a deeper level because it is a form of deontology that is even further from utilitarianism and consequentialism and Hutchesonian sentimentalism than the kind that *merely* distinguishes killing from letting die. For the kind that just distinguishes between, say, killing and letting die can say that this distinction is a distinction regarding *how* one causally affects or relates to or is motivated to act in regard to *another person's well-being*. (It is also possible to distinguish two levels of deontology as between strictures on harming or deceiving to prevent harm or mistaken beliefs from occurring and strictures on harming or deceiving to prevent others from deliberately harming or deceiving—the latter being the more committed or extreme form of deontology. But this distinction of levels or degrees of deontology cuts across or is orthogonal to the distinction of levels or degrees we are focusing on in the present discussion, and I shall simplify things by saying nothing further about it.)

Now the form of deontology that tells us not to kill or lie even if that (to some degree) helps the person who is killed or lied to really does have to be conceived as relating to a rule, as rule-oriented or rule-governed. For the natural way to understand such strictures is to say that a certain rule has a force (of its own) that can in a given case outweigh considerations of human well-being. But (as should now be obvious or becoming obvious) the deontology that arises out of a concern for or caring about human well-being doesn't have these implications or entailments. Apart from taboos or God-given rules, and relying only on a moral concern that focuses on how what we do affects human well-being, there can be no stricture against mercy-killing in certain obvious instances and certain kinds of white lie that a more rule-preoccupied approach to morality would tend to forbid.

But the idea that it is bad to kill one person in order to save others from being killed *can* be seen as involving a concern for how our actions (and motives) affect human well-being. For one thing, we are not defending the idea that it is bad to kill a person when the person herself or himself will be helped by (or have a better overall life as a result of) being killed, as when the person is suffering and without hope of any recovery. I wasn't explicit about the point earlier, but clearly in the light of what has just been said, what I am defending here is the idea or norm that it is bad to kill one (or more) person(s) *in a way that harms their interests* in order to save a (greater) number of others. And it is said to be bad because the motivational willingness to kill one person "harmingly" in order to save others can be said to involve a defective kind of caring, a caring that is (in a certain respect) indifferent to *how* one's actions causally affect *others' well-being*. Concern for how one's actions affect others, and in particular, unwillingness or extreme reluctance (that sheer numbers may overcome) to damage the interests of one to allow those of others to be enhanced, is a morally good or acceptable motive and willingness, etc., a bad motive. But in calling the one motive good and another bad, we are still talking about motives that concern or focus on how one's actions affect the well-being of others (the case of oneself is to be taken up separately). And I want to say that concern as to *how one's actions affect the welfare of other people* is understandable independently of rules.

The uncle case helps us toward seeing this, but the potentially lingering suspicion that rules are nonetheless at the bottom of all "deontological attitudes" and merely obscured or covered over by a putatively agent-based way of presenting deontology will, I hope, finally dissipate when one sees how the kind of deontology we are speaking of pertains to questions of well-being and how it stays clear of the kind of preoccupation with rules—familiar from Ross, Kant, and others—that treats deontology as having a life and validity somewhat independently of issues of how one affects, or wants one's actions to affect, others' well-being.

So deontology really can be given an agent-based, sentimentalist grounding—one that involves taking certain ordinary intuitions about morally good and bad motivation very seriously. And that is good for the morality of caring. For if this weren't possible, it would be difficult to see how such a morality could deny the permissibility of killing a stranger (or two) to save a person one loves, given its own emphasis on caring more for certain people than for others. This would then go against both common-sense deontology and against the moral standard of consequentialism. But I think that in fact we can understand deontology in the above-sketched agent-based terms and avoid the implausible implications of views that emphasize the permissibility of partiality without allowing for deontology.[19]

Moreover, there is a whole other set of considerations that help to secure the idea of agent-based sentimentalist deontology and that have in fact been implicit in our earlier account of balanced caring. (They were alluded to briefly in an earlier footnote). We usually understand deontology as involving some kind of restriction or side-constraint on acts like killing and lying, but there is a wider understanding of the notion that is also somewhat familiar: one is committed to deontology if one thinks that it is (sometimes) wrong to promote or seek what is best from an impartial or objective standpoint. Given such an understanding,[20] partialist views of our obligations to near and dear are committed to a form of deontology, and thus balanced caring and aggregative partialism both count as deontological conceptions of morality: both tell us that we should (sometimes) act against what is best overall, or impartially considered, for humankind.

However, once again, and as we in effect saw earlier, this kind of deontology grows out of our intuitive assessment(s) of certain kinds of partialistic feeling and concern. But if our appreciation and assessment of certain partialistic sentiments[21] lead us into deontology, why shouldn't this happen *in another instance* and, in particular, arise out of our deep sense that a certain kind of difference in *how* one wants or is willing to affect the well-being of others (or oneself) is important to the moral life.

19. I am thinking in particular of Samuel Scheffler's *The Rejection of Consequentialism* (New York: Oxford University Press, 1994).

20. One finds this broader understanding, e.g., in Scheffler, *Rejection*, though Scheffler focuses primarily on the deontology of killing, lying, harming, and the like.

21. Love, benevolence, and compassion have been called moral sentiments. But that doesn't mean that someone who loves or has compassion has to be thinking about morality or that such sentiments are (therefore) grounded in, or take their existence partly from, independent moral principles, rules, or standards. Rather, the term "moral sentiment" seems simply to mean that a given sentiment is thought morally admirable or relevant to being moral. But that is entirely consistent with agent-basing deontology.

6. Caring versus the Philosophers

In this chapter I have been somewhat systematic and theoretical about what an ethic of caring should involve. In doing so, I have in effect imposed some of the typical aims of philosophy on the attempt—at least on my attempt—to understand what caring as an ideal entails, and defenders of caring can easily object to all this. But what is the basis of their objection?

The account of caring I have offered above is not only theoretical, but somewhat complex. Caring, as I have described it, entails a balance between two different kinds of concern about people, and it might well be asked how anyone could be expected to carry such a complicated (or philosophically sophisticated?) view around in her head and guide her life by it. Even if it is possible to do that, wouldn't the attempt to adhere to a certain complex principle or principles interfere with and detract from a caring involvement with or focus on other people?

To be sure, and the point is one that I have been trying myself to make all along here. In offering a fairly structured account of what admirable or decent caring involves, I haven't been saying that people, morally good caring people, should guide themselves by such an account. The account can be used to judge or evaluate the moral quality of people's actions without our having to think that those whose actions are evaluated should themselves have to think in terms of such an account or its standard for right or good action. When a person seeks the well-being of certain strangers, and does so without being concerned about the moral character of her own actions, our theory of caring can say that she acts permissibly and well, but it may also insist that if the person *had* been concerned with moral standards and whether her actions were in accordance with them, her actions would have been less morally worthy. Thus people aren't to guide themselves by the principle (very roughly) that it is wrong to act uncaringly, but such a principle can still represent a valid moral standard against which their conduct and motivation can be measured by those who would wish to do so. So having a correct, but complex philosophical account of a moral ideal of caring needn't interfere with the particularity and sensitivity of concern for others that mark what is most attractive, and indeed compelling, about that ideal.

But even if the moral(ly good or decent) individual isn't supposed to think in terms of balanced caring, her psychology or character are supposed to exemplify the balance spoken of in our theory, and a defender of caring might well want to ask how concern for loved ones and (a different sort of) concern for human beings can generally be *integrated or brought together* within the individual, if the individual *doesn't* make use of a single, unifying moral principle that recommends such balance? However, not all psychological integration has to occur by means of principles, and in particular there seems to be no reason to think that the form of integration known as balance has to occur by way of (applying) a principle. After all, the father who loves both his children deeply will, by virtue of the very psychology of what it is to love, tend to allocate concern, efforts, attention, money toward his two children in a somewhat balanced fashion. Thus if during a given period of time, he for some reason has to see very little of one of the children and a great deal of the other, he will tend to *miss* the first child and want to spend more time with her, and he will also presumably realize that that child may miss him and be concerned about that; and as a result, the balance of his attentions toward the two children will tend to right itself—and, obviously, none of this has to depend on making use of moral principles. Is there any reason why balance as between intimate and humane caring cannot be exemplified or embodied in a similar fashion?

Well, there is at least this. We believe that love toward one's children and the balance that involves can arise naturally, without the aid of moral prescriptions. But balance as between intimate and humane caring is less familiar to us, and indeed at this point, I assume it is known to us *only through an acquaintance with the explicit moral theory offered in these pages*. In that case, it might seem a bit of a miracle to suppose that *this* sort of balance could fall into place without the aid and guidance of moral claims (or a whole moral theory) about its desirability, so I think I need to say something about why I believe such balance *doesn't* depend on explicit moral thinking.

The balanced love a father feels toward his children doesn't require explicit moral underpinnings, but neither does it just fall into place out of the blue. It reflects the father's sense of what it means to have a child and what it means to a child to have a parent (what it means for people to be close or near or related in this way). Similarly, I want to say that if we understand friendship and kinship relations and really appreciate what it means in our lives to have (the) friends and relations (we do), the force impelling us to be concerned with the welfare of (the whole class of) such people *will not be of a different order* from the impulsion toward general humanitarian concern for others that arises from deeply appreciating our common humanity (our common roots and destiny) and the vastness of human suffering and of human problems worldwide. And this constitutes the kind of rough balance I have been speaking of.

I am not sure whether what is appreciated here is objective facts or something relative to our conative/emotional nature (or both). That is a metaethical issue we needn't get into. But certainly we don't have to say that the present view attempts to conjure balanced caring out of thin air, and I think the reader can now see how balanced caring might arise out of a sensitivity to or appreciation of the (differing) ways we are situated with respect to (groups of) others—without specific reliance or dependence on moral thought or theorizing.[22]

Thus the theory of balanced caring seems to be more complex or structured than anything defended or described by (other) caring ethicists, but I think it contains nothing offensive to the (original) idea of caring. It doesn't gerrymander or commandeer caring back toward the faults that feminists and/or defenders of the idea of a feminine morality have attributed to masculine approaches to ethics because it doesn't, for example, tell us (or in any way entail) that we need to or should approach life or people via (a relation to) principles. Of course, the theory of balanced caring does tell us that a person can be morally criticized if she or her actions fail to exemplify a certain sort of balanced motivation, but the original caring

22. In *The Limits of Morality* (New York: Oxford University Press, 1989), esp. p. 320, Shelly Kagan defends utilitarianism by (among other things) emphasizing the importance, to proper moral understanding and action, of having vivid correct beliefs about relevant facts. But the only facts he deems relevant in this connection concern people's needs (interests), not their differing relations or connections to the moral agent. A vivid understanding of the latter facts might well, however, lead one away from impartialism (whether utilitarian or virtue-ethically agent-based) toward a partialistic view like that defended here. (Perhaps this distinction also marks a/the sense in which partialism stresses connection more than any impartialist view can do.)

ethicists—and most notably Noddings—were perfectly comfortable criticizing people for acting uncaringly, and the main difference between the views lies simply in the complexity, the structural character, of the motivation that is taken as the touchstone for such evaluation.

In the present chapter, I have tried to deal with some philosophical issues that aren't much discussed in the voluminous literature of caring, and I have followed through on the philosophical impulse to work out (though I have only sketched) an ethic of caring as a total or systemic view of individual moral motivation and action. But we have yet to see how or whether an ethic of caring can deal with issues of social morality, and that will be the topic of the next chapter.

FOUR

THE JUSTICE OF CARING

Carol Gilligan's *In a Different Voice* famously argued that men tend to conceive morality in terms of rights, justice, and autonomy, whereas women more frequently think in terms of caring, responsibility, and interrelation with others. At about the same time, Nel Noddings in *Caring: A Feminine Approach to Ethics and Moral Education* sought to articulate and defend in its own right a "feminine" morality centered specifically around the ideal of caring (for people one knows).[1] Since then, there has been a heated debate about the reality of the distinction Gilligan drew and about its potential implications for ethical theory. Discussions of the morality of caring have questioned, in particular, whether any such morality can really provide a total framework for moral thought and action. For in order to deal with our obligations to people we aren't acquainted with and address large-scale issues of social morality, any morality of caring seems to require supplementation by typically "masculine" thinking in terms of rights and justice, with the result that caring turns out to be but one part of morality, rather than anything women, or more enlightened men, could find attractive as a total and self-standing way of approaching ethical issues.

---

1. See Carol Gilligan, *In a Different Voice: Psychological Theory and Women's Development*, (Cambridge, Mass.: Harvard University Press 1982); and Nel Noddings, *Caring: A Feminine Approach to Ethics and Moral Education* (Berkeley: University of California Press, 1984).

But the ethic of caring is in a better position than the above worries suggest. Our last chapter pointed out a way for such an ethic to widen its concerns[2] so as to take in our obligations to people we don't know. And in the present chapter, I want to argue that caring can also develop plausible ideals of social justice and of social morality generally. An ethic of caring doesn't have to supplement itself with or embed itself within any traditional ''masculine'' approach like contractualism, Kantianism, and utilitarianism. It can plausibly deal with the larger-scale concerns of such approaches from within a virtue-ethical framework that is far more in keeping with ideals of caring than anything to be found in those other traditions.

1. From the Personal to the Political

We have thus far confined ourselves to discussing the morality of individuals relating to individuals, but we need to speak about how individuals should relate to larger entities like institutions and countries if we want to build on the idea of caring in developing an account of social justice. And a certain analogy between our relations to individuals and our relations to such larger entities may help us to accomplish this. If individuals can care intimately and humanely about other human beings, they can also care about (the good of) their country and about (the good of) other countries as well. If a foreign nation or country is invaded or mistreated by a neighbor, we object morally and are concerned with the fate of the invaded or mistreated nation (this is especially true when television, films, or personal stories make that fate vivid to us). Of course, we typically have stronger feelings about our own country, but the term ''patriotism'' in the dictionary sense, and without the familiar connotations of jingoism and blindness to fault, applies to a devotion to or love of country that (given what love or devotion is) essentially involves some sort of practical (i.e., action-relevant) concern for the welfare of one's own nation or country. Like concern for individu-

---

2. In *In a Different Voice*, Gilligan allows caring to take in our relations to strangers and people we don't know, and to that extent her views are closer to what I have been proposing here than what one finds at least in Noddings's book. (On this point, see, especially, Susan Moller Okin's ''Reason and Feeling in Thinking about Justice,'' *Ethics* 99, 1989, esp. pp. 246f.)

als, such devotion and concern can develop in people in a way that is in substantial measure independent of moral strictures or advice to the effect that one *ought* to love one's country, but there is no need to describe here the various possible routes to love of country.

What is most immediately relevant to our present purposes is a certain parallelism between motives in relation to larger entities and motives that concern particular individuals. For just as we are morally supposed to care more about individuals who are "close" to us, we are supposed to love or care about our own country more than other countries, and just as it is morally deplorable not to have a substantial concern for human beings generally, it is objectionable to treat the fate of other nations as a matter of practical and attitudinal indifference.[3] (For simplicity, I shall ignore cases where one's strongest political ties are to a city-state or other such smaller unit.) So even in regard to larger entities, there can be different moral requirements corresponding to the distinction between intimate and humane caring, and I propose to use this parallelism or similarity to move toward an account of the social virtue of justice that naturally complements the morality of caring.

Intuitively, we think less well of someone who has no feeling for her own country than of someone who has such feeling (and is not jingoistic, unconcerned with other nations, etc.). (The case where one's country is morally corrupt is a special one and I will not discuss it here.) And like our commonsense good opinion of caring more for those people who are near and dear to us, our belief in the virtuousness of greater concern for the good of (the people of) one's own country seems to need no grounding in other ethical considerations; it is an attitude that makes sense to us, that seems plausibly regarded as preferable to treating all countries alike.

In that sense, the morality of special (though far from exclusive) concern with the welfare of one's own country is agent-based. But that doesn't mean it is totally uncontroversial. Impartialists concerning the sphere of personal or private morality can and do question the virtuousness of concerning oneself more with the well-being of loved ones, and impartialists about nations—for example, cosmo-

---

3. By "practical indifference," I mean simply indifference shown or reflected in one's actions. I am in no way taking back what I said earlier about the moral desirability of doing without practical, in the sense of action-guiding, principles.

politans like the Stoics or, nowadays, Martha Nussbaum—would almost certainly challenge what I have just said and so many of us think about special concern for the fate of one's own country. We shall consider that challenge at some length in the next chapter, but for now let us simply assume that it *is* morally better to give (some) preference to one's own country and see whether we can use that assumption to develop a theory of social morality and justice that sits well with what we and/or others have said about the morality of caring about individuals.

If we think better of those who love their country more than other countries, we also think better of people who put their country ahead of personal considerations when dealing with important political issues that largely or exclusively concern the country's welfare. Love of country has both these aspects, but the second is or at least seems somewhat problematic. It is one thing, analogously with intimate caring, to say that one should care more about one's own country than about other countries; it is quite another to say (as so many of us intuitively would) that when one takes a political role as a voting citizen or public official, one should let love of or devotion to country take precedence over the caring partiality toward friends and family that one is supposed to express in one's personal or private life. Why should someone's moral attitude shift in this way when s/he has to deal with political issues?

This is a question Ronald Dworkin poses very forcefully in his "Foundations of Liberal Equality"; and in fact Dworkin finds it so difficult to understand how such a fundamental shift can or should occur that he denies its existence and ends up treating personal and political morality as pretty much of a piece.[4] Dworkin, as I interpret him, models the morality of personal life on that appropriate to the political sphere, and he notes that utilitarianism involves a rather similar reinterpretation of the morality of personal life in impartialistic terms that intuitively seem more appropriate to political morality. But the attempt to treat the personal and political as fundamentally of a piece can also be seen moving in the opposite direction in attempts by Nietzsche, Nozick, and others to reinterpret political

4. See Ronald Dworkin, "Foundations of Liberal Equality," reprinted in *Equal Freedom*, ed. S. Darwall (Ann Arbor: University of Michigan Press, 1995), pp. 199–214.

life in partialistic terms that we ordinarily think of as best *confined* to the personal sphere.[5]

However, intuitively, different principles/attitudes do *seem* to be relevant to personal and political life, and it would behoove us, I think, to try to make sense of that difference, of the moral shift described above, rather than too quickly assume that we can't make sense of that shift and that the same fundamental principles/attitudes must therefore characterize both personal and political life. In order to do so, I think we need to mention some other more or less familiar examples of similar moral shift.

Common-sense morality differs from act-consequentialism in requiring agents to refrain from certain sorts of harmful action, even at some cost to overall optimality of results (not kill one person to save five or prevent five killings). But commonsense also tells us that when the stakes are high enough this deontological permission/obligation is displaced or superseded. If killing an innocent person is necessary in order to avoid a large-scale human catastrophe, then one may and even should perform the killing. In such a case, we think a certain sort of moral shift occurs because large-scale humanitarian considerations enter the picture, because the horrifying fate of so many individuals is at stake, and indeed the term "catastrophe" seems tailor-made to capture our sense of the qualitative moral difference involved. (Quantity "passes over into" quality.)

Typically, this difference is described as a large-scale difference in results, but it is also natural enough to formulate the difference in agent-based terms. We saw in the last chapter that our caring concern for others makes us highly reluctant to harm them, even if people will be (somewhat) better off on the whole, as a result. It makes us both as moral agents and as moral evaluators sensitive to the difference between doing and allowing (harm), and that much, of course, is deontology. But caring concern also worries about *how many* people are going to be harmed by a given action. Thus, if it is a matter of killing one to save three, then in common-sense terms the fact of doing harm may well seem more salient than the loss of life if one doesn't kill; but if the fate of a nation or race is involved,

5. See Friedrich Nietzsche, *The Genealogy of Morals* (Garden City, N.Y.: Doubleday, 1956); and Robert Nozick, *Anarchy, State, and Utopia* (New York: Basic Books, 1974).

then one's attention to deontological considerations (to the differences that deontology is sensitive to) is typically overwhelmed by the enormity of the threat to human life that lies with a refusal to kill. This then means that a fundamental moral shift may occur between deontological situations where a couple or a few (extra) lives are at stake and situations where the threatened difference in loss of life is enormous. And it can be said that the fullest humanitarian concern naturally or inevitably leads to such a shift of thought or attitude.

Now I think something similar happens when one goes from personal life to public life, or from addressing problems in one's personal life to facing political issues as a voter. We spoke earlier of the importance, in personal life, of caring about one's own interests and those of people near and dear to one; and also of balancing (each of) these concerns with humane concern. But one's special or greater concern for oneself and those near and dear to one and thus the idea of (this kind of) balance as well seem morally to go out the window when significant public or political issues are at stake. (To simplify matters, I will largely confine our discussion to issues of national, rather than international or local, politics).[6] And I think what happens here is quite similar to what we have just seen occurring in connection with common-sense moral deontology. For in ordinary life a person may not pay much attention to the future of her country, but when called upon to help decide important issues about the future of her country, the feelings of someone who really loves her country will be engaged, aroused, in a way that drives out or damps down personal considerations (and the related idea of balance).

Now in the case of voting or acting as a public servant, it seems as if the moral shift occurs as a result of a role change that activates an otherwise merely latent patriotism, but when, in the course of one's personal life, or acting as a private citizen, one's aroused sense of the enormity of potential harm overwhelms one's normal sensitivity to the difference between doing and allowing, the moral shift seems to occur without a change of role. But there is actually more

6. Notice that when issues internal to a nation are at stake, the term "patriotism" seems less appropriate than "love of (or caring about) one's country." Also, I am for the moment sidestepping the difficult question of how religious affiliations should bear on one's conduct as a citizen or public servant.

similarity here than may initially meet the eye. For when a person has to decide whether to kill an innocent person in order to prevent a great human catastrophe, it is natural to think of her as having been effectively but unofficially *thrust into* a public or political role by the enormity of the effects of her possible actions. In fact, when the *scale* of action changes in this way, it is as if a person were somehow *entrusted* with the fate of a large number of individuals. In that case, our example of aroused concern for *numbers* of lives at stake is more similar than one might initially think to explicitly political examples of moral shift, and this similarity helps to make it more understandable, I think, that political roles should override considerations of personal or family advantage in those who have a deep and genuine love of their own country.[7]

Moreover, it makes it understandable in terms that are ultimately friendly to a morality that wishes to emphasize and elevate personal (relationships of) caring. For in relation to one's interest in other countries, love of one's own country is analogous to caring for those near and dear to one;[8] and if the shift of perspective that is called

7. One should not, however, imagine that all interesting cases of moral shift involve a move from less general to more general concerns in special circumstances. In the familiar example of miners trapped underground, we recognize or at least typically *feel* the need to help those miners rather than spend an equivalent amount to install safety devices in the mines that will save a greater number of lives in the long run. So if one was contemplating spending money on safety devices but miners suddenly become trapped as a result of an accident, general concern for miners gets displaced or damped down by concern for, compassion toward, *these particular* miners, and indeed one wouldn't normally be considered a compassionate person if one didn't feel this way and act accordingly. It would be interesting to consider how the kind of immediacy or particularity that emerges in the miners example should be taken into account by (a proper attitude or moral theory of) caring, but I won't take the matter up here.

8. In fact, one can and perhaps should push this analogy further than I have so far done in the main text. I believe that concern *either* for one's own country *or* for other countries is only appropriate in the political or public sphere and doesn't really arise in private life. But in that case I think one can plausibly hold that one's political attitudes toward nations should be viewed analogously to one's individual or personal attitudes toward people. So if a morality of caring prizes balance between the class of intimates and the class of all other people when political issues are not at stake, it should probably prize balance as between one's own country and other countries considered as a class or group, when international questions arise. (This places more weight on concern for one's own country than a political analogue of aggregative partialism would presumably commend.) Thus when political issues affect only one's

for when one moves from the personal to the political can be explained in terms of a morally appropriate or desirable activation of the love of country, then we have an account of political action or activity in the same agent-based motivational terms that were earlier used to account for the moral value of partialistic caring. So the morality of caring can be naturally and plausibly extended to deal with the actions of individuals in political or public roles, and thus extended, it has now become a quite general view of the morality of individual action.

But this takes us only part of the way toward an account of social justice and of other issues of social morality. Our next steps require us to draw on another parallelism or analogy that will help us to characterize larger entities like institutions and societies in moral terms.

2. Social Justice

If we think of societies roughly as groups of individuals living under or according to certain institutions, laws, and customs, there is an analogy between the relation the institutions, etc., of a society have to the (membership of the) society and the relation of individual acts to their agents. The laws, customs, and institutions of a given society are, as it were, the actions of that society—they reflect or express the motives (though also the knowledge) of the social group in *something like* the way actions express an agent's motives (and knowledge), though in a more enduring manner that seems appropriate to the way societies typically outlast the individual agents in them. And so just as individualistic agent-basing regards individual acts as morally good if they reflect morally virtuous motivation and wrong if they reflect vicious or deficient motivation, an agent-based account of social morality will treat customs, laws, and institutions as morally good (positively and admirably just) if they reflect virtuous

country, the moral shift to the public sphere entails that one try to do what is best for one's country. But when such issues have broader ramifications, I think the shift entails balanced concern between one's own country and the class of all others. (What to say about United Nations officials and about circumstances in which there is some sort of world government is a more complicated issue that I won't attempt to get into here.)

(enough) motivation on the part of (enough of) those responsible for them and as morally bad (or unjust) if they reflect morally bad or deficient motivation.

But then, given what we said about the importance of concern for the good of one's country in regard to actions taken in the political roles of citizen and public servant, we can say that national public institutions and laws are just when they reflect (enough) such concern on the part of (enough of) those who create (or implement or maintain) them or at least don't reflect a (great) lack or deficiency of this motive. By contrast, customs or institutions in private life or in the private sphere can be said to be just if they reflect a balance between intimate and humane concern for people (and self-concern) or at least don't show a deficiency of such motivation. (If it turns out that certain kinds of well-intentioned individual or private activity lead to collective disaster, then people who care in a virtuous or morally acceptable way about the good of their country will be impelled toward setting up public institutions or passing laws that *counteract* such ill-effects.)

Remember, however, that not every action of a malicious person will count as wrong. Even malicious people have to eat and sleep, and an agent-based morality of caring can treat (some) such actions as morally permissible *because they don't express or reflect the malice of those who perform them.* And something similar can happen in regard to laws and institutions. Morally deficient national legislators who were largely indifferent to the overall good of their country might, for example, pass a law allowing right turns at stoplights, actuated by the desire to make things better for motorists, but also fail to enact legislation that would do away with far more serious social ills. In that case, since the desire to make things better for motorists is, presumably, in no way incompatible with genuine love of country, their enactment of the stoplight law in no way *exhibits* or *reflects* their deficient or lukewarm concern for their country, and an agent-based view can regard such a law as just. What does exhibit their deficient concern for their country (or, as we might say, their almost total lack of public-spiritedness) is their failure to pass, and the consequent absence of, the other, more needed legislation, and this institutional state of affairs *will* count as unjust according to our theory.

However, we have still not said what it is for a society to be just, and we can now do so in fairly short order. On an agent-based view,

if an individual is morally good, that is because s/he has good motives or motivation, and if some pattern of balanced caring for individuals and larger units is the morally best individual motivation,
then the morally best kind of individual is one who is motivated in
just that way. But if a society is a group of people living according
to certain institutions, etc., then an agent-based approach will naturally want to hold that a society's moral goodness, its justice, will
depend on how good the (overall) motivation of the group of people
who constitute it is. So for the kind of view that naturally complements the individual morality of caring, the justice of a society will
depend on whether (enough of) its members have (motivation that
is close enough to) the kind of motivation recommended by the
caring ethic expanded or reconfigured so as to include concern for
one's own and other countries along the lines indicated above.

We thus end up with a view that sees the social virtue of justice
as a function of individual virtue(s), that is, of the virtuousness of
the individuals who constitute a given society. But we should also
point out some of the implications of such an agent-based account
of justice. That account is in a position, for example, to criticize
societies where a ruling elite denies most people a political voice or
doesn't allow workers to form unions; for to that extent the public
institutions/laws of such a society will presumably reflect and/or
express the greed or indifference of that elite, or its desire to retain
its hegemony of power and privilege, rather than any genuine concern for the country's, or the public, good. And similar criticisms
will be available in regard to meritocratic or other societies where
there is no (guaranteed) safety net for the handicapped, the poor, or
the unemployed.[9]

Moreover, what we have just said about particular laws and institutions applies on a larger scale (and more holistically) to the
founding of a state. Where the writing and implementation of a
constitution reflects (is motivated by) greed or indifference to others,
the constitution is not a just one, and the society/state as a whole,
given its predominant actuating motives, isn't just either. But where

9. These sorts of arguments shadow those given by utilitarians in defense of
democratic and equalizing laws and institutions, e.g., Mill's in ''Representative Government.'' This shouldn't be surprising, given the (usually assumed and frequently
existent) connection between good consequences for (the people of) a country and
devotion to and concern for a country's welfare.

there is a morally appropriate level of concern for the good of the nation, the problems of coordination and cooperation that make political institutions (and laws) necessary *can* and, I want to say, *will* be dealt with in a just manner (though, as we shall emphasize below and should already be clear from what we have said in defense of moral agent-basing, justice isn't the same thing as success in one's politically good aims). Moreover, in the light of what was said earlier, it will be clear that laws, institutions, and constitutions motivated by insufficient concern with the welfare of *other* nations can also be criticized as unjust, according to the present conception, and a society where such motivations are prevalent (enough) will not count as just, even if its *internal workings* are entirely just in terms of that conception.

It is also worth considering at this point whether and to what extent the picture of justice offered here favors equality of wealth and/or of well-being, among the members of a society. How well-off a country or society is (largely) depends on how well its various inhabitants or members are doing.[10] But then, because of considerations having to do with diminishing marginal utility, (relatively) egalitarian outcomes will tend to be overall better for a society than inegalitarian ones, and the present sort of agent-based view will then want to say that justice tends to require legislators, citizens, and others dealing with political issues—at least to the extent they are aware of diminishing marginal utility—to favor egalitarian economic (and other) outcomes over unequal ones.

However, nothing in the present view of justice clearly precludes the possibility that the good of a nation or country may sometimes depend on inegalitarian distributions of welfare or utility (consider, just to take an easy example, the effect on certain individuals' welfare of being conscripted during wartime). Moreover, talk about concern for the good of one's country might not translate into any sort of general argument against large inequalities of wealth or income, if, for example, trickle-down or supply-side economics really benefited everyone and was instituted for that reason.

---

10. For purposes of the present argument, I don't think it is important to distinguish countries or nations from societies; nor do we need to consider whether the well-being or good of a society is *completely reducible to* that of its members or of those who live in it.

3. Laws and Their Application

It is time to say (more) about the justice of laws and of penalties, punishments, or benefits that occur through the operation or administration of the law. And this is an area where, at least at first glance, it would seem that agent-based views would run into difficulties.

We are naturally inclined to think, for example, that certain crimes are minor and others serious and that some crimes are (objectively) worse or more serious than others, and it is natural to suppose that a justified or just legal system should reflect such distinctions. Thus a system of laws that punished car theft more severely than murder would seem unjust, and a sentence of death for car theft seems clearly unfair and unjust. But it is difficult to see how any *agent-based* view could capture such apparently external or objective facts about what is just or fair.

For an agent-based view of justice holds that the justice of laws depends on the moral character of the motives they reflect, that is, the motives of the legislators that institute them and perhaps also of the constituents they are trying to represent (and even of the judges who review them).[11] And such a view will also want to hold that punishment in a particular case is just if it results from just criminal laws being justly applied or administered. But it is natural to wonder whether any such view can put enough constraints on legislators and others so as to be able to insure that there will not, for example, be just laws that mandate a twenty-year prison sentence for ordinary car theft. Otherwise, agent-based theories of social justice, by implying the possibility of *just* laws to that effect, will ultimately be very implausible.

But think of what would have to be the case for a (national) law providing for a mandatory twenty-year sentence for car theft to

---

11. There is a complication in cases where certain laws were originally passed for bad reasons (as a result of bad motives on the part of the legislators), but subsequent reformist legislators find reasons for preserving those particular laws. Perhaps we can and should say that such laws were originally unjust, but *become* just when their *continued* existence reflects good reformist motives, rather than the bad motives that originally gave rise to them. Scott Gelfand has pointed out that complications also arise for cases where a bill passes via a majority and most of those voting for it have good motives, but most of those voting *on* the bill have bad motives. It would take too long here to discuss how such cases should be handled.

count as just or fair, according to our agent-based theory. Those passing (and signing) the law would have to be motivated by concern for the good of the country (or at least not be expressing selfishness, indifference, partisanship, and the like), and how could any really public-spirited legislator think she could do more good by instituting such a severe punishment rather than something milder?

Well, you may respond, what about recent "three strikes you're out" legislation concerning felonies? In such a case, the punishment instituted by legislation is very severe. Yes, to be sure. But what about the motives of those who pass(ed) such legislation? Are they really trying to do the most good they can for society or the country or are they not, rather, pandering politically to the prejudices, fears, and resentments of their own constituents (or subject to such irrational attitudes themselves)? It is not entirely implausible to suppose that those who are clamoring for or instituting such laws are motivated by desires and attitudes that are a far cry from anything like concern for the good of the country. Of course, legislators may, to relieve cognitive dissonance, convince themselves that such legislation is good for the country, but if this is self-deception and they really know better, then they are not really, or at the deepest level, concerned with what they tell themselves is their public-spirited objective. In that case, there is no threat that our agent-basing will force us into admitting the justice of "three strikes you're out" laws or laws making twenty-year prison terms mandatory for car theft.

But what if in present social circumstances, three-strikes legislation really is necessary to stem the rising tide of crime? Well, if it is, then it is certainly possible for those who favor it to be motivated by the good of the country, rather than intolerance, vindictiveness, political ambition, and/or indifference toward criminals; and in that case such legislation, if passed, will be just. I simply doubt such a thing to be possible in anything like our present circumstances, and by the same token if there ever, science-fictionally, were circumstances in which twenty-year sentences for car theft were somehow clearly necessary to social well-being, then perhaps such sentences would be socially justified. Given present circumstances and assumptions, however, it is simply unthinkable that there could be just legislation making twenty-year sentences mandatory for car theft in a way that it is not *entirely* unthinkable that three-strikes legislation might be called for.[12]

Of course, if legislators are sufficiently *misinformed* about the facts, they might well mistakenly think that very severe punishment was good for people and for society as a whole. Would our agent-based view of justice then allow for the passing of laws of this kind and be committed to treating them as fair and just? It all depends. There are in fact two different sorts of cases at issue here, and we must distinguish them before we can give a satisfactory answer to this objection.

For someone to count, in the fullest sense, as concerned about or with the welfare of her country (and what I am saying now is similar to points made earlier, in Chapter 1), she must not only be pleased by the happiness and displeased by the unhappiness of compatriots, but must be actively committed to helping them when she can. But a genuine practical desire to be helpful cannot be indifferent to *facts*. A person with such motivation doesn't just throw good things around or give them to the first person or group she thinks of; she cares about *who* exactly is in need of help and about *what kind* of help they need, and such care, in turn, criterially involves wanting and making efforts to know relevant facts, so that one's concern for the good of the country can be really useful. Thus if legislators are fully concerned with the public good, with the good of their country, they will try to inform themselves before passing legislation intended to benefit (the people of) the country. And it seems difficult to imagine, *given obvious facts about the world*, that legislators who bothered to inform themselves could think that legislating a mandatory twenty-year prison term for car theft would benefit their society or country more than other laws that they might institute instead. To that extent, an agent-based view like that presented here

---

12. It is also interesting to consider whether our agent-based account of justice is likely to justify the sorts of excusing conditions the law typically allows. For example, courts sometimes permit a mitigating defense of "provocation" and don't usually hold people legally responsible for causing harms they could not reasonably have foreseen or for actions whose wrongness they lacked the capacity to recognize; and to the extent such features of the law serve a socially benevolent purpose, the present view will almost certainly justify and mandate them. However, present law allows for strict liability, and it cannot be ruled out in advance that our account of justice should in some instances do so as well.

can argue against those penalties and punishments that we intuitively regard as unjust, undeserved, or unfair *without making any sort of independent appeal to the latter notions.*[13]

Except for one possible case. If the public-spirited legislators try to inform themselves and, despite their best efforts, end up with faulty or totally misleading information, then our agent-based theory will (have to) say that the laws they pass as a result of being misinformed are, morally speaking, just, even if they turn out to have unfortunate results that are the very opposite of what the legislators intended. If the society is just, if the legislators are duly elected, if they make their best efforts, and if the laws they pass reflect all those facts, then there is nothing morally to criticize about those laws, on an agent-based view, and I think this conclusion is fairly intuitive. We can and do distinguish moral fault or inadequacy from what is merely unfortunate or even tragic, and our theory tells us we need to make such a distinction precisely in the kind of case under consideration. In normal circumstances, though, it seems clear that the present view allows us the resources to regard certain sorts of highly punitive law as unjust.

Agent-basing also implies that it can be just to convict and punish someone for a crime s/he didn't commit, if just procedures were followed, but the evidence before a court was (innocently) misleading.[14] This conclusion is not, in itself, particularly implausible; and neither does it automatically entail that such punishment is also *deserved*, a conclusion that really would be problematic. Certainly, the Aristotelian conception of justice is grounded in the notion of desert, but modern-day Kantian, utilitarian, and contractarian theories conceive justice *independently* of desert, and the agent-based view of justice offered here is very much in keeping with this trend.[15] Of

13. However, in some circumstances it may be difficult to compare the consequences of different acts of legislation, and different legislators may end up with different conclusions about what would be good for their country, despite good faith efforts to convince one another. Compromise may then be called for, but, unlike some kinds of trade-off among special interests or factions, *this* sort of compromise may well reflect genuine public-spiritedness on the part of all concerned and thus provide the basis for admirably just legislation.

14. But it will also hold it to be unjust to make a justly convicted person serve out his sentence after exculpating evidence is discovered.

15. On these points see, for example, Thomas Hill Jr., ''Kant's Anti-Moralistic Strain,'' in *Dignity and Practical Reason in Kant's Moral Theory* (Ithaca, N.Y.:

course, to complete our picture, we would have to say something more about how, or even whether, notions of deserved reward and punishment apply in social and individual morality. But assuming our ability to conceive justice in quite different terms, the notion of desert becomes much less theoretically important than it was once thought to be, and its consideration may perhaps reasonably be left aside to another occasion.

At this point we do, however, need to say more about the justice of those customs and institutions that are at least somewhat *independent* of political/legal institutions and enactments. Susan Moller Okin and others have criticized Rawls's *A Theory of Justice* for failing to consider issues of justice within the family and to see fully the mutual bearing of family (or other supposedly private institutions) and public institutions, and it is sometimes even claimed, as a result, that we cannot really or in principle distinguish the private or personal from the political.[16] This conclusion would clearly undermine our present approach, but I think these recent criticisms can be more plausibly taken as showing, rather, that private life and public life are *morally relevant* to one another, and our account of justice can speak quite plausibly to this topic.

For example, gender bias in society's public institutions can create or compound gender bias within the family (or other private institutions), resulting in (further) disadvantages for women and children. But the influence can also work in the opposite direction, and the view of justice offered here allows us amply to explain what is wrong or unjust about these forms of influence and about the situations that give rise to them. Thus if husbands are customarily selfish or somewhat indifferent in relation to the well-being of their wives and children (and wives, *mutatis mutandis*, are not), then the

---

Cornell University Press, 1992), pp. 176–95; Sidgwick, *The Methods of Ethics*, 7th ed. (Indianapolis: Hackett Publishing, 1981), p. 284n.; John Rawls, *A Theory of Justice* (Cambridge, Mass.: Harvard University Press, 1971), pp. 103, 314f.; and Thomas Scanlon, "The Significance of Choice," in *The Tanner Lectures on Human Values*, vol. 8 (Salt Lake City: University of Utah Press, 1988), p. 188. (Scanlon's views here about desert seem to entail that an innocent person can deserve punishment, but this repugnant conclusion doesn't actually follow from what he says about *justice*).

16. See Susan Moller Okin, *Justice, Gender, and the Family* (New York: Basic Books, 1989); and Jane Mansbridge and Susan Moller Okin, "Feminism," in *A Companion to Political Philosophy*, ed. R. Goodin and P. Pettit (Oxford: Blackwell, 1993), esp. pp. 271–75.

inequalities of (private) family life exhibit a good deal of morally deficient individual motivation, and our view allows us both to criticize the behavior of husbands as insufficiently caring and to treat (various) families as morally deficient or unjust.

But by the same token agent-basing allows us to regard the elimination of gender bias both within the family and in public institutions (and indeed everywhere) as a matter of just *political* concern. Given reasonably held background assumptions, it cannot be for the good of the country that children are inadequately cared for or that women are treated badly, and (male) legislators who turn a blind eye to the disadvantages of women and children or who deceive themselves about their own bias exhibit a deficient concern for the public good, for the good of the (whole) country. So just legislators under the familiar conditions of our social life will work to eliminate the bias of public institutions and public life, as well as pass laws (or make constitutional changes) that are needed to insure better treatment of women and children within the private sphere.[17] The distinction between private and public or political doesn't, therefore, have to be obliterated in order to do justice to their mutual moral influence;[18] and I think our agent-based conception of justice gives full and reasonable scope to the criticisms that need to be made of particular families and of the institution of the family generally. Indeed, at one and the same time, it allows us to evaluate both public and private institutions/customs *and* how these bear on one another.

17. In *Justice and the Politics of Difference* (Princeton, N.J.: Princeton University Press, 1990), Iris Young points out that justice may sometimes call for us to work against and eliminate inequalities of welfare and opportunity rather than concern ourselves (exclusively) with promoting "the common good" (the good things that society offers to everyone, like defense against a common foreign enemy). But I take it that what is "on the whole" good for a country includes more than this common good, and so (like Young and unlike certain contemporary communitarians) I assume that just legislators will sometimes or often have to concern themselves with something other than, and even in some measure opposed to, the common good (or common "practices"). However, I have used "public-spiritedness" and "concern for the public good" in the wider sense that connotes desire for what is good for a country on the whole.

18. The distinction between the private/personal and the public/political is also challenged—though hardly, I think, undermined—by various conceptions of (the institutions and activities of) so-called civil society; but I won't take up those issues further here.

4. Conclusion

One thing that seems appealing about an agent-based approach to social justice and to other questions of social morality is the way it conceives such matters as dependent on the ethical character of the individuals who make up or constitute a given society. Institutions, for example, are to be judged in terms of their motivational under-pinnings, their human element, and it follows from such a picture that if the people of a just society with just institutions became increasingly selfish or indifferent to fellow-citizens, the society itself would have become less ethically admirable, less just, even if those institutions—the husk or shell of justice—were somehow to remain in place for a while. Thus according to our agent-based view, the justice of a given society cannot simply be "read off" from the way institutions (or laws) are at a given time (from the fact that institutions, or laws, are as they would or might be if the society *were* just). Rather, it depends on the "(ethical) soul" of the society, and it is an attractive feature of agent-based views that they in this fashion treat social justice as a more *deeply human* matter than it is on theories of justice that place primary importance on (mere conformity to) rules, principles, and/or institutional norms.[19]

Of course, (what are in some sense) impartial rules for the adjudication of social disputes are supposed to be easier to come by and maintain than a feeling/motive like concern for the good of one's country, so the present conception of justice, grounded as it is in the latter, may seem less practical, and perhaps, as a result, less valid, than rule- or principle-oriented approaches. But is it really easier to maintain a system of impartial rules and, in particular, laws against the encroachments of powerful human feelings than to encourage and nurture certain kinds of human feeling as against others?

I don't think all the relevant facts are in yet, but I think part of our tendency to prefer impartial rules or principles comes from a conviction or hope that they—and individual motivation to comply with them—can be grounded in pure practical reason. If, as I be-

19. The same point can be made about theories that understand justice as a *state of affairs* or *situation* in which goods or resources are distributed equally or in some other specific way.

lieve, we have reason to wonder whether such a thing is possible, we also have reason to wonder whether the maintenance of a system of principles couldn't depend on underlying human sentiments/motivations (concerning those principles) rather than necessarily functioning as a basis for protection against our emotions. Even pure conscientiousness may draw strength from underlying human needs and feelings more than from some sort of pure reason, and so I think we have every reason to explore the potential of a less rationalistic, more sentimentalist approach to morals and justice of the sort advocated here.

Of course, if psychological egoism were true, then justice conceived in accordance with our present agent-based view might prove to be humanly impossible, and that might (though this is controversial) redound against the *truth* of our theory of justice. (Would Kantian moral and political theory fare any better under such a radical assumption?) But much recent work in experimental social psychology suggests strongly that childhood selfishness has been exaggerated and the capacity of children for benevolent concern for others greatly underestimated in the previous literature of social psychology.[20] And if sympathy with and concern for others come naturally to people and can be cultivated by proper education and forms of social life, then justice as described here may represent a practically attainable conception, a relatively realistic ideal, of social morality.

Note too that our agent-based sentimentalist account of justice doesn't require its own public acknowledgment as a necessary condition of social justice. For reasons rehearsed in Chapter 2, people who are genuinely concerned with the welfare of their own or other countries are likely to focus more on what they can do to help those countries than on whether their society is (in agent-based terms) just or whether they are acting morally or justly.[21]

---

20. See, for example, N. Eisenberg, ed., *The Development of Prosocial Behavior* (New York: Academic Press, 1987); N. Eisenberg and J. Strayer, eds., *Empathy and Its Development* (Cambridge: Cambridge University Press, 1990); J. Kagan and S. Lamb, eds., *The Emergence of Morality in Young Children* (Chicago: University of Chicago Press, 1990); and M. Hoffman, "Is Altruism Part of Human Nature?" *Journal of Personality and Social Psychology* 40, 1981, pp. 121–37.

21. In "The Misfortunes of Virtue" (*Ethics* 101, 1990, pp. 42–63), Jerome Schneewind says that virtue theory encourages people to impugn (the morality of) the motives of those who disagree with them on political or moral questions. But in fact people concerned with the good of their country are unlikely to do this *in most*

An agent-based account of justice will thus want to accommodate a sense of justice and an action-guiding public use of principles of justice no more, but also no less, than it does conscientiousness and obedience to rules in the sphere of individual(istic) morality.[22]

At this point, I also want to say just a bit more about the overall structure of this and other agent-based accounts of individual and social morality. Such views begin by advancing partial or complete theories about how ethically to evaluate individuals (or individual character) and then use these as a basis for larger-scale social evaluations. This way of proceeding stands in marked contrast with Rawls's approach, according to which a theory of the justice of the basic structure of society has to precede any account of individualistic moral norms or virtues. It is also the opposite of Plato's procedure in the *Republic*, where justice "writ large" in society or the state is treated as a heuristic device for understanding justice in the individual.

However, there are other theories of social justice that resemble agent-based views in the way they move from individualistic claims to evaluations of whole situations or societies. Nozick's libertarian conception of justice essentially proceeds in this fashion; and some recent and very interesting work by Kantians also deals with questions of social justice in terms that have their original home in Kant's account of individualistic morality (for example, Onora O'Neill's view that capitalistic institutions can often be criticized for treating workers as mere means).[23]

The present chapter offers no knockdown arguments against utilitarian, Kantian, contractarian, or, for that matter, Aristotelian ap-

---

practical contexts because that would typically be counterproductive to their own aims. However, a moral *theory* needs to show how it can accommodate (most of) our intuitions about particular cases, and given the nature of sentimentalist agent-basing, our argument here has (had) to point to various morally unsatisfactory underlying motives in order to account for various particular kinds of intuitive wrongness and injustice.

22. However, to the extent that appropriate caring for people and countries is known to be a means to the well-being of people and countries, citizens will have reason to promote and preserve (what our agent-based theory regards as) justice, though not necessarily under that very description.

23. See Nozick, *Anarchy*, and O'Neill's *Constructions of Reason: Explorations of Kant's Practical Philosophy* (Cambridge: Cambridge University Press, 1990), pp. 122ff.

proaches to social justice, but it does attempt to show that one kind of agent-based virtue ethics possesses the resources to account for many issues of social morality in plausible or promising terms of its own and to do so within a plausible overall theory of morality. Moreover, our agent-based treatment of social issues is a natural extrapolation from Noddings's original morality of caring—more congenial to it, for example, than any traditional theory of justice could possibly be. Of course, the idea of caring more for particular individuals is *most* naturally extrapolated toward the idea of a society in which everyone is always more concerned about particular individuals than about the overall good of society. But such a view lacks intuitive plausibility as an account of justice, whereas the agent-based theory we *have* been discussing does answer to much or most (though, like other theories, not all) of our intuitive thinking about justice and morality generally. The present approach sits well, then, both with an ethic of caring and with reasonable conditions on a theory of justice, and for that reason I think what we have been presenting may with some propriety be called the theory of justice *of* the ethic of caring.[24]

Of course, what has been offered in this chapter is also just the sketch of a theory, and it would require a book in itself to spell out the present sentimentalist approach to political philosophy in a thoroughly adequate manner. But I hope at least that the general form of such an approach and its distinctive way of dealing with political problems and distinctions are both now clear to the reader.

Defenders and critics of the idea of a morality of caring have worried about how any such morality could be extended to larger moral issues, but we have argued that such an extension is possible and defensible, if we regard the caring ethic as a form of agent-based virtue theory. To be sure, agent-basing is unfamiliar in the recent literature of ethics. But we have seen that such an approach

24. At least, it is a plausible candidate for that title. There have been other attempts to extrapolate from individual caring to social justice (e.g., views emphasizing the mothering relationship and social analogues of mothering); but as far as I know, such views haven't yet systematically examined the questions of individual and social morality (and their interrelations) that an overall theory of caring needs to consider. (See in particular Sara Ruddick's *Maternal Thinking: Towards a Policy of Peace* [Boston: Beacon Press, 1989].)

can deal in a plausible fashion with specific and general moral issues. And the additional fact that agent-basing can be used to undergird and fill out appealing ideas about the ethical importance of caring is a further, perhaps even a stronger, reason for taking such an approach seriously.[25]

25. It is perhaps some measure of the present-day appeal of individual and political ideals of caring that we so frequently see references in the media to "the caring society" and that a Republican presidential candidate like Bob Dole felt compelled to tell us "I am essentially a caring person and I care about America" (quoted in the *Washington Post*, February 20, 1996).

FIVE

UNIVERSAL BENEVOLENCE VERSUS CARING

We have argued that the ethic of caring is best conceived in agent-based terms and have now set out what such a view can say about the structure of individual/personal morality and about social justice. I said earlier that we needed such an account of caring if we were to compare the merits of partialist and impartialist forms of sentimentalist (or warm) agent-basing; and I also suggested that it was easier to formulate (and understand the implications of) an agent-based morality of universal benevolence than to do so with a partialistic morality of caring. The reason, in part, lies with the greater (structural) simplicity of impartialistic views and with the fact—whatever its cause—that a certain impartialist view, utilitarianism, has been elaborated in a more thoroughgoing philosophical manner than anything (I am aware of) that has been done for partialistic views like the morality of caring. In any event, though we said a substantial amount in chapter i about the character of agent-based morality as universal benevolence, we need to say a bit more about that view in what follows. In particular, I think we need to consider how such a view differs from another form of impartial agent-basing we haven't yet considered, namely an ethic of universal or agapic Christian love. Once we have seen why a warm agent-based morality of universal benevolence is superior to one of universal love, I shall go on to explore how the former approach can also deal with political issues of law and justice. We shall next consider a problem that challenges *both* partial *and* impartial sentimentalist accounts of justice: the question whether good (overall) motives like love and humanitarian concern can't lead religious and ideological fanatics to perpetrate gross forms of injustice. Then, finally, we shall come back to the crucial question of whether we should prefer a partial or an impartial approach to agent-based virtue ethics.

1. Universal Benevolence and Universal Love

As we saw earlier, morality as universal benevolence regards actions as right or morally permissible if they reflect or express a motive that is close enough to universal, that is, impartial, benevolence.[1] Such a view treats universal benevolence as in itself (and apart from its consequences) the morally best of motives, and it morally assesses actions in terms of the motives (or overall motivation) they reflect, exhibit, or express (I see no reason at this point to distinguish among these last three notions).

However, given the argument of chapter 3, it is perhaps no longer clear whether morality as universal benevolence really is some kind of internal analogue of direct (or act-) utilitarianism. That is because morally acceptable benevolence seems intuitively to entail or involve "deontological dispositions," and this assumption moves morality as universal benevolence away from utilitarianism. Moreover, since utilitarianism itself often invokes universal benevolence and holds, in particular, that acts are right if they would be approved or chosen from the standpoint of such benevolence, familiar, antideontological forms of the principle of utility will perhaps have to disassociate or detach themselves from the moral psychology of benevolence. This may well weaken direct utilitarianism as a philosophical position, given the way direct utilitarianism has in the past appealed to (the moral psychology of) universal benevolence. But in any event a virtue-ethical agent-based morality as universal benevolence is probably more complicated than we assumed earlier, and that fact needs

1. To simplify the discussion, I shall not specifically consider whether universal benevolence is best conceived in "person-affecting" terms. (See Derek Parfit's *Reasons and Persons* [Oxford: Oxford University Press, 1984], pp. 386f.)

to be noted. However, deontology is part of our intuitive sense of moral right and wrong, and to the extent morality as universal benevolence incorporates it, it may be in a better or stronger position than it otherwise would be.

But in chapter 3, we also spoke of the deontological character of morally approvable love and defended a conception of morality, a morality of caring, that gives love a special place. The assumption was that we love only certain people and are morally permitted to care more about the welfare of those near and dear to us than about the welfare of people we neither know nor love. This assumes we aren't going to love absolutely everyone, but I would like now for us to consider what would happen if we advocated an (agent-based virtue) ethic of universal love. In other words, morality as universal benevolence assumes that it is admirable (and presumably feasible) to have strong and equal concern for all human beings (and/or sentient creatures). But concern is not the same thing as love, as the example of humanitarian concern was supposed to show in chapter 3; so the issue can then be raised why we shouldn't think of universal love, rather than universal (humanitarian) benevolence, as the morally best of motives and why we shouldn't evaluate actions in relation to universal love, rather than universal benevolence. (Universal love, like universal benevolence, involves equal love for everyone and in that sense is an impartial sentiment.)

The idea of an ethic of universal love is more than a little reminiscent of what Christianity says about (agapic) love. However, although Chapter 1 mentioned some reasons for wondering whether various historical versions of the Christian ethic of love are really agent-based, the morality of universal love I would like to consider here is free of any appeal to theological assumptions (about God's goodness or lovingness or commands) and can be stipulated to be agent-based. We then have to consider whether love should be regarded as the morally best or highest of motives, and it will help us here to compare universal love with (the theoretically rival warm motive of) universal benevolence.

We saw earlier that love "thinks" in balanced terms, whereas humanitarian concern for people is aggregative. And there is some tendency in at least some of us to think of love toward an individual as a more admirable attitude to take than a (mere) humanitarian concern that treats that individual as fungible with others. When we love someone, our concern for them remains separate from other concerns and in that measure is more *particular(izing)* (or in some sense more *personal*) than sheer humanitarianism, and it is no accident in this regard that Christianity thinks of God's attitude toward us as particularizing (or personal) in this fashion: he is said to love us as his children. (Indeed, in order to do full justice to this aspect of God's, and ideal Christian, love, and given the argument of chapter 3, we really have to reverse the parable of the lost sheep or at least invent a new "parable of the safe sheep" in which a shepherd or God remains concerned with a single safe sheep even while worrying about ninety-nine sheep that are lost.)

Now it could be argued, as against the above, that God is capable of loving everyone in a way that ordinary humans aren't. But such a reply is two-edged, to say the least, because it seems to concede that Christian love is *more ideal* than any warm attitude (whether of balanced caring or of aggregative partiality or of universal benevolence) that involves a more aggregating attitude toward (some) people and thus leaves itself open to the objection, or countersuggestion, that human beings at least ought to *try* to love everyone in a nonaggregating or balanced way. Interestingly enough, Nel Noddings makes a suggestion very similar to this in her book *Caring*. She urges us to extend the circle of caring beyond those we already care about to strangers and others we don't (yet) know, and since she doesn't want to talk about humane or humanitarian caring for people we don't know, she presumably wants us to have a particular or personal concern for more and more people. And this is somewhat similar to the idea of trying to love everyone.

But (again) can one really love everyone and is this really something we should want or admire? Let me begin with the obvious. It doesn't seem possible to love someone one doesn't know, so even if an omniscient deity can love us all (as her children), it doesn't seem possible for any human being to love all other people. Still, we could try to love as many people as possible or, at least, more people than, at any given time, we do, and so we now need to consider whether such an enterprise makes sense or is morally admirable.

There is or seems to be something very beautiful in the idea of extending to everyone the love one feels to certain particular individuals, but consider this. If a person loves his family and friends, but is constantly looking for other people to become (equally) intimate with, won't the friends and family he already has feel slighted by this? Picture a family where there are already five children and the parents tell their offspring that they want to have another child. Won't the already existent children feel hurt—and to some degree cheated of love—as a result? Won't they ask "aren't we (good) enough for you?" and won't there, really, be reason for them to ask that question?

But the Christian or follower of Noddings may ask, isn't this jealousy a feeling that we shouldn't encourage? Surely, jealousy is a less than ideal emotion, and so, the argument might go, there is something wrong with the attitudes of those who complain in the situations I have just described. But I disagree, or at least such an argument is far from obviously correct. What if the desire to have yet another child or friend is in some sense untrue to the love the parent or friend is supposed to feel? The reactions of the children and friends may not indicate (merely) jealousy, but a real sense that the person involved loves them less or less fully than they had thought (or hoped). If there can be proper pride, perhaps too there can be such a thing as proper filial jealousy (just as we tend to acknowledge the propriety of some sorts of spousal jealousy). And so I would say that if a person involved in loving relationships with family, spouse (or significant other), and friends feels impelled to extend the circle of such intimate concern to strangers, that may well *derogate* from those relationships and from the love the person already has or is supposed to have.[2] Fungible, humanitarian concern for everyone of the sort praised by morality as universal benevolence is not subject to these criticisms and so (apart from other criticism we haven't yet mentioned) such a view seems preferable to one based in universal love. Universal humanitarianism seems more feasible than universal love, and the effort to extend love as far as possible may actually be inconsistent with (the spirit of) love. So, having said as much, I think we should now consider how morality as universal benevolence can ground a theory of social and legal justice.

2. For somewhat similar ideas, see Michael Stocker, *Plural and Conflicting Values*, Oxford, 1990, esp. pp. 313–14. Note too the similarity of the complaints of a child whose parents want (yet) another child and a child whose actual sibling gets a lopsided amount of attention from the parents.

2. The Justice of Universal Benevolence

We can understand the political implications of morality as universal benevolence if we help ourselves to some of the methods and analogies employed in chapter 4. In particular, we can evaluate institutions and laws as expressions of those who create and/or sustain (and/or administer) them, just as acts are assessed in terms of what motivation *they* express; and, using that criterion, we can say that institutions and laws are just when and only when they reflect or express motivation that is sufficiently close to universal benevolence on the part of (enough of) the relevant people. A society, as a group of people, can then be said to be just if and only if those people have good enough motives, just as a person is said to be morally good (or just?), according to an agent-based theory, if her motivation is good enough. So we end up with the view that a just society is one whose inhabitants or citizens are sufficiently benevolent toward humankind.[3] Like utilitarianism (and the justice of caring), this makes people outside a given society relevant to the justice of a given society, but unlike utilitarianism, justice is assessed not in terms of effects on people, but on the basis of motives (that seek good effects). This yields different judgments about justice from those that come out of a utilitarian standard of justice.

For utilitarianism, if a motive like (capitalistic) greed has very good trickle-down effects *but no one knows this or cares about it*, then we have a just society. By contrast, morality as universal be-

---

3. Something like this view can be found in Percy Shelley's "Essay on Christianity" (reprinted in *The Necessity of Atheism and Other Essays* [Buffalo, N.Y.: Prometheus, 1993]). Shelley argues that social justice should be understood in terms of Christian love (among the members of a given society), but assumes that such love is aggregative in the manner of utilitarian benevolence. Interestingly, the idea that the moral goodness of citizens' motives is important to the justice of a given society is also defended by G. A. Cohen in "Incentives, Inequality, and Community" (reprinted in S. Darwall, ed., *Equal Freedom* [Ann Arbor: University of Michigan, 1995], pp. 331–97). Cohen doesn't, however, say that motivation is the *only* thing relevant to social justice, though it is possible, I think, to see some of his arguments as a kind of halfway house on the road to an agent-based view of justice.

In addition, human rights can also be conceived in agent-based terms, but there is no need to discuss this here. For such discussion, see my "Virtue Ethics and Democratic Values," *Journal of Social Philosophy* 24, 1993, esp. pp. 15f., 24f.

nevolence when applied to questions of justice will naturally hold that a society where people are greedy is, morally speaking, less just than a society where people are attempting to help one another and thus are motivated by motives closer to universal benevolence. Here I think morality as universal benevolence comes closer to capturing what we intuitively want to say about such cases than utilitarianism does.

Of course, if universally benevolent people learn from economists that their attempts to help others (via progressive taxation and/or welfare) are doomed to failure and are even counterproductive, they will stop trying to help. But far from showing (as utilitarians assume) that universal benevolence could in some situations be a morally bad or indifferent motive, such examples at most indicate that morally good benevolence can sometimes to some extent be *stymied*. Thus morality as universal benevolence will want to distinguish between a less just society where greed unintentionally produces good results and a more just society where, given conceivable knowledge of economic factors, benevolence impels people to refrain from interfering with the operation of the market (and similar good results occur). And surely the latter society does seem juster than the former—even if utilitarianism seems incapable of capturing such distinctions.

The ideals of justice that develop out of morality as universal benevolence can also handle the problems we spoke of in connection with the justice of caring in chapter 4. It can speak to issues about the exploitation of workers, about inequalities in the family, about the possibility of disproportionately harsh laws, etc., all in terms very similar to those employed earlier, and I will not rehearse these issues here.[4] What I do want to consider, however, is an objection

4. It is sometimes said that an ethics based in sentiment cannot account for our moral and political obligations because " 'ought' implies 'can' " rules out any general obligation, e.g., to love or feel strong concern for people. But if an ethics of love or humane concern only obligates us not to act in ways that *reflect* a lack of love or concern, then these worries are misplaced and such ethics can indeed function as a total theory of morality. Even in situations where mutual love and/or concern are absent, legislators are *capable* of doing their homework about the potential effects of legislation and of passing laws that in no way reflect their lack of these sentiments. (In most circumstances this will require them to pass laws that help people.) This is all that a warm agent-based view need require of them in the name of justice, so despite claims to the contrary (see, e.g., Jerome Schneewind, ''The Misfortunes of

to agent-basing that can be directed both at partialistic and at impartialistic accounts of social morality and justice. It can be wondered whether warm motives/sentiments like universal benevolence, love, and balanced caring don't in some political contexts lead to glaring injustices, and certainly if the sentiments we have been discussing cannot prevent injustice, they can hardly form the exclusive basis for an adequate large-scale treatment of individual and social morality. So let us now consider, in greater detail, the objection that I have just mentioned.

3. Humanitarianism and Religious Belief

Recent defenders of liberal/Kantian approaches to social justice have frequently assumed or presupposed that natural feelings like love or compassion can cut against the grain of social justice. Natural feelings, in Hume's sense, are feelings that are not based in assumptions about social or individual morality in the way that a sense of justice and ordinary conscientiousness presumably are. And recent Kantians (including Kantian contractarians) have held not only that natural feeling cannot by itself account for what we think about social justice, but also that such feeling has a tendency to undermine justice under the conditions of modern life.

One example of such Kantian thinking is to be found in the widespread belief that adherents of (particular sects or branches of) religions like Christianity may seek to impose their faith on others and deny freedom of worship (or nonworship) to others on the basis of the very love and concern for (the well-being of) others that Christianity advocates. After all, or so the argument goes, (one or another sect or branch of) Christianity believes that our salvation, and thus our own ultimate or long-term well-being, depends on having the proper beliefs and adhering to the proper religious practices, so if the (sectarian) Christian loves her fellow humans and is thus deeply concerned for their welfare, she will have every reason to impose her religion on others and prevent their practicing a false faith.

Virtue," *Ethics* 101, 1990, pp. 42–63), such an ethics can function as a criterion of political obligation and just political action even under the conditions of conflict and divided loyalty (much less uncertain concern for others) that exist in modern societies.

But liberals—and other defenders of democratic values—think that such an imposition violates the deepest canons of justice. If justice has any use or validity at all, it must enable us, rather, to maintain peace and toleration among different religions or religious sects (or other groups) within a single state or society, and recent Kantian liberals have generally agreed that justice must contain or involve an ideal or ideals of impartiality or disinterestedness that can enable us—despite the heat of natural feelings—to avoid religious wars and religious intolerance and find a modus vivendi that is acceptable to all members of a pluralistic or religiously divided society. And this is precisely what religious feeling and sectarianism—despite the best of humane or compassionate motives—is thought to threaten.

We see this assumption in much of recent liberal-thinking political philosophy. Thus Thomas Nagel in *Equality and Partiality* treats it as a major task of political philosophy to find a way to rule out the imposition of faith by adherents who are concerned with the well-being and salvation of those whose freedom they mean to limit.[5] And many religious Christians may well agree that Christianity stands in this way opposed to the liberal or secular state, while disagreeing with liberals or secularists about whether it would be a bad thing or unjust for them to try to impose (their brand of) Christianity on society or the state.

But something, I think, has gone wrong here. It is not really as clear as Nagel and others have imagined that love or concern about the good of others *would* lead religious Christians (or adherents of other religions) to try to limit the religious freedom of others in the ways we have seen attempted both historically and in the present day. And though this last statement will perhaps awaken a sympathetic response in the reader all on its own, I hope, in what follows, to offer you some articulated reasons why we should not assume that Christian love and secular benevolence or caring pose a threat to the secular liberal or democratic state.

What then follows, or would follow, is rather interesting. Those who have sought, on grounds of justice, to limit the influence of religious faith and religious feeling in the public sphere may end up

---

5. See Thomas Nagel's *Equality and Partiality* (New York: Oxford University Press, 1991), pp. 154–68.

with fewer intellectual (and practical) problems than they have supposed. Thomas Nagel is at great pains to show us that controversial religious assumptions ought to be barred from public debate or influence, but that *other* controversial assumptions and beliefs can, ought, and indeed must play a role in contemporary public life. But such fine distinctions may not be necessary, if true religious and humanitarian feeling is actually self-limiting in respect to nonbelievers and general public policy. We could then allow that other controversial points of view may have a valid role in our public life, without fearing that this might somehow permit or justify intolerant religious interference in that life.

But although the conclusion about self-limitation, if correct, will help the liberal and others to justify barring religions from imposing themselves over the public sphere, it is not ultimately favorable, I think, to the Kantian/impartialist defense of liberalism that has in recent decades been the main source of its intellectual support. If a religious faith involving love or strong humanitarianism wouldn't seek to impose itself on others or in the public sphere, then a Kantian/impartialist view of public reasons and reasoning isn't *necessary* to the vindication or justification of modern-day public secularism or, arguably, of liberalism itself. And if non-Kantian agent-based sentimentalist accounts of public or social justice can, therefore, justify the contemporary liberal-democratic state as well as more familiar views do, that will certainly redound to their credit.

So why do I think that Christian love and strong humanitarianism do not pose a threat to the liberal or secular state? For reasons of space, the argument will have to be somewhat schematic or sketchy, but I do think there are some aspects of Christian love in particular that have been underplayed or ignored by those who fear its influence on the state or society, and once we recognize these, we may have to revise our easy assumption that unchecked Christianity and other systematic forms of ''warm'' sentiment run counter to justice. The attempt to show that Christian love and the concern for other people are no threat to nonbelievers will proceed in three stages. I want first to discuss some circumstances where it might *not* be unjust for religionists to impose a particular religion on others. I will then say something about why—at least in the circumstances of contemporary life—someone who already had a strong humanitarian concern about the well-being of other people would be strongly motivated *not* to acquire belief in a Christian faith that threatens nonbelievers with eternal damnation. Finally, and to complete the picture, I shall argue that the attempt to impose a particular religion—in salient historical instances and in the present day—itself bespeaks a failure of Christian love and humane concern.

To begin with, then, it needs to be pointed out that not every situation in which people aren't allowed religious freedom is obviously unjust. Widely recognized human rights can sometimes be trumped by conditions of national, community, or family emergency—for example, in wartime or when there is the threat of some natural disaster. And I think we can all conceive—imagine—situations where refusal to grant religious liberty is a reasonable and not an unjust response to a dire emergency. Such an emergency would, in fact, exist, if a group of people acquired real evidence—strong, empirical, shareable, publicly verifiable evidence—that the universe was governed by a being who damned for all eternity anyone who refused to worship in a certain way, and in such circumstances it might well *not* be unjust for those people to deny religious freedom to others who had no access to the evidence or (irrationally) refused to believe it secondhand, if they did so out of concern for the well-being of those others. Similarly, if a being announced his power over the universe, proved that s/he had such power, and gave us reason to believe that s/he would destroy our species or country if anyone ever again ate a tomato, laws forbidding the eating of tomatoes and backed by the severest penal sanctions might easily be just, and the clarity of the present example, where no one proposes to deny anyone their religious liberties (I assume we are not talking of any cult of the tomato), may well make it easier to see the point of our previous example, where the justice of denying religious liberties *is* the issue.

What the typical modern-day liberal fears, I believe, is *not* the above sorts of interference with freedom; for such a liberal doesn't hold that the kind of situations just described—where there is scientifically or evidentially forceful, non-question-begging reason to believe in a certain kind of deity—is at all likely to (have) occur(red). What they tend to fear, rather—and what they seem mainly concerned to condemn as unjust—is religionists' imposing religious uniformity in circumstances like today's: where there is no generally accepted evidence for God or ''miracles'' or any particular religious view and where it is known that people disagree strongly about the validity and/or reasonableness of various religious beliefs. But I want to argue that in these present-day circumstances people who love or are strongly concerned with the good of their fellow human beings would have strong reason to resist belief in a God who condemns those who do not worship in a certain way to eternal damnation and would, in any event and in addition, not impose their views forcibly on others.

Love is not some isolated mental atom, but logically connects with thoughts, dispositions, desires, and other emotions in ways that have become increasingly well-charted since the days of Ryle and Wittgenstein.[6] No one can be said to love another or to be very concerned for their well-being if they aren't pleased by (an increased chance of) the other's happiness, and if they aren't made unhappy by their actual or likely unhappiness. The greater the love and concern, the greater these emotional reactions are apt to be, and given, for example, the myth but also the realities of "mother love," we are not at that surprised to hear (as in Arthur Miller's "All My Sons" but certainly in real life as well) of a mother who, years after her soldier son is reported missing in action, thinks he is still alive somewhere and may "walk through the front door" at any moment.

Someone who cares greatly about the well-being, the fate, of other people will surely be disturbed and unhappy at the thought that a large segment of humankind, indeed most of the people in the world, are going to suffer everlastingly.[7] Now if the person with such feeling doesn't *yet* believe in Christian doctrines about salvation and damnation, she will not at that point have the sort of reason to seek a state ban on other religions that, as we have seen, is so often ascribed to the religious. And it is interesting to consider whether or how easily she can *acquire* such beliefs. Is there some

6. In *A Theory of Justice* (pp. 485ff.), John Rawls describes some interesting connections between love and justice, pointing out, for example, that if one loves someone, one is bound to be indignant at (the injustice of) someone's needlessly hurting that person. But Rawls also thinks that love or benevolence toward all human beings doesn't suffice for justice (pp. 190f.), and the present discussion will attempt to criticize that assumption.

7. Our argument here will remain agnostic about how easy it is for people to be strongly concerned about all other human beings. I am also assuming that it is fairly obvious that most of the people alive in the world at a given time are not going to be converted to (some particular sect of) Christianity (or any other one religion).

understandable way such a person could come to believe in Christian doctrines about salvation while continuing to love or at least be strongly concerned about all human beings?

Remember the loving mother who refuses to believe her son dead. Not all loving mothers, fathers, or spouses are like this, of course, but all do have a strong motive to resist belief in the death of a loved one. Does this mean they are irrational, epistemically irrational? Perhaps it does, but love is, after all and by way of exaggeration, supposed to be blind—or at least less (more?) than objective and impartial. Someone who loves or really cares about another shouldn't be as ready to believe the worst of them as someone who takes a more detached attitude—and it is not just a question of the person who loves or cares knowing the person better and having reason to discount evidence that points to the worst that a more objective or detached observer will simply lack. The love and concern themselves will (in different degrees) make the person resist a negative intepretation of the same evidence that a more detached observer would say pointed to misfeasance, disloyalty, weakness, or inadequacy on the part of the person one loves or cares a great deal about. This phenomenon has been pointed out and discussed by others—and there has been some question as to whether the resistance to thinking the worst is rational or irrational on the part of the person who loves or cares. But whether rational or not, the phenomenon itself is real enough, and it is similar to what we can readily see to be the influence of love and caring on beliefs about the state of happiness or suffering of someone we love or care about.

Just as these feelings/motives can make one unwilling to believe bad things about someone's character or deeds, it can make one reluctant to believe that bad things are likely to *happen* to that person. Indeed, I would go so far as to say that someone who doesn't have these tendencies doesn't fully love or care about a given person. Impartiality, a lack of partisanship, just isn't the way of genuine love and caring;[8] and if—perhaps a big "if"—that means that these

---

8. In saying that love and concern for people are partisan, I don't mean that the latter entails preferring some people to others. Someone with strong (equal) benevolence toward everyone will be partisan only in the sense that s/he will want or tend to think more highly and more optimistically about each person that the evidence (as it would appear to an emotionally detached individual) would epistemically warrant.

feelings are or make us epistemically irrational, so be it. Some will say that that is a reason to try to avoid strong feelings, but others may be content to say that some important human goods depend on being irrational in certain ways. And there is the alternative possibility, defended by Adam Morton, that the influence of certain strongly positive feelings on our beliefs shouldn't be considered irrational as such.[9]

But independently of issues about rationality and irrationality, what we have just said gives us the beginnings of the argument we are looking for. A person who really wants and is concerned to promote the well-being of another will resist the assumption or conclusion that that person is in trouble or unhappy or doomed— whether the issue be one of wartime injury or one of eternal damnation. So how—in the circumstances of modern life—is someone who has strong concern for her fellow humans going to acquire belief in a religion that relegates nonbelievers to hell-fire and damnation?

In those circumstances, we are assuming, there are no publicly verifiable miracles, no uncontroversial arguments for (one) religion (over another), and although some people today may live in sufficient isolation to be ignorant of those very facts, of what I am calling the circumstances of modern life, *such people pose no direct threat to religious freedoms of the liberal democratic state*. Any group that does pose such a threat will need a sophisticated knowledge of technology and science and will obviously have to know about the religious differences that characterize modern times and trigger that very threat. So even if people in isolation might (think they) have acquired special knowledge of particular religious truths, it is more

---

9. See Adam Morton's discussion of this and related issues in "Partisanship," in *Perspectives on Self-Deception*, ed. B. McLaughlin and A. Rorty (Berkeley: University of California Press, 1988), pp. 170–82. Note too—and this complicates our discussion above—that someone whose love or concern makes him somewhat reluctant to think that bad things are happening or going to happen to someone *may have reasons derived from his love or concern to try to counteract that very tendency*. Knowing that (my) love or concern inherently involves such reluctance but realizing too, say, that I am responsible for the well-being of my (physically or mentally challenged) child, I may have reason to force myself to be alert to possible problems and dangers for that child and, more generally, to work against my feelings' tendency toward wishful thinking. But no one ever said that caring about others—or the moral life—was simple or easy.

relevant for us to consider whether people who are concerned with their fellow humans and are also aware of modern-day circumstances might come to believe in the doctrine of eternal damnation. And it is more relevant because the main theoretical/ethical issue our sentimentalist approach is now facing is whether (a group of) loving or caring people might deliberately undermine or undercut the modern liberal state and unjustly deprive people of their (right to) religious freedom.

In modern circumstances, there isn't any uncontroversial *evidence* or *argument* for the doctrine of damnation, anything that someone not committed to or eager for faith would likely find convincing, and, for the reasons mentioned above, a real humanitarian will hardly be eager for—or be impelled by wishful thinking toward— a faith that condemns so many to infinite unhappiness and pain. In that case, such a person is likely to stay with ordinary, intuitive modes of thought and evidence rather than feel the need to make a leap to such a faith. By the same token, those who do believe in religion often defend their faith by questioning (the necessity of) the standards of inference and self-evidence that the nonreligious make use of. And given the will to believe, the desire to have or maintain faith, it frequently happens that such ordinary standards of thought *are* rejected. That rejection is motivated by strong feeling, namely, preexistent religious faith (or desire for faith).

But if such feeling and commitment can lead to a rejection of the (otherwise) intuitively appealing modes or standards of ordinary thinking, then it seems even more likely that those who are genuinely concerned about and devoted to the happiness or welfare of others will reject the unusual modes of inference that are required for the attainment of belief or faith in the doctrine of damnation. Ordinary, secular modes of thought are (apart from the influence of strong feeling) more *intuitively plausible* than the special logic or inferences that religion sometimes insists upon, so if religious commitment or desire can lead us to accept what goes, so to speak, against the grain of plausible thinking, then it should be much easier for a caring individual to *resist* doctrines that go against the grain of such thinking.[10]

---

10. The reader may wonder, at this point, whether I haven't forgotten love's tendency to panic. A parent who loves a child may want and tend to think well of her prospects, but if the child goes off in a bus on a school picnic, and news of a fatal accident involving a school bus later comes over the radio or television, won't

Thus even if a person aware of contemporary circumstances had an experience in which a being purporting to be God told her about damnation and salvation, she would have reason to resist that message, and some of the reasons for disbelief are familiar from Christian thought itself. Priests sometimes tell their parishioners that any dream (or other message-bearing experience) that purports to be, say, from the Virgin, but in which the Virgin tells them to do something that goes against Christian morals is to be treated as false or illusory rather than as a revelation. Given, moreover, the knowledge that many, many others would (think they had reason to) doubt the evidential force of the experience purporting to be about damnation and salvation, I think someone who had such an experience would remain pretty skeptical about it. (For such a person to reject out of hand the doubts of others would be to display an arrogance that, as I shall be arguing below, is not compatible with really caring about the well-being of other people.) So I do not yet see a route, in modern conditions, from strong concern for others to the doctrine of damnation and thence to a threatened injustice that stems from concern for people's (ultimate) welfare.

However, the reader may want to remind me, at this point, of the way in which children acquire religious faith or commitment. They believe the vague or incomplete statements their parents initially make to them, let us say, and then later presumably realize that the faith they are committed to condemns most of humanity to damnation. But when and how does humanitarian concern for people come into existence? It is not easy to imagine it already present full-blown in early childhood when children are given their first formal or informal religious instruction, and if a child who acquired a simple faith and learned to care about all human beings were *then* told

some loving parents tend to imagine/fear/think the worst? Absolutely! But if further information isn't available for hours, wishful, hopeful thinking will also occur in such a parent (e.g., they may bargain with God). Hopefulness will tend to reverse or counteract the initial panic, and at the very least one doesn't expect a loving parent, in the absence of further information, to settle into the firm belief that their child is dead. (This *might* happen if a parent were clinically depressed, but doesn't depression interfere with a person's capacity to love and care about others, to get outside himself?) So a universally caring person might panic upon first hearing of the Christian doctrine of damnation, but at the very least strong doubt about such a doctrine would tend to (re)assert itself in such a person, and that would be especially true, if, as we have assumed, the panic-inducing doctrine can't be supported by epistemically plausible reasons.

that her religion also believed in the saved and the damned, wouldn't she then resist that religion (the way children who come to like animals *start resisting* the idea of eating them)?

But, you may say, if the child is afraid of letting down her parents, then she is likely to go along with the further and less attractive features of their religion, once she learns of them, and couldn't a whole group of people raised in this way and aware of modern conditions pose a threat to religious liberties? Yes, probably so. But this fact is completely consistent with the view I am defending. The strong desire to please one's parents and keep their love might indeed lead a child subliminally to accept a belief in damnation. But such a strong desire is precisely incompatible with a strong concern for all human beings. Someone who (already) cared enough about (the fate of) humanity wouldn't be *predominantly* worried about his or her own comfort, wouldn't be as self-centered as the child eager to please her parents. Someone *not* so self-centered, someone with strong *larger* concerns would not only, I think, be shocked by his parents' or priest's introduction of the idea of damnation, but would resist what they were saying. Not to do so would be a criterial sign of a lack of (Christian or humane) universal concern and of the presence, rather, of the sort of narrow or self-centered concerns that Christianity is supposed to counter or do away with.

Perhaps the reader can think of a way to overcome all these difficulties, but, finding that I cannot, I am led tentatively to the conclusion that there is no clear way in which modern-day people who already really cared about all people could come to believe in certain Christian doctrines. But we must now take the next step in our argument and try to determine whether there is any incompatibility between a (sectarian) Christian faith that seeks to stifle or threaten nonadherents and the universal love or concern for people that is thought to lie at the heart of Christianity.[11]

11. The references in this section to the circumstances of modern life will understandably remind the reader of John Rawls's *Political Liberalism* (New York: Columbia University Press, 1993), and the present argument to a certain extent shadows and draws upon Rawls's view, while at the same time, however, and as I indicated above, it opposes Rawls's general skepticism about justice based in sentiment.

4. Humanitarianism and Intolerance

We have argued that already existent humanitarianism doesn't give belief in the doctrine of damnation much of a place to grow, but it has not yet been shown that concern for all people and belief in damnation cannot come to coexist in some other way, though I have, and I hope the reader already has, doubts about such a possibility. But there is also something suspicious in the idea that belief in the eternal damnation of nonbelievers could lead one, on the basis of Christian love, to stifle their religious freedom or force them to convert. The conviction that one's own religion is so far superior to others' that its doctrines give one good reason not to tolerate other religions is really, after all, rather arrogant.

A person who really loves another or takes that person's interests to heart will be sympathetic with the point of view of that other, rather than viewing herself as the superior of that other or acting arrogantly in relation to that other. And the refusal to tolerate (the practice of) other religions—except, perhaps, where it is just an exercise of power—is a *form of arrogance toward, of assumed superiority over, those not tolerated.* Therefore, I would question whether it really is possible to love or care about humankind and at the same time seek to convert people by force or limit their religious freedom.

A Kantian might say that the use of force would manifest a lack of *respect* for those one sought to coerce.[12] But it seems just as plausible to say that the use of force betrays an arrogant sense of one's own superiority that is simply incompatible with strong *love and concern* for people. However, a clarification is called for at this point because, after all, parents don't give their children much choice about morals or religion (or household duties), and there seems to be no consequent lack of love. It is not arrogant to think one knows more than one's children, and any sense of superiority good parents have is presumably compatible with the highest love. Why, then, must we assume that religious "paternalism" has to be different?

But children's lack of moral and religious knowledge is simply a *fact*, whereas the assumption that the adult adherents of other religions or sects are one's inferiors in those central aspects of human

---

12. See Joshua Cohen, "An Epistemic Conception of Democracy," *Ethics* 97, 1986, pp. 26–38.

existence betrays arrogance and a lack of sympathetic concern for others. To be sure, "advanced" civilizations have confronted "primitive" ones and sought to impose their religion by force. But if the evidence for advanced status is supposed to be superior weaponry or scientific knowledge, isn't it arrogantly paternalistic to assume, and act on the assumption, that such superiority automatically translates into moral and religious superiority? Would anyone who loved or greatly cared about another make such quick inferences and snap judgments or decisions?[13]

Moreover, even if we were willing to grant that certain religions are superior morally or as religions to others, the person who in modern circumstances seeks to establish a state religion and proscribe all other worship (as well as the agnostic or atheist's refusal to worship) isn't just thinking his religion superior to "primitive" religions but, so to speak, to all comers (including any that might emerge in the future). And this attitude also means intolerance of atheists, whose position, however else it may be regarded, is not generally thought of as *primitive*. Atheism may be dangerously sophisticated or sophistical, but it is not *naive* or *childlike*, and in such nonprimitive cases, the analogy with children and childhood breaks down and the case for arrogance is pretty clear. Those who think religious persecution and repression compatible with Christian love or caring concern for others have simply failed to notice how these concepts interact with the notion of arrogance.[14] By the same token, some (though hardly all) paternalistic legislation reflects real arrogance on the part of legislators, the electorate, or some power elite and would be condemned, on our account, for similar reasons. To that extent, what we are saying clearly favors liberalism and (a desire to preserve) autonomous decision-making.

13. The kind of paternalism most of us find objectionable involves a disregard of other people's own sense of what is good for them. But to impose things on others without attempting, sympathetically, to understand their beliefs and values, is arrogant and shows a failure of caring concern.

14. There are also arrogant ways of trying to *persuade others noncoercively* of the truth of one's (religious) beliefs, and a caring individual will presumably not feel arrogant or "superior" about people and views she disagrees with and wishes to argue against. Cf. Amy Gutmann and Dennis Thompson, "Moral Conflict and Political Consensus," *Ethics* 101, 1990, pp. 64–88 (esp. p. 76).

In addition, and this begins a new part of our argument, those who think Christian love and caring might lead to religious repression have also failed to notice certain interrelations among (the concepts of) caring, religious intolerance, and prejudice. As we saw earlier, someone who cares about another person is predisposed in favor of that person. One wants to think the best one can of someone one really cares about, so if those who want to exclude other religions have a tendency (or desire) to think of the differences between their own religion and other religions as very much to the disadvantage of the others, they arguably lack caring's tendency to see good in those one strongly cares about, a tendency which, when there are differences between oneself and a person one cares about, *translates into a tendency (or desire) to put those differences in the best possible light.*

For example, parents of the professional class who love, say, their daughter and have spent a great deal on her education will perhaps be surprised when she tells them one day that she wants to spend the rest of her life as a farmer in Maine. Indeed, they may at first attempt to argue her out of it, and do so largely because they love her. But if they eventually (let themselves) become convinced that this is what she is likely to want over the long term, then, if they really love her, they will warm to the idea of this very different life she has chosen. Rather than seem to reflect some sort of defect or deficiency in her, their daughter's new life will be or become interesting to them, and her doing well in it (or being satisfied with it) will become a source of satisfaction to them too.[15] And something

---

15. But there are limits here. If the daughter wants to go in for Russian roulette, the parents won't warm to the idea, and paternalistic opposition to her plans will be far from arrogant or intolerant, if (they realize that) no sane, mentally undamaged adult could go in for such an activity. Here (and elsewhere) there needs to be room for what we can call "tough caring."

Incidentally, the idea that love or humanitarian concern makes one value differences has interesting connections with the Rawls/Humboldt idea of a "social union" in which each person can enjoy the distinctive benefits of participating in a larger scheme of cooperation with people who have skills and assets s/he lacks. (See Rawls, *A Theory of Justice*, pp. 520–29.) And note too that if we treasure love and caring, then Romantic ideals of passion and feeling are at least to some extent vindicated *against* the Enlightenment ideal of total openness and impartiality in all one's thinking.

like this ought to be true if one loves or cares about people who practice another religion (or are importantly different in various other ways).

The tendency to see other religious practices in a bad light, indeed as unacceptable and even revolting, indicates, then, a lack of love and caring and, moreover, the presence of prejudice. Prejudice, by its very definition, involves a disposition or tendency to think badly of someone or something independently of knowing relevant facts, and what else, then, is prejudice but an unfavorable emotional predisposition? But unfavorable emotional predisposition involves (at least) dislike or a tendency to dislike. As Jorge Garcia has forcefully argued,[16] it is a matter of the heart. But it is the heart set against someone or something, rather than, as with caring, pointed in their favor.

So I am saying that religious intolerance not only represents a failure of love and caring, but constitutes prejudice that by its nature *runs contrary* to these sentiments. What we find in religious intolerance is a predisposition to find fault and, at the very least, the lack of any tendency to find good. By its very nature, then, strongly felt concern for people cannot exist side by side with prejudice against them or with a practical attitude of intolerance. Of course, someone might argue at this point that the tendency to think ill of other religions and their practices may sometimes reflect a desire to be in the right, rather than any sort of (emotional) prejudice. But even if one were to grant this, the incompatibility with love and caring would still be evident, since the desire to be in the right *as against others* is clearly egotistical, self-centered, and even selfish.

We have now argued against the idea that loving, caring, humane people might try to impose their religion, by force if necessary, on other people. But the case, if proved, has been made without reference to any independent considerations of justice (or moral impartiality). Rather, certain feelings/motives were themselves found to be incompatible with active religious intolerance, and so the idea that a sentimentalist virtue ethics cannot account for the injustice that occurs through a group's imposing its religion on others and is inadequate for that reason is highly questionable.

16. See Jorge Garcia, "The Heart of Racism," *Journal of Social Philosophy* 26, 1996.

To be sure, we have acknowledged that in some (logically) conceivable situations it might well be *just to impose* a single religion. However, in the circumstances of modern society (or the modern state) that liberals worry about, circumstances characterized by ethnic and religious diversity and by a general disagreement about religious doctrines, it would be unjust for one group to deprive others of religious freedom, and virtue-ethical sentimentalism can explain why.[17] Such sentimentalism can also explain why certain historic attempts to impose religious uniformity were also very clearly unjust. If our view couldn't account, say, for the injustice of the Spanish Inquisition (and other such notorious attempts to limit religious freedom), it would lack credibility as a general conception of justice. But in fact when one considers the actual motives—and, to use John Locke's memorable phrase, the "dry eyes"—of the inquisitors who tortured, maimed, and killed people "for the sake of their souls," one has every reason to doubt that they were (primarily or even in most cases substantially) actuated by strong humane concern for the welfare of others, and that gives us an argument, in agent-based terms, for the conclusion that the Inquisition was (an) unjust (institution).[18]

It is also worth pointing out that if a case can be made along the above lines that caring people would not want to deprive others of their (right to practice their own) religion, then many other such presumptive civil rights may likewise be assured through sufficient humane concern for others. And the possibility then looms that all the other ingredients of (liberal) democratic justice might be assured in the same fashion.[19] Why would people who cared about other

17. Whether agent-based sentimentalist justice allows or requires a special place to be made for particular religious, ethnic, and other (minority) groups within the modern-day state is an important and complex issue that I want to leave aside for another occasion.

18. A primitive tribe may occasionally quash religious doubts or alternative religious practices, but somehow the charge of injustice and of "denying rights" seems less forceful here than in (modern) circumstances of entrenched diversity and disagreement. I am not sure I understand why this should be so, but the issue is one that Kantian, consequentialist, and sentimentalist virtue-ethical theories may all wish to consider.

19. However, agent-based (and utililitarian) views of justice leave the door potentially open to possibilities that many liberal and rights-based views would wish to preclude in all circumstances. For a concern for (human or one's compatriots')

people and their welfare *not* be willing to grant them rights of free speech and assembly, the assurance of decent work and wages, full political participation, etc.? But this vindication of (warm or senti-mentalist) agent-based virtue ethics against the suspicion that it leaves the door wide open for intolerance and injustice doesn't yet tell us which form of such agent-basing—partial or impartial—is preferable, and it is to that issue that we must now, finally, turn.

5. The Choice between Caring and Universal Benevolence

Morality (and justice) as universal benevolence is simpler, less com-plicated, than the (particular form of) caring ethic we have described and (partly) defended, but this theoretical virtue is presumably not all-decisive when it comes to choosing between moral theories, and I think caring has some strong intuitive advantages over universal benevolence. We think highly of love and tend to think less well of someone who doesn't love, say, her own children or spouse. But if loving and loving concern are morally called for in regard to people who are near and dear to one, then morality as universal benevolence has a problem, because of the way it mandates equal concern for everyone.

If one loves certain people, but not others, then, by the very nature of love, one will be more concerned about their welfare than about the welfare of those others. But we saw earlier that one can't really love people one doesn't know, so given the size of the human species and the conditions of human life as we know it, someone who loves some people will invariably be more concerned about them than about (many) other people. But this is inconsistent with

---

well-being might, in certain social conditions, lead to the legal barring, say, of a pro-Nazi march that a rights approach or liberalism might insist on allowing (there is still the question whether the freedom to express racial hatred through a public march actually is included in a maximal set of equal civil and/or political liberties/rights/powers). To that extent, justice conceived in terms of caring or in terms of universal benevolence (or in utilitarian fashion) may not deliver everything that some modern-day liberals want to justify. But it delivers enough so that we can still speak of a defense of liberalism in these terms, and perhaps *some* aspects of liberalism really should be questioned within an overall defense of modern-day democracy.

being equally concerned with everyone's well-being, and the conclusion then seems to follow that if love is morally appropriate and called for, then so too is differential concern for (other) people's well-being. (Unless morality is incoherent, but let us leave that possibility aside.) So our high moral opinion of love is inconsistent with accepting morality as universal benevolence, and I take that to constitute a strong reason to favor caring over universal benevolence.

Certainly, our ethic of caring is more complexly contoured than morality as universal benevolence, and its emphasis on a very specific idea of balance is philosophically unfamiliar. But I hope the reader has seen the intuitive moral appeal, in private or personal life, of treating particular loved ones and the whole class of those we love in a nonfungible (or one-on-one) fashion, and this would certainly then support caring, as conceived and described above, over the aggregative attitudes and treatment that morality as universal benevolence prefers in both the private and the public sphere.[20]

So I somewhat tentatively prefer the caring, partialistic mode of warm agent-based virtue ethics and will assume it from now on. Having outlined a general individual and social morality, we can use our results to address some other important questions of ethics. In the second part of this book, I hope to show you, in particular, how the previous account of morality can help us to frame an agent-based conception both of human well-being and of practical reason.

20. In "Interpersonal Virtues: Whose Interest Do They Serve?" (*American Catholic Philosophical Quarterly* 71, 1997, pp. 31–60), Jorge Garcia criticizes agent-based morality as universal benevolence for the "collective" (i.e., aggregative) way in which it treats virtuous concern for people's well-being. He argues that virtuous motivation needs to be "distributed" toward each individual *via the role relationships in which an agent stands to that individual*. In one respect, this suggestion clearly moves in the "personalistic" direction of (morality as) balanced caring. However, the idea that we are morally related to people only via roles threatens to deny a moral significance to what I have been calling humanitarian caring, i.e., concern for human beings generally. To be sure, Garcia says that each of us has a "morally constitutive role relationship" with everyone else, but the meaning of "role" in this context needs to be clarified.

PART II

Practical Rationality and Human Good

SIX

THE VIRTUE IN SELF-INTEREST

In this chapter, I will be taking the first steps toward an agent-based (what we shall eventually have reason, in fact, to call "hyper-agent-based") account of human good or well-being. In the chapter following, I will go on to develop an agent-based conception of practical reason, and the latter, along with our earlier views about agent-based morality, will make possible the further steps necessary to a fully agent-based account of well-being. For the moment, though, we shall explore some differing ways in which ideals of virtue can connect, or fail to connect, with considerations of human good. Virtue ethics offers, or can offer, a distinctive theory of such connection, but we need to place such a theory, and the motivation for it, in a wider context of possibilities.

As a motive, self-interest is constituted by a certain kind of concern for oneself, but we also use the term "self-interest" to refer to the object of such a motive, to the well-being or good life sought for herself by a self-interested agent. In this chapter, I want to concentrate on self-interest in the latter sense and say something about how self-interest or well-being relates to virtue. One reason to be interested in this relationship stems from our concern to know whether virtue pays, that is, is in the moral agent's self-interest, a question Plato notably asks in the *Republic* and that has been of concern to moral philosophers ever since. But the importance for ethics of notions like virtue and self-interest is hardly exhausted by their role in the debate over whether virtue pays, and indeed any large-scale ethical theory will presumably have something to say about how these major notions relate. So we have reason to want to understand this relationship independently of the particular desire to show that morality or virtue is in the self-interest of the (virtuous) agent.

Moreover, it will also be assumed here that some ways of connecting virtue and well-being/self-interest redound to the advantage of the larger theories that incorporate them. If, in particular, we believe in the bona fides of ethical *theory*, then unifying power is a desideratum in ethics and it stands in favor of utilitarianism (and epicureanism) that, as we shall see, it offers us a way of unifying our understanding of virtue and well-being. To be sure, that advantage may to some extent or ultimately be dissipated if unification leads to unintuitive ethical consequences. But if theory is appropriate in ethics, then utilitarianism stands to gain from its ability to *reduce* all notions of virtue to the coinage of well-being and self-interest.

In what follows, however, I hope to show you that the ability to unify is not unique to reductive theories like utilitarianism. Many other ethical views may be "dualistic" about the categories of virtue and self-interest and thus at an initial disadvantage vis-à-vis utilitarianism, but certain forms of virtue ethics are also capable of unifying virtue and self-interest, and what I have in mind here is not reductive virtue-ethical theories like epicureanism, but forms of virtue ethics that effect the unification in an entirely different *direction* from the way in which both utilitarianism and epicureanism proceed.

1. Unification in Utilitarianism

One of the main strengths or attractions of act-utilitarianism is that it allows for a reduction of all our ethical ideals and standards to the ethical notion of well-being or welfare. Actions count as right, roughly speaking, to the extent they bring about the greatest possible well-being. And utilitarianism also reduces other moral notions to the notion of well-being suitably supplemented by appropriate causal and other concepts. An act counts as blameworthy, for example, if the act of blaming or negatively reinforcing it will have best or good enough consequences for human or sentient well-being, and a trait counts as a virtue if it generally leads to well-being rather than its opposite. In addition, utilitarianism tends to treat terms of *rational* appraisal like "prudent," "rationally acceptable," and "good choice" as reducible to the category of personal good or well-being taken together with other, nonethical concepts (though different utilitarians effect this reduction in different ways).[1] So it is, I think, safe to say that utilitarianism reduces all prominent ethical notions to concepts of well-being or self-interest.

But then the fundamental ethical category of well-being is treated by the utilitarian as further reducible to empirical or nonethical notions like preference-satisfaction or pleasure/pain. So utilitarianism not only reduces the major concepts of ethics to a single ethical notion, but then reduces the whole realm of ethical value and evaluation to naturalistic or value-free facts. However, this unifying reduction occurs at a considerable price, since utilitarianism notoriously clashes with commonsense judgments about what is morally right or admirable. Even apart from this "price" I think we also need to be a little clearer about the character of the double reduction that utilitarianism seeks to effect.

In philosophic parlance, one kind of reduction occurs or is attempted when one seeks to understand the macro in terms of the micro (the whole in terms of its elements or parts), as, for example, when we identify salt with sodium chloride. But another form of reduction takes place when an attempt is made to understand what is "higher" in terms of what is "lower."[2] Thus when the utilitarian identifies well-being or doing well in life with pleasure or desire-fulfillment, this is plausibly regarded as a *reduction*, because the realm of value seems in some way *higher* than the merely empirical and natural (is that perhaps because it involves *standards for judging* what actually occurs or might occur in human life?). For the same reason, it makes sense to say, for example, that Freud and Adler *reduced* all higher activities and aspirations, respectively, to mere sexual strivings and desire for power.

When utilitarianism seeks to understand all rationality, virtue, and morality in terms of facts about well-being, that also counts as a reduction, because it is natural to think of the ethical category of

1. See my *From Morality to Virtue* (New York: Oxford University Press, 1992), ch. 4.

2. One can also try to reduce the number of entities or concepts one refers to or makes use of in a theory, but this notion of reduction cuts across the distinctions I am making in the text, and I shall ignore it in what follows.

well-being as in some sense *lower* than the ethical categories utilitarianism seeks to understand in terms of it. To that extent, the unification utilitarianism seeks *within* the realm of the ethical is reductive in character quite apart from the further attempt to reduce well-being (and thus all other ethical concepts as well) to naturalistic concepts, but I think we need to say a bit more about why well-being is regarded as *lower* than virtue, etc.

The first point, I think, to be made in this connection is that what counts as an element in our well-being or as good for us may in no way be admirable. For example, in the *Eudemian Ethics* (1248 b17–27) Aristotle makes the common-sense point that unlike the virtues, (sheer) health is good but not praiseworthy.[3] And a similar point can be made about pleasure and common enjoyment. These involve something good happening to us, but because they do not seem to require any virtue, rationality, or morality on our part, there seems to be nothing admirable about the capacity for and occasions of pleasure, enjoyment, or, for that matter, health.

But the distinction between what is *merely* enjoyable, pleasurable, and good (for us) and what is admirable seems to involve a distinction between lower and higher ethical values (what else can the word "merely" be doing in this sentence?). Claims about rationality, morality, and what is admirable in other spheres express *ideals*, and in becoming generous or prudent or trained in physics or philosophy, we would normally be thought to be realizing certain actual or possible ideals of character or human aspiration, in a way that enjoyment or feeling secure or a healthy constitution do not require. Of course, it is also possible to be immoral, irrational, vicious, but even these negative attributes, like their positive counterparts, seem to involve more *highly evolved* capacities than those required for well-being and its opposite. So in understanding rationality, virtue, moral goodness, and their opposites as (mere) means to well-being and its opposite, utilitarianism is reducing (what is intuitively and antecedently taken to be) the ethically higher to (what is intuitively and antecedently taken to be) the ethically lower. And to that extent utilitarianism deflates ethics internally by telling us that there is

3. Health can perhaps be thought of as praiseworthy when it is regarded as the result of prudent exercise and self-controlled dieting, as an *achievement*. But a sheer state of good health, or a healthy constitution that owes nothing to one's efforts, is presumably not praiseworthy, and this may be what Aristotle had in mind.

nothing to the apparent distinction between higher and lower ethical values, telling us that the virtue and rationality, etc., that we tend to think of as higher than mere or sheer well-being is really at the same level as (what we regard as) the lower.

But isn't this an inevitable effect of any attempt to unify the major concepts of ethics, a price we have to and should be willing to pay if we value theoretical systematization and unification highly and are willing to pay the price of rejecting many of our ethical intuitions? I think not. There is another mode of intraethical unification that involves just the opposite of reductionism, and it will be my main purpose here to try to demonstrate its philosophical promise. In order to understand how such a different mode of unification is possible and even plausible, we would do well first to consider the difference between Stoicism and Epicureanism.

2. Elevation versus Reduction

Epicureanism is reductive in the manner of utilitarianism, though on an (arguably) egoistic, rather than universalistic or agent-neutral, basis. What is antecedently regarded as higher is understood in terms of what is antecedently thought of as lower via its claim that practical rationality and (the) virtue(s) generally are nothing more than effective means to—and thus exist at the same level as—a person's well-being. (Like utilitarianism, Epicureanism then effects a second reduction by treating well-being as a matter simply of pleasure or, more accurately, freedom from pain.)

But if Epicureanism, like utilitarianism, assimilates the admirable and putatively higher to the desirable and putatively lower, Stoicism works in just the opposite direction, understanding the putatively lower values of well-being or self-interest in terms of the supposedly higher ones of rationality and virtue. If the term ''reduction'' is useful for conveying the first sort of assimilation, we need a convenient term for the opposite mode of assimilation or identification that Stoicism advocates, and there is none readily available in the philosophical literature. (It is quite odd that there should be no such generally available expression, since, as we shall be seeing in a moment, many kinds of theories both inside and outside ethics assimilate levels in the manner of Stoicism.) The best we can do, I think, is to say that Stoicism *elevates* human well-being to the level of human virtue/morality/rationality (unfortunately, I haven't been able to find any more idiomatic, natural, or attractive way of conveying the opposite of *both* higher/lower *and* macro/micro reduction).

For the Stoics, human well-being *consists* in being virtuous. Virtue or the virtues taken together are the sum and substance of human well-being: nothing beyond (the attainment of) rational virtue is required for us to be well-off or have good lives, and nothing that fails to improve us in virtue/rationality can be, therefore, of any real benefit. A virtuous individual bereft of wealth, friends, bodily pleasure, and good health—indeed even on the rack and in great pain— can be as well-off as it is possible to be, and so on a Stoic account human well-being is regarded very differently from the way it ordinarily is. For common sense, whether or not virtue, or various virtues, are part of a good life, certain enjoyments and activities that seem neither admirable nor the means to anything admirable are definitely seen as constituents of living well, of a good life, of personal good or well-being. But Stoicism denies the intrinsic personal goodness of so-called worldly and appetitive goods, and it doubts even the universal instrumental goodness of such things because it questions whether they usually lead to the virtue of those who enjoy them. And so the following contrasts can be drawn between the Stoic and Epicurean treatments of the relation between personal goods/ well-being and the virtues.

The Epicurean deflates our ideas about virtue and admirability by regarding the latter as simply a matter of what is conducive or not conducive to the well-being (or happiness) of individuals. What is normally seen as higher than mere personal well-being (as being, e.g., admirable in a way well-being or enjoyment isn't and/or as depending on evolutionarily higher capacities than well-being depends on) turns out, on the Epicurean account, to be of a piece with, at the same level as, facts solely about human well-being and its causes or effects.

But rather than reduce virtue/admirability to personal well-being (or happiness), the Stoic inflates or elevates our ideas about personal good (or well-being or happiness) by regarding the latter solely in terms of (what constitutes) human virtue or admirability. What is normally seen as lower than (ideas of) virtue turns out, on the Stoic account, to be of a piece with facts about virtue. And if, for the Epicurean, virtue is nothing more than a factor in personal good or happiness, then, for the Stoic, happiness and well-being are nothing *less* than virtue or virtuous living, and these contrasts should at this point make it understandable that Stoicism should be deemed a form of elevationism if Epicureanism is regarded as a form of reductionism.

But having set elevationism and reductionism at odds, I think it is important to note what they have in common. It is well-known, for example, that reductions needn't preserve meaning—"salt is sodium chloride" is not an analytic or a priori truth. Similarly, neither utilitarian nor Epicurean reductionism need claim for itself an analytic status, and the same holds true for Stoic elevationism. These are *theories*, and they can be true in the way theories are true rather than definitionally or by virtue of some form of ethical mathematics.

In addition, the idea of reducing one kind of entity or property to another is often clarified by invoking the notion of certain *distinctions* being reducible to certain others. For example, we naturally think of the mental as in some sense higher (evolutionarily and perhaps spiritually) than the purely physical, and if the mental then turns out to be reducible to the physical, then every valid mental distinction can be reduced to or identified with some distinction made in physical terms. According to such reductionism, then, where no physical distinction obtains, no distinction will (be able to) occur at the mental level either. But none of this entails that every physical distinction will be accompanied by some mentalistic one. As long as the mental is a function of the physical, the reducing relation can obtain even if no function from the mental to the physical can be found, and so, more briefly, we can characterize typical reductions of the mental to the physical as claiming that physical distinctions are *necessary but not sufficient* for the existence of mental distinctions.

By the same token, when Epicureanism (or utilitarianism) reduces virtue to well-being, it treats all distinctions of virtue as accompanied by distinctions in (causal, relational, and other) facts about individual well-being or happiness. But it need not claim that every distinction in facts about the production of well-being (distinctions, e.g., about *who* certain dispositions benefit) will be accompanied by or give rise to a distinction having to do with virtue.

Elevation can be understood in essentially similar terms. When the Stoic elevates the personally good (up) to the virtuous or admirable, he or she is committed to saying that every distinction with regard to the former can be thoroughly understood or accounted for in terms of distinctions relating to the latter, just as, when the Epicurean reduces the virtues or virtue (down) to matters of well-being, he or she is committed to saying that every distinction with regard to the former can be thoroughly understood or accounted for in terms of distinctions involving the latter. The only difference between the two processes or results lies in the respective *heights* of "the former" and "the latter" in the two cases. In elevations, distinctions with regard to the presumptively lower are always correlated with distinctions that involve the presumptively higher, but the reverse need not be true. In reductions, distinctions regarding the presumptively higher are always accompanied by distinctions relating to the presumptively lower, though, again, the reverse need not be true. So in some sense reduction and elevation are the same thing operating in *opposite* (vertical) directions.

Moreover, the distinction between reduction and elevation also applies well beyond the confines of ethics. For example, just as in ethics we can be dualistic about virtue and well-being or else identify these concepts either reductively or elevatively, one of our main choices in metaphysics is between mind-body dualism and monism of an either reductive (materialist) or elevative (idealist or phenomenalist) character. Indeed, quite a number of disputes outside ethics allow of historiographic clarification through these categories. We think of concepts, for example, as higher (as depending on more highly evolved capacities) than percepts or sensations, yet British Empiricism basically reduces all concepts to percepts, whereas Continental Rationalism treats sensation/perception as a matter of obscure conception and thus counts as a form of elevationism. Kant's insistence on the distinction between percepts and concepts would then represent the "dualistic" option in this area of philosophical thought.

Similarly, thinking now in terms of wholes and parts (rather than in terms of the higher and the lower), the choice among reduction, elevation, and dualism can also be seen to apply in the area of social philosophy. Social atomism is the reductionistic option regarding the relation between individuals and the societies of which they are members, whereas an organicism that treats the individual as a mere aspect or reflection of society constitutes a form of elevationism, and the view that the social and individual levels need to be differentiated represents dualism in this area. But however historiographically significant these extraethical applications of our distinction may be, we have more than enough to occupy us in considering its relevance, and, in particular, the relevance of elevationism, to the field of ethics.

3. Is Elevationism Viable?

Stoic elevationism is implausible as a theory of human well-being. It notoriously considers ordinary appetitive pleasures to constitute no part of human well-being, and it regards (nonmoral) pain as in no way intrinsically contrary to human well-being or good. Such conclusions about human good and ill are highly counterintuitive, perhaps more counterintuitive than anything utilitarianism commits us to, and although the Stoics offer a variety of arguments for their views, those arguments are widely regarded as unpersuasive and will not concern us here. Let us see, rather, whether any other kind of virtue-ethical elevationism can avoid the excesses of the Stoic view of human good and ill.

At first glance, this might seem to be impossible. If a virtue ethics is to be elevationistic, it must understand all distinctions relating to well-being in terms of distinctions having to do with virtue. Doesn't this mean that how well off one is will depend on how virtuous one is and doesn't this precisely deliver us up to the forbidding conclusion that pain is no evil for the virtuous person on the rack? It is certainly natural to think so. It is natural to think that if virtue and well-being don't, so to speak, coincide, then neither can be understood in terms of the other (suitably supplemented by nonevaluative notions), and it is interesting, in this connection, to consider what Kant says about Stoicism and Epicureanism in the *Critique of Practical Reason*.[4]

Kant recognizes that these ancient views are not merely inconsistent with one another, but are in an important respect opposites— his discussion to some extent anticipates, though in a less general fashion, the distinction we are making between elevationism and reductionism. Kant holds that individual virtue cannot be identified with what effectively serves the well-being or happiness of the in-

4. See especially the *Critique of Practical Reason* part I, book I, ch. 2.

dividual, in the manner of Epicureanism, but also that individual well-being or happiness cannot, in the Stoic manner, be identified with the individual's (consciousness of his or her own) virtue. (He refuses to accept the Stoic's claim that pain is for him no evil.) Kant is in fact a dualist about our higher and lower values, about the admirable and the personally desirable, and he claims that well-being and virtue are "entirely heterogeneous" concepts.

But it in fact doesn't follow from the fact, assumed by Kant, that virtue and well-being don't coincide in either the way Stoics believe or the way Epicureans believe that these notions are entirely heterogenous. Kant doesn't say that this follows, and he seems to have independent reasons, to be discussed briefly in a moment, for holding that we cannot understand virtue in terms of well-being or vice versa. But what is most important at this point is to see why "entire heterogeneity" doesn't follow from noncoincidence, since that will precisely leave open the possibility of an elevationism that avoids the problems of Stoicism. And we can see this most easily, I think, if we consider utilitarianism (which isn't mentioned in Kant's discussion).

Utilitarianism at one and the same time denies the coincidence of virtue and well-being and insists that the former can be understood in terms of the latter, taken together with nonethical, empirical notions. For under utilitarianism, the virtuous individual is one who contributes to the general well-being at the possible *expense* of her own, and the familiar criticism that utilitarianism is too demanding is based on the realization that utilitarian morality puts at considerable risk, rather than insuring, the well-being of the virtuous individual. Yet utilitarian reductionism treats virtue and morality as understandable in terms of well-being rather than as "entirely heterogenous" with the latter notion, and in that case there is room in ethical/conceptual space for an elevationistic (virtue) ethics that understands well-being in terms of virtue without assuming, in the way so damaging to Stoicism, that virtue and well-being coincide in individuals. It must be possible for there to be a view or views that bear to Stoicism something like the relation that utilitarianism bears to Epicureanism, a possibility that I myself have sometimes ignored in writing about elevationism and that Kant doesn't seem to regard as a serious option for ethical theory.

I believe that the overall Critical Philosophy gives Kant a reason to ignore this option and to look askance at all monistic theorizing about virtue and personal well-being, a reason emerging from the approach to metaphysics and epistemology taken in the First Critique. Kant thinks that in ethics well-being represents or corresponds to sensibility and virtue represents or corresponds to the understanding, and to the extent the Critical Philosophy rests on a dualism of sensibility and understanding (and of percepts and concepts), Kant seems to want a corresponding dualism in ethics; and that may be why he insists that well-being and virtue are entirely heterogeneous. So Kant's larger or more systematic dualism seems to predispose him not only against any form of reductionism, but also against the possibility I want to defend here, the possibility of understanding well-being in elevationistic terms but not as *coincident* with virtue. (Sam Kerstein has pointed out to me that Kant's position here may have in part also derived from an intuitive conviction that virtuous people are sometimes very unhappy and the wicked sometimes "flourish as the green bay tree.")

But doesn't the drive for a unifying system actually favor the Kantian ethical dualism at this point over any form of elevationist monism? To be sure, monism allows us a greater unification within ethics than dualism does, but to the extent Kant's ethical dualism allows him to dovetail his ethics with his metaphysics in a way that ethical elevationism doesn't claim to do, doesn't Kant's *ethical* dualism come out ahead of any monistic elevationism virtue ethics can deliver?

It depends, I think, on what one says about the First Critique. If one has doubts about the way Kant treats concepts and percepts and about his general metaphysical and epistemological conclusions in that context, then that may actually rebound *against* the approach Kant takes in ethics. Basing an ethics on an epistemology-cum-metaphysics is a double-edged sword, but rather than attempt here to investigate all the epistemological and metaphysical issues that we would need to examine in order to determine which way the sword cuts, it seems reasonable to explore the possibilities of monistic, elevationist virtue ethics in order to see whether, quite apart from any connection to metaphysics and epistemology, such an ethics can fulfill the (somewhat independent) criteria of a good systematic ethical theory. Those criteria are demanding and interesting enough, so that it seems worth our while to see whether any form of elevationist virtue ethics can meet them, and I shall proceed accordingly.

4. Aristotelian Elevationism

A more plausible example of virtue-ethical elevationism than Stoicism offers us can be found, I think, in a certain way of understanding Aristotle's views in the *Nicomachean Ethics*. The so-called function argument of Book I of the *Ethics* concludes that the good life for human beings consists in a long and active life of virtue. But Aristotle immediately qualifies this claim by pointing out that how pleasant or painful, successful or unsuccessful one's life is also helps to determine how good it is. This further point seems to take Aristotle away from any attempt to understand human well-being in terms of the higher categories of virtue and rationality and toward some sort of dualistic conception of the ethical. But that interpretation is not actually forced on us, because of some of the things Aristotle says later about pleasure. In Book X (chs. 3–5), he says that pleasures deriving from perverted or morally unworthy sources are not good, not desirable, and it is possible to interpret this as meaning that a person who gains money or certain enjoyments through injustice or betrayal gains nothing good for himself, fails to have his well-being (even momentarily) enhanced. Sarah Broadie interprets the relevant passages in something like this manner,[5] and once one does so, there is an obvious way to treat Aristotle as an elevationistic monist.

For if Aristotle is saying that pleasure and success count as elements in our well-being only if and when they can be obtained consistently with being virtuous, then his conception of well-being or the good life will at every point have to refer to virtue. The good or best life will then, roughly, be a life full of virtuous activity and of pleasures and successes that are consistent with virtue—and lacking in pains and failures that virtue doesn't require. And on such a picture there are no purely natural personal goods and evils: that is, everything that adds or subtracts from our well-being must do so *in relation to higher moral or ethical values*.[6] We have ended up with

5. See Sarah Broadie, *Ethics with Aristotle* (Oxford: Oxford University Press, 1991), p. 376.

6. I stress this last phrase because it may be useful to us in answering the following objection due to Thomas Hurka. Aristotelian elevationism allows two people to be equally virtuous yet differ in well-being, but how, the objection goes, is this

a form of elevationist monism, but one that is less extreme and less implausible than Stoicism because it allows many ordinary pleasures and achievements a role in constituting human well-being and allows many ordinary pains and failures a similar role in making lives worse than they otherwise could or would be.

However, as I indicated earlier, this is not the only way one can interpret Aristotle's views about the good of pleasure and achievement. In Book X Aristotle also says, for example, that the good man is the measure of what is truly pleasurable, so that what appears pleasant only to a spoiled or perverted taste is not really pleasant. Perhaps he is here making the quasi-linguistic point that what is pleasant only to a perverted taste cannot properly be called pleasant *tout court*, while at the same time being willing to grant that such things can be pleasant to—and perhaps then even good for—the perverted individual. On such a reading, a vicious person can get something good-for-himself, something that enhances *his* well-being at least, from vicious actions, and this then leaves some natural or lower human good outside the orbit of (specification in terms of) virtue. It makes Aristotle into a dualist about virtue and well-being.

No matter. We are trying to see whether any plausible form of elevationistic monism can be found, and the form of monism we have just unearthed—whether it is actually in Aristotle or not—seems more promising in its own right than Stoic elevationism. So let us consider whether it enables virtue ethics to achieve a unification of virtue and well-being that can rival anything utilitarianism has to offer.

Because "Aristotelian" elevationism, as I shall call it, allows individual well-being to depend on more than virtue and virtuous actions, it claims no coincidence between individual virtue and in-

---

possible if all distinctions in well-being are to be understood in terms of distinctions in virtue? There is a difference, however, between distinctions in virtue (in one obvious sense) and distinctions having to do with, or having reference to, virtue. Remember that Aristotelian elevationism treats differences of pleasure (e.g.) as creating differences of well-being only if the pleasures are consistent with virtue (not ignoble). In the case, then, where two individuals differ in well-being because one has more virtue-consistent pleasure than the other, the two don't perhaps differ in virtue, i.e., in how virtuous they are; but there is still a distinction between them having to do with, or having reference to (or bringing in facts about) virtue, namely, the fact that one of them has more *virtue-consistent* pleasure than the other.

dividual well-being and avoids the worst implications of Stoicism. But it has other implications that I think ought to bother us. It entails that the pleasures (or achievements) that a vicious person obtains only through being vicious are no part of her good, so that, for example, the pleasure of eating food she has stolen is no sort of good for the thief. But intuitively, and here I am following Kant as well, one wants to say that though it is not a good thing *that* someone should benefit from wrongdoing, what is bad here is precisely that a person actually *benefits* from acting viciously.

Aristotelian elevationism will also seem implausible for what it has to say about personal evils. To maintain a thoroughgoing and essential connection to virtue in each aspect of its account of human well-being, the view has to maintain that the pain that virtue requires an individual to suffer involves no diminution of her well-being. If virtue requires someone to remain silent under torture, then the pain and suffering that occur during and result from such an episode will count as in no way making the individual's life worse, and, if anything, this seems even more implausible than what the Aristotelian theory has to say about the well-being-irrelevance of pleasures gained through vicious actions. In the end, I think Aristotelian elevationism is seriously counterintuitive, though certainly less extreme and counterintuitive than Stoic elevationism. (Here I ignore what these views have to say about the content of virtue and refer only to how they connect virtue with well-being.)

But the possibilities of elevationistic ethical monism are not yet exhausted, and if we take the proper lesson from the assumed failure of Aristotelian elevationism, we may yet learn how to construct a plausible form of elevationistic virtue ethics. At this point I would like to see if we can avoid the unwelcome consequences of Stoic and Aristotelian elevationism by *weakening our assumptions about the connection between well-being and virtue*. Stoicism says that virtue and well-being coincide in the individual, Aristotelian elevationism says, in effect, that all elements of personal well-being must be compatible with *virtue taken as a whole*, and we have reason to criticize both these assumptions. But what if we say, instead, that every element of human well-being must be compatible with or involve at least some *part* of virtue or one or another *particular* virtue? Such a claim might be entirely in keeping with the goal of elevationism and yet enable us to avoid the untoward implications of both Stoic and Aristotelian elevationism. For it allows us to deny that virtue and well-being coincide and to hold that a pleasure that a virtuous individual wouldn't choose or desire, a pleasure incompatible with *virtue as a whole*, might still count as part of someone's well-being *as long as it bore an appropriate relation to some particular virtue or part of virtue*. Better still, I believe that the beginnings of a theory that actually meets these requirements can be found in Plato's *Gorgias*.

5. Platonic Elevationism

Plato notably holds that all good things possess a common element or exemplify a common property or pattern, and Aristotle famously criticizes this fundamental view in the *Nicomachean Ethics*. But Plato makes a somewhat more specific claim about the things that are good in a rather neglected passage in the *Gorgias* (S. 506), where he says that "all good things whatever are good when some virtue is present in . . . them." Leaving aside judgments about functional goodness (but remembering that good knives and good doctors are commonly spoken of as having their "virtues") and focusing solely upon judgments about intrinsic personal good or well-being, Plato's claim implies that all personal good or well-being contains an element of virtue and thus has something in common with the virtues themselves. If this thesis were correct, then we would have all the help we need in establishing elevationism, but what Plato is saying clearly sounds odd, to say the least, so let us at this point see what can be said in its defense.

What we need to do, I think, is find a plausible way of arguing that even common pleasures and enjoyments, in order to count as an intrinsic part of our well-being, must contain or be accompanied by some form or instance of virtue, and at this point such a view seems perilously close to the idea, previously rejected, that pleasure is a good thing in someone's life only if it is achieved compatibly with the dictates of moral virtue. However, the Platonic view mentioned above in fact allows that a person who viciously steals food and then enjoys it may, contrary to the Aristotelian and Stoic views, have his well-being enhanced *as long as he exemplifies one virtue in the course of that enjoyment*; and what I want to argue in what follows is that appetitive pleasures and enjoyments must be accompanied by at least some degree of moderation, a quality we admire and think of as a virtue, in order to count toward a person's well-being.[7] The idea that appetitive goods demand some sort of virtue is far from obvious and represents the largest stumbling block to any acceptance of the Platonic approach I am proposing. But before we consider more closely what can be said about the relations between appetitive satisfactions and the virtue of moderation, let me say a bit more about other sorts of personal good or well-being whose connection to one or another virtue seems far less problematic. (Later on, I shall also say something about how Platonic elevationism treats personal ills or evils.)

For the rest of this chapter, I shall simply assume some relatively plausible "objective list" theory of personal well-being. An objective list view assumes that not all aspects of well-being are reducible to subjective factors like pleasure or desire satisfaction, and it treats a plurality of things in human life as intrinsically (rather than merely instrumentally) adding to the goodness of lives. And what I hope to show you is that if one assumes some such reasonable or intuitive pluralism about personal goods, about the sorts of things that inherently contribute to human well-being, one ends up with a short list of highly plausible candidates all of which (with the exception of appetitive and other pleasures and enjoyments) have an obvious and essential relation to particular virtues.

Different objective lists of intrinsic personal goods have been offered by different philosophers, but it seems to me that almost everyone who favors this sort of approach will include certain conspicuous examples: enjoyment/pleasure; achievement/accomplishment; love, friendship, and certain other relationships; and certain kinds of knowledge or wisdom. Now the connection between putative goods of relationship, goods like love and friendship but also less intimate forms of interaction, and various virtues is not difficult to see. Love and friendship essentially depend on loving or caring about the welfare of one's friend or loved one. Intuitively, a relationship doesn't count as love or friendship if its participants are entirely selfish in their relations toward one another. Even some of the less intimate social ties we might regard as elements of a given

---

7. Actually, I shall only argue that appetitive goods require that one not be *totally immoderate*, but for simplicity's sake I shall continue to speak as I have in the text above.

individual's well-being—for example, "civic friendship"—seem to require some connection to virtue, some degree of concern, for example, for the well-being of (other members of) a community, association, or nation. Where there is no concern for others, we simply have people using one another, and though, arguably, various personal goods can *come from* such interaction, the interaction itself is not commonly regarded as an independent and substantial personal good on its own, the way friendship, love, and membership in a genuine community (etc.) tend to be.

The goods of personal interaction or relationship—goods like love and (civic) friendship—thus seem to require certain virtues, and (relative to the conception of morality we have been defending in these pages) the virtues in question are other-regarding ones like love and benevolence. However, other goods on our objective "short list" are not essentially interpersonal and, therefore, not surprisingly connect only to more self-regarding virtues. Almost anyone who thinks there are elements of personal well-being other than pleasure would mention achievement or accomplishment as an example. Notoriously, achievements can require great suffering and great personal sacrifice in the course of their accomplishment, and anyone who believes achievement represents a personal good in itself will want to hold that despite all the suffering and sacrifice, a life can be made good or better through the achieving of the goals that required all the suffering and sacrifice.

But what kind of virtue or virtues does achievement require? A certain degree of talent or aptitude is certainly necessary to most achievements, but talent and aptitude are arguably not virtues, whereas strength of purpose, or perseverance, pretty clearly is a virtue, and I think any genuine achievement will essentially depend on the presence of some degree of perseverance. Even Mozart, in whom musical invention seems to have arisen spontaneously, had to write down the tunes that occurred to him, and orchestrate and develop them, in order to produce his actual compositions. Talent itself doesn't depend on effort and perseverance; indeed, one needn't at all develop a talent one knows one has, but, interestingly, most of us are much less inclined to treat the presence of raw talent as in itself a personal good in someone's life. If the talent isn't developed, is left fallow, then it doesn't seem to represent any sort of life good for the individual who has it, and so the case of talents contrasts intuitively with what we think about achievements, about successfully making something out of and with a talent or ability. Achievements seem to qualify a life as better in a way mere unused talents do not, and I think part of what leads us to such a distinction is our sense of the effort and perseverance that go into actual achievements. Talent doesn't require any application of virtue, but achievement always requires some degree of perseverance, and the latter fact influences, I think, our willingness to treat achievement, but not sheer talent, as a genuine life good somewhat independent of pleasure and enjoyment.

But what about knowledge or wisdom? Do these putative personal goods also require the presence of virtue? Now knowledge, at least of deep or important facts, and wisdom may themselves be thought to be virtues, intellectual virtues, so once again, and fairly straightforwardly, there is a connection between what we tend to think of as personal goods and certain possible virtues, in this case a relation of absolute identity. But more can be said about the connection between wisdom or deep knowledge and at least one familiar *ethical* virtue: courage.

Nowadays we tend to think that some of the deepest and most important facts about the universe and our relation to it are frightening or at least highly unpalatable. In consequence, we also think that it takes a certain kind of courage to face those facts rather than deceive ourselves or think wishfully about them (or avoid thinking at all about certain topics). I say nowadays, because (for reasons it would be very interesting to pursue on another occasion) very little of this attitude is to be found, for example in ancient thinkers like Plato and Aristotle, despite all their emphasis on the virtue of wisdom.

Consider one famous example of the courage it takes to face facts about the universe. In the nineteenth century (though not merely then), accumulating evidence of the age of the earth and cosmos and of the evolutionary origin of plants and animals led many people to doubt the Biblical account of things and reexamine their religious beliefs. But it took some courage to face and "take in" this evidence against the Biblical account of human life and human destiny. It is much easier and more comfortable, in the main, to believe that there is a God who has a plan for human beings, and one (Whiggish, I admit) way to interpret the struggle that occurred in the nineteenth century (and is not over yet) between secular science and religious tradition is to see it as a test of the courage of human beings.

But the test of courage vs. self-deception and wishful thinking occurs in a host of other areas. It takes courage to face some of one's own deepest fears and desires, and to the extent wisdom as a life good requires facing one's inner demons, the important connection between wisdom and courage is further underscored. Finally, it can take courage to face the results of philosophical argument. What we initially hope for from philosophy, philosophy in many instances proves itself incapable of providing: Hume, Goodman, Quine, and Wittgenstein all show us that philosophy can run out of justifications more quickly and more irrecusably than we hope or desire. And it is interesting that Wittgenstein himself seems to be noticing the connection between philosophical understanding or wisdom and moral virtue when he says: "You could attach prices to thoughts. Some cost a lot, some a little. And how does one pay for thoughts? The answer, I think, is: with courage."[8] I think Wittgenstein is basically right here. Many of the conclusions philosophy tends toward are unsettling and uncomfortable, and it requires courage rather than wishful thinking to accept them. More generally, Platonic elevationism will say that knowledge constitutes a distinctive form of personal good, and counts as wisdom, only when it takes courage to acquire it.[9]

It would seem, then, that some of our best candidates for status as personal goods have an intimate connection to one or other virtue or set of virtues, and so to make good on the form of elevationism I think most promising, we must now establish a similar connection between appetitive (or other) pleasures and human virtue. We can do this if we can show that someone totally lacking in the virtue of moderation, someone insatiably immoderate in her desires, gains no personal good from the pleasures she frenetically or restlessly pursues and obtains.

A moderate individual who is enjoying food or drink will at a certain point decide that she has had enough (enjoyment) and stop

---

8. See Ludwig Wittgenstein, *Culture and Value* (Oxford: Blackwell, 1980), p. 52e.

9. We are then committed to saying that sheer information, however instrumentally valuable, is not intrinsically good for people. Note, however, that where knowledge doesn't require courage *but is difficult to attain*, it can still count as a personally beneficial *achievement*. (Something similar may even be true of the insatiable person who gains more and more power or pleasure through persistent efforts.)

pursuing, perhaps even turn down, further gustatory enjoyment(s). But the totally insatiable person will never feel she has (had) enough and will remain thoroughly unsatisfied no matter how much she has had or enjoyed, and it is not counterintuitive to suppose that such an individual gains nothing good (at least noninstrumentally) from her pursuit of pleasure or power or whatever. We feel sorry for someone who is never even partially satisfied with what she has or has obtained, and in feeling thus, I don't think we are necessarily assuming that the insatiable pursuit of power, gustatory sensations, sexual pleasure, or whatever is automatically frustrating and painful; rather, it seems somewhat plausible to suppose that we feel sorry for such people because their frenetic pleasure and desire for pleasure are never "rounded off" by any sense of satisfaction with what they have or have had. When people gain something good for themselves from pleasure, it is, I am arguing, because the pleasure is part of a "package" containing both pleasure and satisfaction with that pleasure. (We shall say more just below about how the elements in this package may relate to one another and to the personal good that requires them.) And in that case Plato's claim in the *Gorgias* appears to be vindicated. For the idea that some degree of moderation is a requirement of all pleasure-related good or well-being, while Plato never explicitly states it, is one that resonates both with the statement we quoted from the *Gorgias* and with Plato's frequent invocation of the virtue of moderation in his discussion of the appetites and of the desire for power, etc. The total elevationist view I am maintaining may not be explicit in Plato, but I think it gains impetus from things Plato says.

Moreover, I am assuming that there is nothing *unintuitive* about the supposition that (some substantial degree of) satisfaction with pleasure is necessary for an appetitive (or any other pleasure-related) good to occur in someone's life. I am assuming, in effect, that the pleasure or enjoyment we take from an activity in some (perhaps metaphorical or analogical) sense *anticipates* some measure of satisfaction and that where the satisfaction, the sense of having had enough, never comes, the pleasure seems empty, the activity not worth it. There is something pitiable about insatiability that reminds us of Sisyphus but also of Tantalus. (Everyone knows about Sisyphus, but Tantalus, according to mythology, was condemned by the gods to stand under luscious grapes that always eluded his reach and in water that always receded when he tried to drink it.) For surely we can say that the insatiable individual wishes to have or obtain something good in her life, yet, on the view I wish to defend, personal good seems always to recede from the insatiable individual as she seeks to approach and attain it. So the appetitively insatiable individual may not only fail to be admirable, because of her immoderate, indeed unlimited, need for and dependence on appetitive (or other) pleasures, but, in addition and as a result of that lack of virtue, act self-defeatingly in regard to her own good.[10]

But why not say, rather, that the insatiable individual does get something good out of his restless and insatiable pursuit of more and more pleasure, namely, whatever pleasure he obtains along the way? Is this view really so contrary to common sense? I think not; but neither, as I have been saying, is the claim that the appetitively insatiable individual gets nothing good from his appetitive pursuit. I don't think common sense is really decisive on this issue, and so I propose to let theoretical considerations resolve the issue for us. If we say that pleasure needs to be accompanied by some measure of satisfaction with it in order for an appetitive good to occur in someone's life, then there is some chance for an overall elevationist account of human good.[11] Such an account unifies ethics in a desir-

10. Our elevationism assumes that the virtue status of the virtues that are essential to various personal goods doesn't depend on their having good consequences for people. Otherwise, we would be saying, circularly, that these virtues both ground and are grounded in facts about human well-being. But Part I argued that caring is morally good even when unsuccessful; and in chapters 7 and 8 we shall see that the virtues essential to other human goods also don't depend on consequences. Note too that to equate virtue with a desire to promote well-being is *not* to reduce facts about virtue to facts about well-being. Utilitarianism does attempt such a reduction: it explains facts about people's virtue partly in terms of the assumption that well-being consists in pleasure, something which, if true, would be a fact about well-being. But warm agent-basing makes no assumptions about what well-being consists in, and although the idea that someone desires to promote well-being contains the *concept* of well-being, the fact that someone desires to promote well-being is no more a fact about actual well-being than the fact that the number of the planets is not necessarily an odd number is a fact about the actual number of the planets. Such intensional contexts are not *de re*. I am indebted here to Shelly Kagan.

11. Of course, someone might claim that nothing *counts as pleasure* unless the individual is in some degree satisfied with it. But this assumption clearly makes it easier for platonic elevationism to hold that appetitive goods require some degree of

able way, and in the name of such unity, we may wish to make assumptions which, though not counterintuitive, are not over-whelmingly obvious apart from such theoretical considerations. (Compare the way linguists like Chomsky have allowed considera-tions of theory, sometimes in different directions depending on the theory then being espoused, to decide the syntactic status—that is, grammaticality or nongrammaticality—of "don't care" sentences like "Colorless green ideas sleep furiously.") If we assume in ap-petitive cases that virtue needs to accompany personal good, we can easily make a similar assumption across the entire range of goods that objective-list pluralism tends to accept, and we end up with a more satisfactory elevationist account of human well-being than Sto-icism or Aristotle provides. In that case, accepting the idea that plea-sure is not a sufficient condition of personal good seems a small price to pay for the unification we achieve as a result (smaller, one could certainly say, than what utilitarian reductionist monism forces us to relinquish in the form of lost intuitions).[12]

If we accept this kind of Platonically inspired elevationism, we have to reject hedonism, of course, but, more interestingly perhaps, we have to reject an idea that many hedonists and nonhedonists *share*, namely, that if pleasure isn't the sole personal good, it is the *most typical* of personal goods and that friendship, achievement, wisdom, and the like are at best somewhat *problematic* examples of such goods. This view represents a kind of half-way house in the direction of hedonism, and the elevationist account we have offered constitutes a direct challenge to it. For Platonic elevationism regards

virtue, and it is in any event very questionable. The French use the term "alumette" (literally "match") to refer to hors d'oeuvres that are supposed to inflame one's appetite, and this more than suggests that such appetizers are pleasurable yet the very opposite of satisfying.

12. Our elevationism entails not only that pleasure may not give rise to an ap-petitive (or other) good, but that appetitive desire-fulfillment may also fail to result in any good for an individual. Someone insatiably seeking a certain kind of pleasure may have an open-ended desire that is never fulfilled, but will certainly have partic-ular desires along the way: the desire for a given piece of pâté de foie gras, for example. That desire is certainly fufilled, but on the account offered here, the insa-tiable person gains nothing good thereby. (We also speak of the desire being "sat-isfied," but if the *individual* is in no way satisfied with the resultant state of affairs, then she has gained nothing good from the fulfillment or satisfaction of the particular desire. I am indebted here to discussion with Richard Wollheim.)

it as essential to and characteristic of human well-being that it should involve an intimate connection to virtue, and personal goods like friendship and achievement show their connection to virtue *much more clearly* than do appetitive (or pleasure-related) goods. Thus the present view requires us to renounce the somewhat tempting belief that pleasure is the most typical of human goods and indeed *to learn about the character of appetitive goods from the example of other, more spiritual forms of well-being.*

In addition, we have still not addressed certain issues about the metaphysics of human goods. We have said, for example, that appetitive (or pleasure-related) goods require both pleasure and satisfaction with pleasure, but that doesn't yet tell us whether the satisfaction with pleasure that is necessary to the emergence/existence of an appetitive good is part of that good or merely its necessary accompaniment. One might hold, in other words, that when appetitive goods occur they consist merely in a certain kind of pleasure or enjoyment, but that such an enjoyment doesn't constitute a personal good for someone unless it possesses the relational property of being accompanied by satisfaction with it on the part of the person in question. But there is also the alternative of saying that appetitive goods *contain* both pleasure and satisfaction with pleasure. Similarly, with regard to the personal good of achievement, one can say that it consists merely in the attaining of the goal one has sought, but that that attaining doesn't count as a good unless its way is paved by a virtuous perseverance or persistence that makes it possible. Or one can say that both the attaining of one's goal and the persistence one shows in doing so are elements in (the good of) any achievement.

However, if we say that satisfaction with pleasure is part of any appetitive good and likewise say that persistence is part of (the good of) achievement and so on for the other goods on our shortlist, then Plato may turn out to have been right in claiming that for something to be good, there must be virtue *in* it. Wouldn't it be interesting and lovely if, in such an unexpected way, Plato turned out to be correct on this issue? Yes, but are there good philosophical reasons for agreeing with Plato?

Consider, for example, the possibility that pleasure and satisfaction with it don't merely accompany one another, but *interpenetrate* one another, so that the character of pleasure differs to the extent one is satisfied with it (or the pleasure one has already had). If this were the case, then it wouldn't make much sense to separate the two phenomena and say that the pleasure constitutes an appetitive good, when one is satisfied with it, but the satisfaction lies outside the good thus constituted. But the ''interpenetration thesis'' is hardly obvious, and I don't think this argument is enough to persuade us that we should regard ''satisfaction with'' as part of the appetitive goods that require it.

But what about the widespread assumption that pleasure, wisdom, and the like are *intrinsically good*? Doesn't this require us to hold that such goods can't depend, for their constitution or existence, on entities outside themselves? Not necessarily. A number of philosophers have recently defended the view that various good things may be *noninstrumentally* valuable (to us) even if that value exists *only in relation* to certain other facts or entities. So the idea that wisdom, pleasure, etc., are more than (mere) means to our well-being (are ends sought for their own sake) can arguably be accommodated without insisting that such goods depend on nothing external to themselves. In addition, it has been plausibly maintained that noninstrumental goods or ends that are constituted in relation to external facts or objects can naturally be regarded as having (a certain kind of) intrinsic goodness.[13] So I don't think we really have to regard the personal goods that require certain virtues as containing those virtues as parts of themselves. It would perhaps be nice if Plato were right, but nothing requires us to assume that he is, and in what follows, therefore, I shall remain agnostic on the question of metaphysics we have just discussed.

Having focused almost exclusively on personal well-being, it is time we said something about the Platonic elevationist account of personal ills or evils. That account, in fact, works symmetrically with what we have said about personal goods and holds, in particular, that nothing counts as intrinsically bad for a person unless it involves some degree of vice (or an absence of total virtue). Thus

13. See, for example, Christine Korsgaard, ''Two Distinctions in Goodness,'' *Philosophical Review* 92, 1983, pp. 169–85; my *Goods and Virtues* (Oxford: Clarendon Press, 1983), ch. 3; Shelly Kagan, ''Rethinking Intrinsic Value,'' *Journal of Ethics* 2, 1998, pp. 277–97; and Thomas Hurka, ''Two Kinds of Organic Unity,'' *Journal of Ethics* 2, 1998, pp. 299–320. The last two articles make a fairly persuasive case for saying that noninstrumental, but relational goods can make some claim to being regarded as intrinsically good.

on such a view pain is a (constituent of a) personal evil only if there is something less than fully virtuous or admirable about how one takes or reacts to the pain, and just as it is best to be in some degree *satisfied* with substantial pleasure, so too does it seem appropriate and admirable—a kind of strength—not to be *dissatisfied* with, but, rather, to *accept* unavoidable, and perhaps also even (some) avoidable, pain. For that reason, I want to claim that where (a) pain is totally accepted, it doesn't constitute anything intrinsically bad for a person. Only when someone *minds* his pain or is (to some extent) *bothered* by it, does the pain enter into or count as something intrinsically bad for the individual.[14] (Of course, there may be kinds of pain that no human being is capable of accepting, and our view will regard such pains as entailing personal evils.)

Thus it takes a "package" of pain (or discomfort) and the vice or nonvirtue of nonacceptance for there to be a personal evil, and this implication of our Platonic elevationism strikes me as by no means implausible. Certainly, it is far less implausible than saying, with the Stoics, that pain is never (part of) a personal evil, but it also seems somewhat intuitive to suppose that a person who so totally accepts a pain that he doesn't (any longer) at all mind it is suffering no intrinsic ill. (Of course, if one wants to claim that something can't count as a pain if it is totally accepted, that makes things easier, not harder, for the view that every personal ill requires some measure of vice.)

Moreover, when one applies Platonic elevationism to more spiritual forms of human ill, one arrives at a view with some obvious attractions. Given present assumptions, failure to succeed in one's goals doesn't amount to a personal ill *unless some vice was involved in the failure.* But this means that if someone fails, despite valiant efforts and through no fault of her own, that failure merely constitutes the absence of something good rather than a positive personal evil; whereas if someone fails through a total lack of virtuous effort and perseverance, the failure really does amount to a personal evil. And this distinction has some intuitive force, since it is natural to

14. In and of itself, then, accepting a pain may be no worse for a person than being rid of the pain, but there may be instrumental reasons to get rid of a pain rather than accept it, if it takes energy to accept it or if its presence somehow interferes with having certain good things happen to one. I am indebted on this point to discussion with Sam Kerstein.

think there is something far more pathetic and unfortunate about a life where failure results from fecklessness than about one where it is due to bad luck. By the same token, it seems acceptable to suppose that a lack of wisdom that results from sheer cowardice is to that extent more unenviable and pathetic than a lack of wisdom that results from the cultural unavailablity of certain kinds of knowledge, and this is precisely what our Platonic elevationism claims.

6. Conclusion

If the above discussion has been on the right track, then intraethical elevationism in a form inspired by Plato is capable of avoiding the problems that beset Stoic and Aristotelian versions of elevationism, while at the same time offering us an account of the relation between virtue and well- or ill-being that has some of the unifying power we find in reductive utilitarian (and Epicurean) accounts of that relationship. I say "some" because Platonic elevationism of the sort we have discussed leaves virtue in a more pluralistic condition than the utilitarian account leaves the notion of well-being. (For simplicity's sake, let us again leave ill-being to one side.) If well-being is understood as pleasure or desire-satisfaction, then utilitarianism is capable of reducing all virtue (as well as rationality and morality) to well-being conceived in a unitary fashion, whereas Platonic elevationism relates different goods to different virtues and offers no immediate prospect of treating all those virtues—moderation, caringness, perseverance, and courage—as forms of some underlying single "master virtue." But still, the present account does allow us to see all forms of well-being as dependent on (and possibly containing) forms of virtue, and such a conception of well-being substantially unifies our ideas about what well-being really is.

Many objective lists of what constitutes human well-being have been based simply on intuitions about what things count as goods, but the objective shortlist we get from Platonic elevationism at least offers us the beginnings of an explanation of why some things count as personal goods and others do not. Its insistence that all personal goods essentially involve some virtue explains, for example, why unused talent and frenetic pleasure are naturally thought of as making no inherent contribution to human well-being, and the theory

also helps to explain why, unlike virtue-involving love and friendship, forms of personal interaction in which people are merely useful
(or just plain indifferent or hostile) to one another are not typically
thought to contribute as such to the well-being of those involved in
them. This is hardly a complete story, but at least it takes the objective list approach beyond its usual aspirations and grounds a particular shortlist in a more general understanding of what makes
things good for us. And our discussion of practical reason in the
next chapter will prepare the way for a complete or completer account of why some things are good and others not that I hope to
nail down in our final chapter.

In the way they deal with virtue and self-interest, ancient ethical
theory and modern moral philosophy often seem like ships passing
in the night. Modern views (and here I am thinking not only of
utilitarianism, but of Kant and certain virtue ethicists, like James
Martineau, as well)[15] tend to separate well-being from virtue and
understand the former on largely hedonistic lines. So understood, a
person's well-being won't contain any virtue, but most ancient views
of ethics have the opposing tendency of making it difficult to understand how well-being can consist of *anything but virtue*. The
present form of elevationism avoids the extremism of Stoic conceptions of well-being and the exaggerated role in the constitution of
well-being that even Aristotelian elevationism imputes to virtue.
Rather than assume that virtue is well-being or that what is incompatible with total virtue makes no contribution to well-being, the
present form of elevationism assumes only the weakest of connections between virtue and well-being. By supposing only that well-
being in all its instances has to involve some particular virtue or
other, Platonic elevationism scales down the aspirations and avoids
the implausibilities of more extreme versions of elevationism. This
leaves the basic enterprise of elevationism intact, but accommodates
our strongest modern-day intuitions about the importance of pleasure
and enjoyment in constituting human well-being. We have to sacrifice the idea that every instance of pleasure constitutes a human
good, but that is an idea whose hold over most of us is tenuous at

15. See James Martineau, *Types of Ethical Theory*, 2 vols. (Oxford: Clarendon
Press, 1891).

best, and the theory we arrive at by rejecting it thus represents a kind of compromise between extreme forms of elevationism, on the one hand, and reductionism, on the other.

In recent centuries we have faced a choice between reductionism and dualism in regard to the relationship between virtue and well-being: ancient forms of elevationism, to the extent we have been aware of them, have seemed too wild and implausible to be taken seriously in our attempts to understand that relationship. In that case, the weaker, milder, more intuition-friendly version of elevationism offered here may show not only that the options we have been considering in this area are too narrow and limiting, but that a revival of the ancient idea of treating self-interest or well-being as a function of virtue has much to recommend it.[16] We shall now see that an agent-based account of practical reason can help us to provide a more thoroughgoing explanatory account of what is good and what is bad for human beings than anything offered in the present chapter.

---

16. I have here been speaking of intraethical elevationism; but an elevationism that seeks to understand well-being in terms of virtue might ultimately attempt to understand or account for the virtues in purely naturalistic terms. Thus elevationism within the ethical is compatible with reductionism respecting the entire sphere of the ethical.

SEVEN

AGENT-BASED PRACTICAL REASON

In this chapter, I want to work out an agent-based conception of practical reason or rationality that complements what we have said about individualistic moral questions and that can be used, along with that picture of morality, to give a fuller explanatory account of human well-being, of the basic kinds of things that are intrinsically good for us. However, since the present book has (at least this far) been developing virtue ethics along moral sentimentalist lines, it is worth noting that some of the most important eighteenth-century sentimentalists, notably Hume and Hutcheson, were skeptical about the rational status of morality, and that Hume, at least, seems to have been a skeptic about practical reason as such. This stands in marked contrast with the enterprise of the present chapter, where I shall be defending an agent-based conception of practical reason that helps to show why we are rationally justified in being moral.

1. Conceptions of Practical Reason

An agent-based theory of rational action or choice must treat the rational evaluation of certain inner states or processes as ethically fundamental and then use such evaluations (together with nonethical facts) as the basis for assessing the rationality of choices or actions. Of course, understood in one sense a choice is an inner state, but as theorists of rational choice typically understand the notion, choices (or acts of volition, if you will) correlate one to one with actions. According to this usage, a mere decision or intention to act in a certain way doesn't necessarily give rise to an agent's actually acting, or actually choosing (willing) to act, in that way; and this means that for all practical purposes choices *are* actions.

An agent-based theory evaluates such things via the rational assessment of (if you will) *deeper* psychological dispositions or processes that may help to explain actions, but are not so immediately connected to actions as choices are. (Such inner processes and dispositions in effect help to explain choices as well.) In addition, however, any theory that bases the rationality either of actions/choices or of more central aspects of the agent's psychology in assumptions about what would serve the agent's well-being is also not agent-based in the above sense. If rationality is said to depend on how much a certain action or disposition will (expectably) benefit a given agent, then assessments of (the agent's) well-being come in prior to claims about her rationality and in effect *ground* such claims. But I said above that agent-based views of rationality treat assessments of inner rationality as ethically fundamental, and given the ethical character of claims about well-being or the good life, this rules out consequentialistic views that base practical rationality in the achievement of certain good consequences.

Of course, there also are consequentialistic theories of rational choice that tie rational choice to preference-maximizing consequences without assuming that such rationality is to be (further) explained in terms of (actual or expectable) consequences *for the agent's well-being*. Gauthier's view in *Morals by Agreement* appears to meet this characterization, for example, but it clearly doesn't count as agent-based because its most fundamental ethical evaluations are rational evaluations of *choices or actions*.[1] But what about a theory that avoided all claims about well-being, anchored claims about the rationality of certain motives or inner dispositions (solely)

---

1. See David Gauthier, *Morals by Agreement* (Oxford: Oxford University Press, 1986), ch. 2. However, later, in ch. 6, Gauthier argues (roughly) that it can be rational not to maximize the satisfaction of one's preferences if such nonmaximization is required to carry out a prior intention that was preference-maximizing as an intention and thus, on his view, rational. If Gauthier's account of act-rationality is in this way partially grounded in independent facts or assumptions about the rationality of intentions, then it would seem to count as agent-based in the sense specified above.

in facts about the agent's preferences, and then assessed the rationality of choices or actions in terms of the rationality of motives, etc.? Such a view would, strictly speaking, be agent-based, but I in fact know of no one who has ever defended such a conception of rationality, and it doesn't, in itself, seem very promising. I think we would do better to look elsewhere for a plausible agent-based theory of practical reason.

Does Aristotle, then, or perhaps Kant have such a theory? Well, in the case of Aristotle, choice lying in a mean between vices is according to (what is sometimes translated as) "right reason," and a rational and virtuous individual has a disposition to make such choices. But here (as analogously elsewhere in Aristotle's ethics) the disposition seems to be virtuous or good because of the way it leads to rational, virtuous, or "noble" choices, so rather than in agent-based fashion understanding the rationality of choices in terms of independently characterized rational motives or dispositions, the status of the latter would appear at least partly to derive from that of the former, so that the theory isn't agent-based.

Kant, then, may seem a more likely example of rational agent-basing, but Kant's views are difficult to interpret, and I hope may be excused for leaving this issue to other venues.[2] It may be that there are no absolutely clear examples of rational agent-basing in the entire history of philosophy, and of course one—very reasonable—response might be to conclude that the whole idea of such agent-basing is a nonstarter. However, even if rational agent-basing is hard to come by, some very familiar and commonplace *kinds* of practical irrationality seem to be a matter, most fundamentally, of the irrational character of an agent's inner states or processes; and their example may point us in the direction of a plausible agent-based virtue-theoretic account of practical reason as a whole.

2. Agent-Based Rationality

Consider one familiar form of irrationality, self-deception. Self-deception involves a rift or inconsistency within the self that we

2. It has been suggested by Marcia Baron (in her essay "Kantian Ethics" in M. Baron, et al., *Three Methods of Ethics* [Oxford: Blackwell, 1997]) that Kant is an agent-baser about rational morality; however, I have argued against this interesting claim in my reply to Baron et al., *Three Methods of Ethics*.

think of as irrational *quite independently of consequentialistic con-siderations*. We don't think self-deception irrational because of its bad consequences for the agent or in general, and indeed we think that some instances of self-deception may actually have good con-sequences. As I have already mentioned, if someone has cancer, it may be easier on himself and others if he deceives himself about his symptoms and what the doctors are trying to tell him. What motivates self-deception in such a case is arguably a desire for men-tal or psychological self-preservation or comfort, but that precisely means that our opinion that self-deception is irrational (even) in such cases has more to do with the inherent nature of the state the self-deceiver is in and/or the psychological process that causes him to be in it than it has to do with the consequences of that state.

Now we say that such a person *deceives himself*, using an active form of words that might seem to indicate the performance of an action. But unlike cases where we intentionally deceive others, self-deception is not an ordinary intentional action. Even if there is in-tention behind it, the act or process of self-deception isn't conscious and lies deeper within the mind. These facts are, of course, con-nected to some of the problematic and even paradoxical features of self-deception, but my point is that to the extent self-deception in-volves a desire for psychological comfort or peace of mind leading one at some deep level to misread evidence of unpleasant facts, it is a psychological phenomenon that lies *behind* overt actions and activities. So when we characterize someone's overt actions (the self-deceived cancer victim's canceling of a doctor's appointment because he thinks he is perfectly healthy) as irrational because they are based in self-deception, but characterize someone else's overt actions as rational because they are *not* based in self-deception, we appear to be deriving claims about the rationality of ordinary, overt actions from claims about the irrationality of the internal state or internal dynamics of self-deception, and as far as it goes, this is an example of agent-based practical (ir)rationality.[3]

It is plausible to conceive the irrationality of self-deception in such agent-based terms, because the most obvious alternative, an explanation in ''consequentialistic'' terms, seems so unintuitive.

---

3. I am not sure whether wishful thinking should be regarded as irrational and have tried to leave the question open.

Consequentialistic theories of practical reason see the rationality of actions or choices as depending solely on whether they lead to good or preferred consequences. But we saw above that self-deception is generally considered irrational even when it leads to good consequences or consequences that the agent and others prefer. Self-deception is *motivated* irrationality, clearly, and as such has the sort of bearing on how we lead or should lead our lives that elements of the practical "sphere" are supposed to have. But when we characterize self-deception as a form of irrationality, that criticism is based not on its (variably good or bad, preferred or dispreferred) consequences, but on (structural) facts about self-deception as an inner state or process. Agent-basing thus makes sense in regard to such examples, and similar things can be said about other aspects and instances of practical irrationality.

I have in other contexts spent a great deal of time talking about the virtue/rationality of moderation and the vice/irrationality of insatiability; and I hope I will be excused for entering into this topic one more time, because the arguments I shall be making here are in fact different from any I have used previously. But I think the phenomenon of insatiability is another area where our judgments of irrationality with regard to actions seem to depend on what we take to be the irrationality of inner states. That is, unceasing active pursuit of food or some other appetitive good is an irrational way to behave to the extent it is due to insatiability.

By its very nature an appetite seeks satisfaction from its object(s), but such satisfaction must remain forever at a distance if a person's appetite for something is insatiable. So insatiable appetite as an internal state is essentially self-defeating. (We didn't have to rely on contingent considerations about consequences to explain above why such a desire undercuts its own aims.) Thus, the person who seeks to appease his hunger but through insatiability is unable to do so is on a kind of treadmill. And when he takes more and more food, we can characterize those acts as irrational because of the irrational (and undesirable) motivational state they causally derive from. A self-defeating desire is irrational, and that is precisely what insatiable appetite for one thing or another is.

By contrast, a consequentialistic view of rationality might hold that insatiable appetite is irrational because it is *frustrating*, painful, and unpleasant. And insatiability may indeed often lead to frustration. But, conceptually, neither the state of not yet being satisfied nor insatiability itself need be painful. The person who has *not yet* had enough cookies needn't feel pain or frustration while eating them, since (pace Schopenhauer and much of ancient Greek and Indian ethical thought) there is nothing about desire per se that entails that it must be either frustrating or painful. And, by the same token, there seems to be no conceptual reason why the child who insatiably eats more and more cookies and who gets pleasure from doing so has to be feeling pain or frustration along the way.

However, we can still, in nonconsequentialist fashion, argue for irrationality here if we distinguish pleasure from satisfaction with that pleasure and recognize the inherently self-defeating character of the insatiable person's appetite.[4] And clearly not all pleasure *is* satisfying. As I mentioned in the last chapter, we have a good example of this phenomenon in the "alumettes" that restaurants in France provide as hors d'oeuvres in order to "inflame" one's appetite, for no one has yet suggested that eating alumettes isn't pleasurable. But it is a very different question whether the pleasure derived from them leaves one satisfied (with that pleasure), and French restaurants are betting precisely that it does not. Thus the consequentialist attempt to derive the irrationality of insatiable appetite and appetitive activities from their contingent consequences cannot deal with all relevant cases, and if we think that insatiability is always rationally problematic, that is because there appears to be something *inherently* irrational about it. I have argued above that that irrationality is largely or basically a matter of the necessarily self-defeating character of insatiable appetite, and so, once again, we have an example where the irrationality of actions seems ultimately to derive from that of the inner motivational states that help to cause or explain them.

Nor can one defeat such a picture by claiming that ceaseless activity of *any kind* is irrational *irrespective* of how it is motivated. That would undercut our example's tendency to support agent-basing, but when one thinks about it, I believe one can see that we don't regard infinite activity as irrational by its very nature and apart from its causes or motivational objectives. If, for example, one un-

---

4. However, it is in keeping with agent-basing to allow that desires may count as insatiable, and consequently irrational, not "in themselves" but in relation to other (psychological) facts about agents.

ceasingly pursues some object because an evil scientist has convincingly threatened to kill many people if one doesn't, then one's action is arguably not irrational; and notice that the rational acceptability of what one does here is clearly influenced by one's reasons for doing so. Having reasons, or rationally acceptable motivations, does, then, play a role in determining the rationality at least of certain kinds of action, and if we can plausibly extend this notion to cover practical reason as a whole, we will have the agent-based account of rationality that we are seeking.

Let us consider some other possible elements, or necessary conditions, of full practical rationality. Instrumental rationality, taking appropriate means to one's ends or goals, is often said to constitute the whole of practical rationality, and if it isn't, it is probably at least the most important or prominent part of practical rationality (outside the realm of the moral). But means/end or instrumental rationality would appear to be most naturally understood in consequentialistic terms. To take means that likely (or expectably) serve one's end(s) is to perform an act or actions with certain likely (or expectable) consequences, so if instrumental behavior *is* practically rational (something that, as I have said, Hume seems to have denied), then that rationality seems best understood or unpacked in terms of the consequences of one's choices or actions.

In that case, it may at this point seem as if we have all along been putting off the inevitable, dealing with cases of practical (un)reason that might admit of agent-based treatment, but delaying the discussion of the one kind of practical rationality that cannot be understood in such terms. But I believe that this conclusion would at the very least be premature.

To begin with, agent-basing has the resources to handle, to understand, instrumental rationality as such, because even when instances of such rationality involve (expectably) producing certain desired or desirable results, they also involve a distinctive *psychological* (or *inner*) relation between intentions: one intends the means to one's intended ends. However, in this connection it is also worth noticing that instrumental rationality is part of a *larger motivational virtue*, strength of purpose. Strength of purpose can be demonstrated in the taking of effective means to ends, but there are other elements in strong purpose as well, and *all* these elements turn out to be necessary to full practical rationality, yet essentially understandable in agent-based terms. So the argument that instrumental reason can be accounted for in agent-based terms is best embedded, I think, within a larger view of strength of purpose as an agent-based requirement of practical reason; and at this point I would propose to consider first an aspect of strength of purpose that *isn't* immediately involved in (the standard or narrowest sort of) means/end rationality, but whose status as an element in practical reason can clearly be accounted for in agent-based terms. I shall then go on to argue that other elements of strength of purpose—including what normally goes under the name of means-end rationality—can in a rather similar way also be understood in agent-based terms.

Consider, then, to begin with, the tendency to change or drop purposes or intentions abruptly and without reason: as we say, "at the drop of a hat." Such an inner tendency, disposition, or state of character is often described as flighty, fickle, capricious, or (diachronically) inconsistent, and the use of such terms, especially the last, strongly suggests that we think of this sort of tendency, or character trait, as irrational from a practical standpoint. Indeed, the idea that inconsistency of purpose over time is a form of irrationality goes all the way back (at least) to the Stoics,[5] but for our present discussion what is interesting about the suggestion that flightiness or inconsistency is irrational is its potential for elaboration in agent-based terms. Whether one keeps to one's earlier purposes or intentions may causally depend on many facts external to the mind or person, but considered in itself, it is clearly an internal/psychological matter. So if the disposition to retain purposes is rational (rationally required), a pattern of actions that reflects flightiness and (internal) inconsistency on someone's part may for that agent-based reason count as irrational.[6] (An agent-based view here can hold that a flighty disposition

5. See Cicero, *Tusculan Disputations*, translated by J. E. King (Cambridge: Harvard University Press, 1950); and J. M. Rist, "Zeno and Stoic Consistency," *Phronesis* 22, 1977, pp. 161–74.

6. An agent-based view will presumably also require synchronic logical (and other kinds of) consistency among one's purposes as a condition of strength of purpose and of full practical rationality. For how can one be said to be strong of purpose in regard to one's intention to do *a*, if all the while one also intends to do an act *b* that (on the evidence available to one) would make it impossible to do *a*.

However, an inconsistency merely among one's desires or hankerings (tonight I have some desire to eat Italian, but also some desire to eat Chinese) seems not to be rationally criticizable, and for that reason the present account has focused only on

is irrational apart from considerations of consequences and that the term ''inconsistent'' is a partial indication of that fact.)

Now clearly the putatively agent-based virtue of (diachronic) consistency with respect to intentions and purposes is one, but only one, element in the larger virtue of strength of purpose (or perseverance). The latter seems to require not only that one tend to *retain* one's purposes but also, for example, that one appropriately *act on them*. Thus someone who intends to do something, doesn't change her mind, but ends up not doing the thing can be accused of *weakness of will*, and such a person can, in addition, be charged not only with lacking strength or firmness of purpose, but very clearly also with being irrational. (In order to avoid confusion, I shall for the moment ignore the fact that such a person may also be accused of being inconsistent.)[7]

But weakness or infirmity of purpose also seems attributable to someone who intends a certain end, but inexplicably (e.g., the proposed means is not immoral or likely to undercut some other end) lacks any intention to do what he takes to be a (necessary) means to that end. Such an internal state is a paradigm example of means-end or instrumental irrationality, and it doesn't in any obvious way involve either weakness of will or flighty purpose(s). (We may also use the term ''inconsistent'' in such a case, but, once again, I want to put off for a moment our discussion of the implications of that usage.) So the rational virtue of strength of purpose (or perseverance) seems to require or involve three different psychological elements: retention of intentions/ends (other things being equal); intending the means to one's ends (other things being equal); and nonweakness of will (which latter involves appropriately *acting* on one's intentions). These three phenomena may ultimately be analyz-

conflicting intentions and purposes. (On this point, see Michael Bratman, *Intentions, Plans, and Practical Reason* [Cambridge, Mass.: Harvard University Press, 1987], pp. 15f.) Note too, finally, that when outside forces *interfere* with the exercise of practical reason—e.g., when someone has a fever or has undergone a lobotomy—we don't consider the alteration or loss of purposes to be flighty or irrational (on the part of the agent).

7. For simplicity's sake I am also ignoring putative cases of weak will where the agent doesn't do what she thinks best (or good enough), but *never intended* to do so.

able into two or even one, but prima facie at least they are separable elements in paradigmatic strength of purpose. (Even if not, they seem to exhaust the content of that virtue.)

We have already seen that the retention of purposes is a fact of the inner life that is rational (a condition of rationality) as such. But whether one fails to intend what one takes to be the (sole) means to one's (sole) end is also an internal or psychological matter, and if, as seems plausible, the actions of someone who displays that irrational inner psychology count as irrational *because* they display or reflect such psychology, then we have yet another agent-based element in our account of practical reason.

Thus although it may be somewhat natural to think of means-end rationality consequentialistically, that is, as a matter of doing things that make certain other things more likely, I am suggesting that such rationality is more illuminatingly regarded as involving an (inner) psychological relation between intentions. In effect, this involves turning the consequentialistic view ''outside in,'' but such a treatment of the requirements of means-end rationality is not historically unfamiliar. It is perhaps already visible in Kant's treatment of ''hypothetical imperatives'' as primarily a matter of *willing* the means *whenever one wills* an end. And it is more clearly evident in the idea (which may well be Kantian and is certainly explicit in Sidgwick) that means-end rationality involves avoiding the situation where one wills an end but doesn't will the necessary means, but *doesn't* require one positively or categorically to will a certain (possibly immoral) means just because one already wills a certain (possibly immoral or even inherently or relationally irrational) end. In other words, means-end irrationality simply involves a certain sort of incoherence or inconsistency with regard to one's intentions or purposes.

Indeed the fact that the term ''inconsistency'' applies so readily here is some indication of the naturalness of an agent-based, as opposed to a consequentialistic, account of means-end rationality. Having inconsistent *beliefs* is (epistemically) irrational because of the inconsistency and, presumably, independently of the (good or bad) consequences of such beliefs; and in general the charge of inconsistency is supposed *in and of itself* to explain, or justify a claim of, irrationality. But, as I mentioned above, the charge of inconsistency (or incoherence) also seems applicable to cases of flighty purposes and weak will, and that is a further indication of how natural an agent-based approach in this area is. Of course, as we have just seen, the agent-based or at least the nonconsequentialistic character of means-end rationality is anticipated in certain historical views. But I believe it is easier to see the nonconsequentialism and the agent-basedness once one recognizes that means-end rationality can be grouped together with nonweakness of will and nonflightiness under the larger rubric of strength of purpose. For what is rational about both these latter doesn't seem to be a matter of their consequences, and the systematic invocation of agent-basing helps, therefore, to nail down what is rationally unacceptable about willing the end without willing the means.

As has been noted, however, weakness of will involves a failure to *act* as one intends or has intended, and what is irrational here is thus not entirely a matter of inner psychology, but rather involves a certain sort of connection—or failure of connection—*between* a choice or action and the deeper psychology of intention or purpose. But this sort of irrationality gives priority to what is psychologically deeper in the following sense. One's will is weak and one counts as irrational on a given occasion because one's actions fail to conform to one's purposes (or intentions), *rather than because one's purposes don't conform to one's actions*. That is, the "direction of fit" is from actions to purposes, not from purposes to actions. So if the irrationality of not doing something is due to or attributable to irrational weakness of will, the explanation, even if it involves a reference to the nonperformance of an action, *operates from a fixed point within*. This is different from our earlier characterization of agent-basing, but it is close enough so that my proposal now to widen the boundaries of agent-basing to include such cases will not, I trust, seem arbitrary or unreasonable. Even thus enlarged, agent-basing is a rather distinctive way to think of rationality, and at the moment, too, we can say that every putatively necessary condition of practical rationality we have so far considered in this chapter—including instrumental rationality conceived as covering much, but not all of inner strength of purpose—seems capable of being accounted for in agent-based terms.[8] Have we missed anything?

---

8. For the sake of argument I am willing to grant that the tendency to shift purposes arbitrarily doesn't count as *instrumental* or *means-end* irrationality. Also,

3. Practical Reason and Self-Interest

Consider one implication of supposing that what we have so far described is all there is to practical rationality. None of the elements of strength of purpose dictates *any particular purpose or intention*, and this remains true when we add non-insatiability and non-self-deception to the requirements of practical reason. So if there is reason to think that certain purposes or motives are required by practical reason as such, then what we have so far said about the conditions of practical rationality is far from complete—and what has to be added may well turn out to evade agent-based foundations.

However, what is most likely to be considered missing from the picture we have offered so far is some form of self-interest or self-concern, and I shall now try to show that the latter can naturally be conceived in agent-based terms. Then later, I shall explain why I think *moral motivation* follows out of a properly conceived self-interest and is therefore required by practical reason. The task of showing that and why moral motives and behavior are rationally required has been taken up by ethicists as diverse as Aristotle, Kant, and Sidgwick, and although there is no general agreement about how to make the connection between morality and practical reason, the desirability of making such a connection in philosophical terms has almost never been questioned. We shall see here that an agent-based understanding of rationality allows in interesting ways for such a connection, but let us first say what needs to be said about the role of self-interest in practical rationality.

Whenever (other-regarding) moral standards or motives are not at issue, it seems rational to pursue one's own self-interest (at least to some extent), and irrational not to do so, yet, as I have mentioned, our characterization of practical reason so far doesn't entail any rational requirement to promote one's own well-being. Or, if we think of self-interest as a motive, then nothing we have said in agent-based terms about practical reason entails that one must adopt or have this motive, or the purposes it may involve. This means that, for all we have said so far, a person can in all rationality fail to care

---

for reasons of space, I am ignoring the tension that exists between treating the in-tending of means to ends as a rational requirement and the not implausible supposition that such intending is criterial of actually *having* a certain end.

at all about her own well-being—and not just a person who already has a pretty good life and may be moderate in her desires, but even someone who is totally unhappy. Surely, one may say, that doesn't make sense.

But notice this. Kant too argued that (the motive of) self-interest is not a direct or immediate categorical requirement of practical reason, but he also allowed that one might have indirect reasons to be concerned with one's own happiness. If unhappiness makes one gloomy and uninterested in helping others, then the rational moral requirement to help others can indirectly require concern for one's own happiness as a means of fulfilling one's other, more basic rational duties.

Something similar can be said in connection with our agent-based view as we have so far sketched it. Strength of purpose is likely to be difficult to maintain if one is miserable and unhappy (and fretting about it), so, *given that one has purposes at all*, one might have reason to promote one's own happiness to a substantial extent. (This is also similar to the utilitarian idea that the attempt to do the best we can for humanity as a whole may as a matter of causal fact require us to take some time off from that task for rest and recreation.)

However, this sort of indirection is unlikely to satisfy those who believe it makes no rational sense to lack the motive of self-concern or self-interest. Anyone who thinks this way is likely to reject any purely formal conception of practical reason and to hold, rather, that certain consistent, non-self-defeating, etc., sets or patterns of purposes are simply irrational. Among these, it is natural to think, are imagined cases where someone is completely or largely indifferent to her own well-being, to how good her life is or will be. And anyone who thinks this way is unlikely to be satisfied to understand self-interested motivation as rationally required *only to the extent* it is necessary to the entirely optional purposes of one's life. Since I am myself very sympathetic to the idea that full rationality contains a material requirement of self-interest, I would like, at this point, to show you how this idea can be accommodated within an agent-based conception of practical reason (that already contains formal conditions of the sort elaborated above).

Consider, then, first the difference between doing what actually serves one's self-interest or promotes one's well being and doing what expectably will have this effect. Utilitarianism frequently presents itself in an actualistic version that treats right action as a matter solely of actual consequences, but even utilitarians—for example, Smart in his contribution to his volume with Williams—wouldn't want to claim that practical rationality is a matter of actual, rather than expectable, good consequences.[9] Being rationally self-interested, then, doesn't entail anything about actual consequences, but at most about expectable consequences for an agent. But I now want to introduce a further distinction: between acts whose consequences are expectably best or good for the agent and acts motivated by an agent's concern for her own (greatest) well-being.

It seems to me that if self-interest or self-concern is a condition of practical rationality, then that condition must be understood as a form of motivation rather than merely of expectation. Being rationally self-interested will require that one act out of concern for one's own well-being or self-interest and not just with the expectation that what one is doing will serve one's self-interest. (Note how "self-interest" is naturally used to refer either to a motive or to the object or goal of that motive.) Thus a person who knows that a certain action is necessary to his own survival or minimal happiness might be totally unconcerned with such facts and perform that action merely on a whim or haphazardly. The practical motivation or attitude of such a person will surely be accounted irrational by someone who wants to insist on the rational claims of self-interest, and this means that a person's motives aren't acceptably rational if he is indifferent to his own well-being—whatever his expectations concerning, or the expectable consequences of, his actions.

By the same token, a motive cannot be rendered rational by *its* actual or expectable consequences, and in this respect the situation in an agent-based theory of practical reason is quite parallel to that within agent-based moral theory.[10] We saw earlier (in chapters 1 and 5) that the moral praiseworthiness or goodness of a motive like universal benevolence is not plausibly conceived as a function of its consequences, and a very similar point applies to concern for one's

9. See J. J. C. Smart, "An Outline of a System of Utilitarian Ethics" in Smart and Williams, *Utilitarianism: For and Against* (Cambridge: Cambridge University Press, 1973), pp. 47f.

10. The idea that motives and/or intentions are to be rationally assessed in terms of (some aspect of) their consequences can be found both in Bratman, *Intentions*, and in Gauthier, *Morals by Agreement*.

own self-interest or the lack of it. For example, a woman relatively indifferent to her own welfare might have a rich uncle who learned of that fact, took pity on her, and, without her knowing it, helped her to be better off than she otherwise could have been. Her indifference in that case will actually result in good, even optimal, consequences for her, but it is none the less irrational by our common lights. Similarly, if the woman learns that the uncle is helping out in this way *and is indifferent to that fact as well*, then her lack of concern for her own well-being has *expectably* good or best consequences for her, but would still, intuitively, be regarded as an irrational state or form of motivation.

So self-regarding consequentialistic considerations seem less than decisive in determining the rationality or irrationality of (well-being-oriented) motives. We have intuitive reason to hold that a lack of self-concern is *inherently* irrational, and in that case, an agent-based theory of practical reason can include the particular motive of self-interest or concern for one's own long-term well-being among the necessary requirements of being rational.[11] But if, in addition to the agent-based virtues of non-self-deception, strength of purpose, and noninsatiability, practical rationality requires self-interested motivation, we need to be able to say how much or what kind of self-interest sets limits on rational choice. After all, the egoist possesses self-interested motivation and may exemplify our other agent-based rational virtues, so why not say that the strongest kind of self-interested motivation is necessary to being rational, that one is rationally required to be an egoist?

This is in fact something I think we should (and will want to) resist saying, and the argument of the next section will indicate why egoism isn't rationally permissible (optional), much less required. But if totally enveloping self-concern or self-interest isn't a dictate of practical reason, it doesn't follow that *minimal* (a modicum of) self-interest is all that practical reason requires. Indeed, it seems far more reasonable to suppose that if self-interested motivation is rationally required, what is required is that one be concerned to have

---

11. Note further that treating self-interested motivation as necessary to practical rationality doesn't commit one to any particular theory of human well-being or attribute any one theory of well-being (indeed any *theory* at all) to everyone who is motivationally self-interested (cf. similar points made about morality as universal benevolence in Chapter 1).

or obtain a full and good life for oneself. I don't have an *argument* for this conclusion, but, as I indicated, it seems fairly reasonable in itself as a condition of practical rationality, and it is further worth noting that nothing in this way of seeing things is incompatible with the moral ideals of caring defended earlier in this book.

We earlier argued that self-concern, intimate caring, and humane caring can permissibly, and perhaps should, be balanced against one another in a morally good person, and I am simply now adding that a certain sort of self-concern, even if not necessarily to moral good-ness, *is* a necessary condition of counting as a (practically) rational person. The person who wants/seeks a good, rich, full life for herself may also want/seek to be of substantial help to intimates and other people generally in *their* lives, and for our remaining purposes, I shall assume that *at least* this degree of self-concern is an agent-based requirement of practical reason. This is prima facie consistent with rational egoism, and it is, as I just said, also seemingly consis-tent with the moral requirements that can be derived from an agent-based morality of caring, as sketched earlier. However, I hope now to show you that the assumption that one should in all rationality be concerned to have a full and good life actually *undercuts* egoism and gives us reason to regard balanced moral caring as *rationally required*.

4. The Rational Requirements of Morality

To show you why practical reason yields substantial requirements of morality, I shall have to borrow from our previous account of the morality of caring and also from chapter 6. In chapter 6, I defended, among other things, the view that the intrinsic (or, if you prefer, noninstrumental) personal goods of friendship and love (and of com-munity, etc.) essentially require the moral virtues of caring. That is, it is possible to obtain the good of love or of friendship only on the basis of caring deeply about the person one is involved with in that relationship, and the goods of larger association—for example, of political, ethnic, religious, or even sporting community—in similar fashion require and are grounded in nonintimate fellow-feeling and in concern about the welfare of (those with whom one participates in) such larger groups.

In making these claims I am, among other things, assuming the antihedonistic view of human well-being that was defended at considerable length in chapter 6. But apart from any philosophical arguments, surely the assumption that one can gain the good of friendship only through loving or caring deeply about the friend is plausible in its own right. If one doesn't care in that way, the relationship presumably isn't a friendship to begin with, but, in addition, the relationship that does obtain isn't the kind of relationship we normally or naturally regard as good in its own right. Certainly, people can use one another or one person can dominate another who cares for him, but (as I mentioned in chapter 6) we aren't inclined to think that, apart from the pleasures or profits obtained from such relationships, the relationships themselves add to the overall good of the lives of those involved. But this is just what we tend to think *is* true of friendship, and I shall presuppose as much in what follows.

At this point, the contours of the argument for the rational requirements of morality I want to give may be coming into view. If friendship and love are among life's great goods (and philosophers as distant as Hume and Aristotle, as well as many others, have believed this), then it is plausible to hold that a life devoid of these goods (and similarly for the goods of larger association) is not a full and good one. But the motive of self-interest or self-concern as formulated above is a concern to have or attain a full and good life for oneself, and if such concern is endemic to practical rationality, we are now in a position to give a rational justification for the moral motivation of caring.

Earlier, we saw that the psychology of insatiate desire is inherently (and thus in agent-based terms) irrational. An insatiable appetite seeks satisfaction and is unable to obtain it—and, as we saw, such a psychology is self-defeatingly irrational. But the same can now be said about an ineradicably selfish desire for a good and full life. If one seeks such a life for oneself but is incapable of the motivation necessary to one whole important area or kind of human good, then one's motivation is self-defeating and irrational as such. To the extent one is incapable of caring, noninstrumentally, for others, one's psychology undercuts the possibility of realizing one's desire for a full and good life. Given such a psychology, one may (somehow, or dimly) recognize that friendship and love are important goods and one may seek love and friendship with others. But if one never develops a caring attitude, the relationships one ends up with will at best only appear to be love or friendship and will at worst constitute using or dominating over people or some other such *distorted* relationship.

But more needs to be said. For a caring or at least a concerned attitude may be lukewarm or weak, but love and close friendship require much stronger attitudes of concern and flourish as special or distinctive personal goods only when nourished by such attitudes. What they require, in particular, I think, is that one's concern for near and dear not be *dwarfed* by (typical, strong) self-concern, or, to put things slightly differently, that the person's concern for friends and loved ones should motivationally *counterbalance* her concern for her own interests (as well as her humanitarianism).

By the same token, I think people are unable to reap the distinctive good(s) of belonging to or participating politically in large(r) groups or units of association if their concern for those groups or units cannot substantially counteract self-concern and concern for near and dear. If, as Aristotle and a good many others have held, we are basically political-social animals, then we need the fulfillment of political participation and of sharing in and with larger groups, and our lives are impoverished where community is no longer possible and where political participation is not allowed.[12] But if that is so, it will also be true that where our own psychology undermines the possibility of partaking of such larger goods of association, our desire for a full and good life will be incapable of being realized. However real and powerful that desire may be, its irredeemably selfish character will render it self-defeating and irrational as such.

But if a self-defeating motive or set of motives is irrational from a practical standpoint, then the rational requirement of self-concern expands to a requirement that we be self-concerned or self-interested

---

12. I am assuming here that a permanent hermit cannot have a full or fully good life, however full his solitary life may otherwise be, and more generally I want to say that the kind of life we have reason to aspire to requires all the basic (types of) goods we have been and shall be discussing. But having such a life doesn't necessarily involve being "well-rounded," and I in no way wish to assume that someone with a full, good life tries, say, to be versatile and accomplish things in many different areas of human life rather than concentrating her accomplishments in some single direction. Compare and contrast Thomas Hurka, *Perfectionism* (Oxford: Oxford University Press, 1993).

in a non-self-defeating way. So our argument thus far, if successful, shows that practical rationality requires that each person be concerned with having/attaining a full and good life, but also be capable of (exemplifying a) psychological balance between such self-concern and two kinds of noninstrumental concern (or care) about the well-being, the good lives, of others: concern for (the group of) those near and dear to the person and concern for (the class of) those whose larger association with the person makes possible the goods of community and social groups generally. And it also shows that we must be capable of the kind of concern for larger political units we described in chapter 4.

But at this point I can see someone objecting: "Yes, I can understand how participation in (the) politics (of one's own country) is an important ingredient in a full, good life and how a person cannot gain the personal good of political participation if they simply use fellow-citizens and lack strong concern for the good of their country. But the assumption that merely sharing a common humanity with (a vast number of) other people is also an important personal good is far less plausible, and in that case we have no reason (analogous to what we have seen in connection with love and friendship) to think that rational self-concern requires (the exemplification or cultivation of) *the humanitarian side* of balanced caring."

But think of what our shared membership in the human race actually involves. It involves living on the same planet, our Earth, and having common origins and (to a large extent) a common history and common problems; and I think our common tendency to ignore the good (for each and every one of us) that may be at stake here stems from the tendency of such facts to be far from salient and, like the air we breathe, to fade far into the background of our awareness, most of the time. Perhaps we need what Daniel Dennett felicitously calls an "intuition pump" in order to reconnect with or more clearly envisage what each of us finds, or may find, of value, and even, I think, precious, in our shared humanity. And perhaps the following will do.

Think of books or films in which the human species has largely died out or been obliterated and in which a very, very small group survives and hopes to continue into the future. If you or I were part of such a group, I think we would feel *bereft* of something very important to us, and what we would be bereft or robbed *of* would (among other things) be the personal good of belonging to a (much) larger humanity (of belonging to what can be seen as a large human *community*). So if it makes no sense in self-interested rational terms to want to live in such a vestigial human world, I think we have reason to acknowledge that shared humanity is an important (though rarely salient) good in human lives.

But consider now what is involved in such a good. Our sense of bereftness in a holocaust situation would at least partly reflect our anguish at what had happened to everyone else, and someone lacking in humane concern for others wouldn't feel such anguish or, I believe, a sense of *bereftness* either, at the loss of so much of humanity. So I think that that loss is a great personal loss only for someone who really cares about other people, only for someone who exemplifies the virtue of humanitarian caring, and the parallelism between the good of shared humanity and goods like friendship, love, and political participation thus seems fairly complete.

If I am not mistaken, then, an agent-based conception of practical reason that includes an appropriate requirement of self-interest or self-concern yields, under certain accompanying assumptions, a further rational requirement that we be capable of both balanced caring and love of country. And lest the reference to capability rather than actuality be thought to render this conclusion fairly empty, consider its implication that sociopaths and others presumed incapable of genuine concern for others are practically irrational. For according to what we have said, the motives, the motivational psychology, of such people will be inherently self-defeating *if they have a rationally appropriate level of concern for their own well-being*. This is in itself, I think, an interesting substantive conclusion, but it doesn't yet explicitly tell us whether *actual* caring motivation is rationally required of us.

However, once we understand the reasons why a sociopath has to be considered irrational, we can see that there generally is reason for us and for others to remain or try to become caring moral individuals, since *actual* caring has turned out to be a necessary means to (or ingredient in) fulfilling a practical concern (or purpose) that is rationally incumbent on us, the concern to have a full and good life.[13] In other words, knowing what we have learned from the above

---

13. I use the qualifying word "generally" because I think there can be circum-

argument, we are rationally required to seek or work toward a good and full life for ourselves, and it would demonstrate irrational weakness in that purpose if we simply let ourselves not care (appropriately) about other people. So we have arrived at a rational justification for being, or trying to be, caring, morally and politically decent individuals, a justification grounded in the agent-based conceptions of morality, of practical reason, and of the goods of friendship, community, and political participation that I have sketched above.[14]

One last step, however, remains to be taken. For even if we are rationally required to care about people (in different ways or degrees), it may be wondered whether that automatically means that *action* on behalf of others is also rationally required or rationally justified. Of course, some philosophers (notably Gauthier, *Morals by Agreement*) think that the justification of certain intentions or other practical attitudes automatically translates into a justification for acting on those intentions. But many consequentialists and others have disagreed, and I propose that we look at this matter afresh from the perspective of our agent-based conception of practical reason.

The question we need to consider is whether someone who has been rationally led to become or remain concerned about (the well-being of) certain individuals will then have reason actually to help those individuals when they need help. And it may seem obvious at this point that the person does have such reason. After all, one could

---

stances in which a selfish individual probably *wouldn't* have reason, on balance, to try to become (more) caring. A self-knowing sociopath or someone near death who had never cared about other people might reasonably think it was *too late* for him to become moral or reap the benefits of doing so. In addition, the desire to lead a full and good life may itself become practically irrelevant and inoperative in someone who knows she is close to death.

14. The reader may wonder why I haven't (again) appealed to self-defeatingness in arguing that actual caring is rationally demanded of us. But the notion of self-defeatingness that applies in this case is much weaker than the one I have been appealing to. For I have argued that where motivation has internally inconsistent or incongruent aspects or elements that make it impossible for its aims to be realized, such motivation is self-defeating and irrational. But an egoist who merely *doesn't* care about others *might* realize the aims of his selfishness by somehow managing to eliminate that selfishness in favor of a more caring attitude. His pure self-concern is self-defeating only as long as it remains in existence, but that is also true of the desire to fall asleep or to quench one's thirst, and it is far from clear that such weak self-defeatingness justifies a charge of practical irrationality.

hardly count as deeply concerned about the well-being of another unless one were ready to help them in time of need, and although such readiness may not amount to an actual (conditional) purpose or intention, something like weakness of purpose would seem to characterize anyone who cared about a friend and was prepared to help her, but failed to do so when help was actually needed. (Some may wonder whether this description is logically coherent, but the tentative assumption that it is makes things harder, not easier, for my account.)

So one demonstrates something like weakness of purpose if one cares deeply about someone and doesn't act accordingly, and this would seem, then, to offer us a rational justification for acting in the caring ways that, I have argued, morality requires. But there is one problem. Sometimes acting in such ways involves *self-sacrifice* and goes against self-concern. For even if love and friendship constitute part of our well-being, it seems possible for someone who, for example, helps a friend out of financial straits to end up worse off than if she hadn't helped. So if someone has to decide between helping a friend avoid absolute poverty and maintaining her own somewhat comfortable lifestyle, she must choose between acting out of concern for her own well-being and acting out of concern for that of her friend. But then, if, as I have argued, both concerns are rationally required, does this mean that anyone having to choose between these concerns is in some sort of rational dilemma where whatever she does will be rationally unacceptable?

I don't think so. For one thing, even if one sacrifices one's comfort for one's friend and is to some extent worse off than one could have been, one's overall life may still be (likely to be) a full and good one, and in that case one's self-sacrifice may not display any lack of the rational concern to have such a life. (Remember that a good full life isn't the same thing as the best life one could possibly lead.) But what about cases where helping one's friend would actually (or probably) make it impossible for one to have an overall good life? Wouldn't rationality, as I have described it, at least require one to avoid making *such* a sacrifice?

Not necessarily. For if, as I argued above, practical reason requires some sort of inner, motivational balance between self-concern and concern for loved ones, then on a given occasion it may be rationally *optional* whether one helps one's friend or oneself. So self-sacrifice may sometimes be rationally required and in any event often makes rational sense, from the standpoint of the present theory.

5. Conclusion

The idea that self-interest requires us to be moral goes back at least as far as Plato, and over the millenia and up until the present day there have been many attempts to defend the rationality of morality in such terms. But these efforts have not always been entirely convincing, and, in any event, since Kant a quite different way to defend the rationality of being moral has become prominent. Instead of tying morality to the self-interest, the well-being, of the moral agent, Kant and his followers have argued that morality is rationally required by the conditions of practical *autonomy* and *consistency* and quite independently of any (grounding) connection to the well-being of the moral agent.

The argument of this chapter in a sense combines these two approaches. Above, I included a condition of self-interest in the requirements of practical reason, and the argument we used to show that morality is rationally required depended, in a most un-Kantian fashion, on appealing to a connection between rationality and self-interest (conceived as a motive rather than as the actual well-being of the agent). But the argument also had to invoke a requirement of consistency, since self-defeatingness and weakness of purpose are both instances of practical inconsistency, and to that extent it resembles the arguments Kant and some Kantians have used to defend the rational status of the moral.

What the above argument resembles most of all, however, is the set of ideas that lies behind the familiar paradox of egoism (and the connected paradox of hedonism). Since Butler, and earlier too, it has been seen that unselfish concern for others may be a component or source of human happiness, and it has been recognized that if one is too (or exclusively) concerned with one's own good, one at the very least *runs the risk* of undercutting that good. The other side of this coin, moreover, can be seen in the embryonic paradox of *unselfishness* that we find in the Biblical injunction to cast one's bread upon the waters and in the related idea that in order to live (or flourish) one must first die (hate the world). Such views make assumptions about the actions of God: for example, that only if one sacrifices worldly things or has faith, will one be rewarded with eternal life. But I think they at least foreshadow the idea that developing or preserving (a substantial degree of) unselfishness is what an enlightened selfishness or egoism would itself recommend quite apart from theological assumptions.

The argument offered above puts new flesh on the idea of there being a paradox of (or in) egoism (or unselfishness), and it does this in agent-based terms. If agent-based practical reason requires substantial self-interested motivation, it also requires the kind of caring for others that an agent-based morality of caring holds to be the essence of or the basis for all morality. But this then clearly rules out egoism as a rational attitude to life.

Of course, we have attempted to accomplish this by deriving rational concern for others from premises that include a fundamental rational requirement to care about having a full and good life oneself. (As with morality, this requirement doesn't kick in, or kick in fully, for children or the mentally limited.) We have in effect reversed the order of ethical explanation one finds, for example, in Kant, where the categorical rational requirement and duty to promote the happiness of others (together with other requirements/duties) provides us with our most stringent reasons to seek our own happiness. But, intuitively speaking, Kant's argument gets the order exactly wrong. We don't normally think concern for one's own happiness requires *rational* support from morality and are inclined rather, like Sidgwick, to treat the rationality of such concern as fundamentally obvious and as categorical in its own right.[15]

By contrast, it is not initially obvious that a lack of concern for others is *irrational*, as opposed to *immoral*. This much any ordinary person will or can tell you, and it is the reason, indeed, why so many philosophers have sought to provide a rational justification for altruism and morality generally. But the very existence of such efforts tends to show that the rational status of altruism and morality is *not* ethically fundamental; and there is no reason why an agent-based virtue ethics shouldn't, therefore, be comfortable treating the rationality of self-concern as a basic ethical fact and treating the

---

15. See Sidgwick, *The Three Methods of Ethics*, pp. 7f., 15, 35ff., 112ff.

rationality—*though not the morality*—of other-concern as derivative.

However, having said as much, I want to caution against a misinterpretation of the previous discussion. As Prichard and many others have pointed out, a fully moral person doesn't need or seek the reassurance that morality is rationally justified or in her self-interest, and it is certainly no part of my purpose here to suggest otherwise.[16] It is well known that a virtue like benevolence needn't call attention to itself, and nothing, therefore, in the morality of caring dictates that the caring moral individual will be concerned about the moral status of her actions. Rather, as was argued earlier, in chapter 2, she can act from concern for others without considering whether she is acting rightly or wrongly or, for that matter, caringly or uncaringly. Although she *might* consider these matters, the highest degree of caring seems to entail thinking solely in terms of what will make certain people better- or worse-off.

But by the same token such an ideal caring person also won't worry or think about whether it is (in general or on a particular occasion) rational or in her self-interest to act caringly, and too much concern with the latter issues seems to constitute a failure of or imperfection in unselfish (which is not the same as selfless) caring. The argument offered in this section thus has *more* practical relevance to an uncaring or egoistic individual who still has a chance to change her ways, and in effect it *is* addressed to such a person. But this then raises the issue whether the account of practical reason offered in this chapter is action-guiding in a way that our agent-based conception of morality is not, and I would like now to spend some brief time clarifying this question.

In this book, I have been defending the idea that the ideal moral individual exemplifies a certain pattern of benevolent caring and that such caring doesn't involve concern with the moral status of one's own actions. But the agent-based picture of ideal practical rationality sketched in this chapter seems likewise not to require a concern for the rational status of one's choices or actions. According to the view defended here, the ideal rational individual is (nonegoistically) con-

16. See H. A. Prichard, ''Does Moral Philosophy Rest on a Mistake?'' in *Moral Obligation* (Oxford: Oxford University Press, 1949).

cerned to have a full and good life, but such a person needn't think that this kind of motivation is rationally ideal nor worry about whether she is rational in her choices. She may simply seek a good and full life, and the standards of rational evaluation defended above may not enter into her consciousness or her motivation. If concern for others needn't be morally self-conscious and can simply aim at the good of others, then a person with a (nonegoistic) desire for her own good may simply aim at *that* good without being *rationally* self-conscious.[17]

In addition, the above account of practical reason stressed strength of purpose and non-self-deception, but there seems to be no reason why either of these further conditions should require rational self-consciousness. A person with real strength of purpose keeps to certain purposes over long stretches of time, but if such a person has to remind himself of the irrationality of capricious changes of purpose in order to stay on course with given purposes, then the person seems precisely to exemplify less strength of purpose than someone whose purposes kept him on course by their own inner momentum. And non-self-deception is in and of itself the furthest thing from an action-guiding notion: no one ever (well hardly ever) abstained from self-deception out of a consideration of how irrational it is to deceive oneself or out of some sheer imperative not to deceive oneself.

I thus believe that our agent-based view here of practical reason has nothing essentially action-guiding about it. However, when we applied it to the question whether there is a rational justification for being moral, we did invoke various aspects of that conception and address them in an action-guiding way to immoralists and moral skeptics. Like so many before us, we were trying to show such people the rational error of their ways, and in doing so, we addressed

---

17. Earlier we saw that the use of moral principles and the having of explicitly moral thoughts can get in the way of one's concern for others and distance one from others in a way that is less than morally ideal. But by the same token someone who has to invoke principles of rationality in order to be concerned with or act on behalf of her own needs, interests, or happiness is in some measure distant or even estranged from her own needs, etc.; and this too seems less than fully rational (and a bit unhealthy as well). I therefore strongly disagree with the account of practical rationality offered by Thomas Scanlon in *What We Owe to Each Other* (Cambridge, Mass.: Belknap, 1998), which treats the self-conscious or conscientious application of rational principles as the core of rational motivation and choice.

to them various general claims about what is rational or irrational. We said, for example, that a rational person seeks to have a good and full life; that such a life requires various political and personal commitments; and that someone with such commitments shows irrational weakness of purpose if they fail to follow up on those commitments in their actions. And at least the first and last of these assumptions are explicitly assumptions about the general requirements of rationality.

I believe that the ideal rational individual doesn't need arguments like these: such a person doesn't need to be convinced, through the evocation of rational principles, of the need to follow through on commitments, such a person doesn't need to be reminded that self-concern is rational, that insatiability is irrational, that self-deception is irrational. But just as we earlier left some moral room for conscientiousness, we can allow that someone who guides herself to some extent by rational principles can embody a substantial degree of rationality. I don't want to go into the details of this idea here, but they would be analogous to what was said in Chapter 2 about moral conscientiousness. And having said as much, there is an issue of terminology that now needs to be addressed.

I am saying that the ideal rational individual doesn't guide herself by principles of practical reason, and the conception of practical reason offered in this chapter is thus not intended as action-guiding. But one might well sense a contradiction here, because "practical" can mean "action-guiding" and because it is therefore natural to think that practical reason or rationality must contain or be constituted at least in part by rules or standards that guide agents and their choices. Some clarification seems in order.

A contrast with *epistemic* or *theoretical* rationality is absolutely essential to standard usage of expressions like "practical reason" and "practical rationality," and my own usage of these terms picks up on this contrast rather than relying on any assumptions about action-guidingness. On my usage, in other words, a description or theory of practical rationality or reason offers (and defends) standards for evaluating voluntary actions and other entities having to do with such actions, but there is no assumption that these standards have to guide any agent who conforms to or meets them. And this is really not far from what is typically meant by "practical reason." Given the Greek root of "practical," it seems plausible to use that word in the noncommittal way I am proposing, and so, rather than deny that there is such a thing as practical reason, because I think standards of rational evaluation don't essentially guide action, I prefer to say that the present agent-based view offers us an alternative way of understanding (what philosophers and others have been talking about all along when they spoke of) practical reason and practical rationality.[18] This terminology needn't confuse or mislead us, I think, and I therefore hope that what I have sketched here will indicate something of the promise of an agent-based approach to practical rationality.

In effect, I am saying that the question of the rational justification of morality is philosophically important independently of its practical bearing on most people's lives. Practical rationality is an important human endowment, and it is, therefore, very much worth our philosophical while to consider, as we have here, whether and to what extent morality speaks to that side of our nature. I believe, then, that the above discussion shows us (at least one reason) why the immoralist and everyone else should be moral. But it does so without distorting the character of morality in the way Prichard warned against. A caring moral individual isn't worried about, and doesn't feel a personal need to answer, the question "why should I be moral?" But that doesn't mean that that question doesn't have an answer.

18. Actually, one can, even in agent-based terms, distinguish between practical reason (as a body of standards) and practical rationality (as a quality of those individuals, choices, motives, etc., that meet those standards), but we needn't expand on this here.

EIGHT

EXTENDING THE APPROACH

1. Hyper-Agent-Basing

Agent-basing involves grounding the moral or rational assessment of actions in moral or rational claims about motives or other psychological states. But this characterization leaves questions about human good or the good life out of the picture, and agent-based theories need not, therefore, have anything to say about human good/ welfare. Or they may treat questions about human good as a side issue, defining or explaining the latter notion in terms entirely independent of what they have to say about morality and/or rationality. However, someone who believes in agent-basing might also seek to ground claims about welfare and the good life in an agent-based view of morality and rationality, that is, in a particular conception of moral and rational *virtue*. And this last possibility is of particular interest here, given what has been said in the last two chapters.

If it makes sense to ground claims about what is good in life in claims about virtue (as we argued in chapter 6) and if (as argued in chapter 7) it is possible to give an agent-based account of both morality and practical rationality, then we may wonder whether all claims about human good cannot ultimately be reduced to or based in claims about ethical human character and motives. And for convenience's sake, we can describe any view that explains all human good (or welfare or well-being) in terms of morality and/or rationality understood in agent-based terms as *hyper-agent-based*.

There hasn't been a great deal of agent-basing in the previous history of philosophy, but one fairly clear proponent of agent-basing, James Martineau, is also pretty clearly *not* an advocate of hyper-agent-basing. Martineau may ultimately understand all morality in terms of an ethical ranking of motives, but he treats human well-being in a manner fairly reminiscent of utilitarianism. He is close, that is, to being some sort of hedonist about the things that are good in life (and not as such morally good), and if the reader wonders how someone so ethically high-minded as Martineau could "descend" to hedonism in his theory of the good life, remember that even Kant is some sort of hedonist about well-being: about *das Wohl*, as opposed to *das Gute*.

Now, as we saw in chapter 6, the Stoics attempt to understand human good or well-being in terms of virtue, but it is difficult to attribute agent-basing to the Stoics, so their views probably aren't either agent-based or hyper-agent-based. However, given the terminology we applied, in chapter 6, to the Stoic account of human good, we have now an additional way to characterize hyper-agent-basing. We can say that a view is hyper-agent-based if and only if it is (in a coherent way) agent-based and also elevationist about good or well-being. Of course, we have argued that, like the Stoics, Aristotle can profitably be regarded as some sort of elevationist, but, once again, since Aristotle is no agent-baser, we cannot regard his overall theory as hyper-agent-based in the sense we have given that term; and in fact I don't know of *any* hyper-agent-based ethical theories other than what I am about to propose. But in order to proceed further, we need to make some adjustments or additions to what was said earlier in chapter 6.

Chapter 6 was written to be independent of the arguments and conclusions of chapter 7, but since chapter 7 has now provided us with an agent-based account of practical reason or rationality, it is worth seeing whether we can explicate or explain all human goods, all the basic elements of human well-being, in terms of the overall conception of morality and rationality we are now, finally, committed to. I am therefore proposing that we revise or update chapter 6 to a small extent in the light of our now completed theory of moral and rational virtue, and in fact the modifications I shall make really are quite modest. So let us see what a hyper-agent-based theory based on the main conclusions (so far) of this book has to say about human good.

The elevationist account of human well-being offered in chapter 6 constituted a version of the "objective list" approach, *but one with larger aspirations than many or most objective list theories*. As an alternative to the more unifying (but arguably more simplistic) "desire-fulfillment" and hedonistic accounts of what makes a life good, a given objective list theory can seem to be a bit of a hodge-podge; for there need be no deep explanation of why the things on a given list are on that list, and this has certainly been true of most (recent) objective list theories.[1] Indeed, the typical reason why a given author puts a given item on his or her list of the elements of human well-being is that the item in question intuitively seems to be good in itself for human or other sentient beings, but since such intuitiveness is epistemic rather than constitutive, the inventors of lists have typically not offered any general or overarching explanation of why any or each given item on their lists really is intrinsically good for people.

However, chapter 6's elevationist account of our well-being takes us further than (most) previous objective list theories (if "theories" is indeed the right term for them) by offering a (constitutively) necessary condition for being listed. It says that only things that involve one or another virtue can properly be elements of our well-being, and most other objective list theories don't even offer necessary conditions, much less a full explanation, of what is intrinsically (or noninstrumentally) good for us. So the account offered in chapter 6 is more explanatory than the usual objective list account, but, given our now completed agent-based picture of moral and rational virtue, I think we are at this point in a position to offer a fuller explanation (of a slightly expanded list).

We can now say what the chief moral and rational virtues are, and we could, on that basis, go on to claim that every item that

---

1. I am understanding "objective list theory" with the emphasis on "list," but if the distinction among hedonist, desire-fulfillment, and objective list theories of well-being is meant to be exhaustive, then Aristotle and the Stoics also have objective list theories, and what I am saying about the hodgepodge of the latter certainly doesn't hold for those theories (which we criticized on quite different grounds in chapter 6). Nor does it hold for certain objective list accounts that seek to explain and unify various human goods under the rubric of (developing or perfecting different aspects of) human nature: for example, Thomas Hurka's *Perfectionism* (New York: Oxford University Press, 1993).

deserves to be on the objective list of human goods corresponds to and requires its own distinctive rational or moral virtue. We could say, that is, that the good things in life correspond one-to-one with the main rational and moral virtues specified in our earlier accounts of these matters, and we would then be able to state more than a (one) necessary condition of intrinsic or noninstrumental goodness/ well-being. We would be in a position to offer both necessary and sufficient conditions for something's being on the objective list of basic human goods, and so we would be able, in fact, to offer a full explanation of why any given human good is a human good.

The account of practical rationality in chapter 7 identified four major rational virtues. They were: noninsatiability (or minimal moderation), strength of purpose, non-self-deceptiveness (the courage to face disturbing facts), and self-concern (desire for one's own well-being). And apart from self-concern, about which it took a rather ambiguous or hedged stance, the agent-based caring morality we ended up tentatively endorsing in Part I treated two kinds of caring about individuals plus concern for the good of one's country (or some other appropriate political unit) as the three principal moral virtues.[2] So we have in fact distinguished seven main moral and rational virtues, and I want to suggest at this point that our objective list of human goods should contain seven items that correspond to these seven virtues. Most objective lists of goods contain a greater or lesser number of items offered for their intuitive plausibility, but the seven items derivable from our present assumptions not only are plausible in that sense and similar to what other objective list theories have said about the things that are good in life, but *can be fully explained relative to those assumptions*. Let us see more particularly how this can work, and let me begin by saying a bit more about the personal goods associated with moral virtue, goods like love, friendship, shared humanity, and political participation.

These goods, these basic elements, as our theory takes it, of human well-being, can all be called goods of connection, because of the way they involve us with something (someone or someones) beyond ourselves. And I want to say that each good of connection only counts as such because it involves or contains that part of

---

2. We weren't absolutely explicit about this in previous chapters, but the structure of our argument now calls for (greater) explicitness.

virtuous caring that is relevant to what the personal good in question involves a relation with. For example, the good of love or friendship depends on and involves intimate caring, because intimate caring is the part of virtuous caring that is specifically relevant to how we treat friends and loved ones; and, for exactly parallel reasons, the personal good of political participation within a given society requires and involves caring about the good, the welfare, *of that society*.

Goods like friendship and love thus correspond to and require virtuous intimate caring and as such constitute one basic class of human goods, one of the seven items on our list. The good of shared humanity analogously corresponds to and requires virtuous humanitarian caring; and, similarly, by corresponding to and requiring virtuous concern for political entities, the good of participation in politics also enters our list.

Let us turn next to rational virtue. Corresponding to and requiring the rational virtue of noninsatiability are various appetitive and sensuous goods of pleasure;[3] and by virtue (excuse me!) of a similar relation to strength of purpose, achievement also gets to be included on the list. Wisdom about deep matters then corresponds to the rational virtue of non-self-deception and enters the list on that basis. Finally, I believe there is a good corresponding to and requiring self-concern or self-interestedness that also belongs on the list, and that good, the only item I didn't previously mention in chapter 6, is self-esteem or a sense of self-worth.

So we have seven listed goods corresponding to seven major virtues (or aspects of virtue),[4] and they are, to bring them together

---

3. Noninsatiability may be necessary to appetitive goods, but, according to the present view, it isn't necessary to the goods of achievement: for someone insatiable about achievement(s) in a certain area may still (may *especially*) demonstrate the rationally virtuous strength of purpose that *is* necessary to the good of achievement. In fact, given our argument in chapter 7, insatiability may be irrational and a vice only when and where it is inherently self-defeating.

4. If there are, as I suspect, virtues that are neither forms of rationality nor of morality (e.g., fortitude and modesty), they don't give rise to corresponding human goods, given what I have been saying above. This seems a more than acceptable result, given the special importance we philosophers have traditionally and typically attributed to the moral and rational virtues (as opposed to others, if we are willing to concede that there are any). For the present hyper-agent-based account of human good, by limiting the good things in life to items that correspond to rational and

and slightly simplify: appetitive and other goods of pleasure; achievement; wisdom; love and friendship; shared humanity; political participation; and self-esteem. This list is quite similar, as I have said, to many of the objective lists that have recently been offered, but the present theory, unlike (almost all) those others, gives an explanation of why those and just those plausible candidates for the status of intrinsic human (or personal) goods really do qualify as such. And it does so, let me just say, by assuming that to each and every (basic aspect of) moral and rational virtue there corresponds one and only one human good whose status as such derives from the way it corresponds to the relevant virtue and by then assuming, more particularly, that love/friendship is the (one and only) good that corresponds to and requires inimate caring, that wisdom is the (one and only) good that corresponds to and requires non-self-deceptiveness, and so on through the other good-to-virtue correspondences we have subscribed to just above.[5]

None of these assumptions, of course, is sacrosanct, but neither is any of them particularly outré or implausible in itself. The use of these assumptions allows us, furthermore, to account for all (non-instrumental or intrinsic) human good in a hyper-agent-based (and elevationistic) fashion, and the fact that the theory we end up with doesn't *seem* to have any particularly implausible implications either theoretically or for our judgment of particular cases (what things we call goods, what things we call virtues) strengthens the present approach (and may encourage us to develop it further).[6]

moral virtues, offers a (further) reason *why* the rational and the moral are more important than any other kind of virtue that may exist.

5. Any ethic of caring will think it important to establish a link between the moral goodness of (an attitude or motive of) caring and the (personal) desirability of certain caring relationships. But, as we saw in chapter 1, Noddings's attempt to explain the former in terms of the latter leaves the moral difference between caring and being cared for unaccounted for. Elevationism as applied to goods of connection reverses that order of explanation, viewing the desirability of caring relationships as based in the moral status of caring, but this conclusion seems to fit the phenomena better than Noddings's approach.

6. Tom Hurka has pointed out to me that, rather than see human good(s) as containing or accompanied by virtue(s), we could in elevationist and hyper-agent-based fashion see it/them as the intentional object(s) or goal(s) of (the) virtue(s). One can find the potential beginnings of such a view in Stephen Darwall's "Self-Interest

But does the present account really have no implausible implications? Doesn't it contain, for example, one candidate for status as
a human good that wasn't even mentioned, much less argued for, in
chapters 6 and 7, namely, self-esteem? Yes, to be sure. But self-
esteem is something several previous objective lists have included,
and there is no particular intuitive reason to think that it *isn't* one
of the basic good things in life. I didn't originally mention it in
chapter 6, in part because it seems to be mentioned on fewer objective lists than the other personal goods discussed there, but also
because the virtue I believe it entails, namely, self-concern, was left
with an ambiguous moral status in Part I (chapter 3) and only
emerged as a clear-cut *rational* virtue in chapter 7.

But is self-concern, concern for one's own welfare, really a necessary condition of self-esteem? In a word, I think yes. For someone
who always, for example, helps others when he can do the least
good for them and never does anything for himself, someone who
always chooses lesser goods for others over greater goods for himself, shows himself lacking in self-esteem. To present ways of thinking, such a person seems masochistic or burdened by inordinate and
presumably misdirected guilt, pathetic. As I mentioned earlier, the
Victorians may have admired selflessness and self-abnegation of the
sort just mentioned, but we nowadays don't admire these traits, and
think a certain measure of self-assertiveness, of the individual's, to
some extent, asserting his or her rights and interests against those
of others (when they conflict), is a sign of health, not something to
deplore or feel guilty about. (We also think the Victorians were
relatively naive, self-deluded, or unsophisticated about such moral-
psychological matters.) So for many of us a lack of real concern
with one's own happiness or well-being is a sure indication that
something has gone wrong with a given individual and, more particularly, that the individual has an unhealthy lack of self-esteem (is
burdened by inordinate, irrational, unhealthy guilt).[7] I think, then,

and Self-Concern'' (*Social Philosophy and Policy* 14, 1997, pp. 158–78), where it is
proposed that we understand what is good for someone in terms of what a person
who cares about that person would want for them.

   7. In ''Servility and Self-Respect'' (*The Monist* 57, 1973, pp. 87–104), Thomas
Hill treats certain sorts of deference, of servile behavior, toward others as indicative
of a lack of (moral/rational) self-esteem, but he insists, nonetheless, on upholding

that it makes sense to treat self-concern, that is, a substantial measure of concern for one's own interests, as necessary to proper self-esteem.

But that is not to say that self-concern is all that self-esteem involves or consists in—far from it. One is lacking in self-esteem, or a sense of self-worth or self-respect, if one is inclined (for the right price!) toward sycophancy or (for the right master!) toward submissive, blind obedience or (for the right authority!) toward needy credulity. These traits indicate a measure of servility and a lack of autonomy that by their very nature derogate from (the attribution of) full or desirable self-esteem, and it is interesting, in this connection, to note that autonomy in something like this sense is sometimes mentioned on objective lists of intrinsic human goods[8] but has not previously been mentioned by us.

However, the account of goods offered above, while it doesn't treat autonomy as a basic good, does treat self-esteem as one. So at the very least, our view entails that autonomy is a necessary element or aspect of an important human good, and that seems close enough to saying it actually is a good to satisfy, I think, even those who have made the latter claim. The idea that autonomy is a good isn't so overwhelmingly obvious and the distinction between good-status and being an element in a good isn't so overwhelmingly important to trouble those who would like to find a place for autonomy within an objective list theory. Or so, at least, it seems to me.

Still, there are one or two other items sometimes mentioned on objective lists that I have decidedly left no place for, and in order to test the strength or weakness of the present objective-list approach, I think we ought to consider just how much is lost in intuitiveness when we omit them. One of these items is power, something many people pursue and dream about for their lives. It is not

---

the Kantian view that there is nothing morally or rationally untoward or inappropriate about being uninterested in one's own happiness (except insofar as one sees it as helping to promote the happiness of others, etc.).

8. See, for example, Brad Hooker, "Is Moral Virtue a Benefit to the Agent," in *How Should One Live?* ed. R. Crisp (Oxford: Clarendon Press, 1996), esp. p. 145. For other discussions of the objective list approach, see, e.g., James Griffin, *Well-Being: Its Meaning, Measurement, and Moral Importance* (New York: Oxford University Press, 1986), and David Brink, *Moral Realism and the Foundations of Ethics* (Cambridge: Cambridge University Press 1989). The term "objective list" comes from Derek Parfit's *Reasons and Persons* (Oxford: Clarendon Press, 1984).

enough here to say that power is a means, not an end, that it is only valuable for the good things it can get you, because many people really do seem to want and be satisfied (to the extent they are not insatiable or greedy) with power—over others and especially political power—*as such*. And why can't this be? The analogy with money and miserliness is actually a double-edged sword here, since wealth too is often pursued for its own sake, and wealth doesn't mean a pile of gold coins in a miser's keep, but something less physically anchored and, well, *akin to a kind of power*.

Moreover, if one says that power and wealth are mere opportunities and that opportunities are valuable to us only for what they allow us actually to do or obtain, one fails to reckon with a certain human tendency to find even opportunities satisfying (to some extent) in themselves. Why else do so many people like (and value!) living in a large metropolis where there are myriad cultural opportunities, even when they (unlike many others, of course) don't take advantage of those opportunities and perhaps know they have no real intention of doing so? There is something comforting and even exhilarating, for some people, in knowing they *could* do various exciting or interesting things, and from the standpoint of such individuals, opportunity and opportunities really do constitute something inherently or noninstrumentally valuable. And do we really have a good argument to the contrary?

In that case, there are a whole number of possible goods that an objective list could well include, but we have ruled out as goods. Among them—and all these things can be considered opportunities for other, clearer examples of intrinsic life-goods—are: power (including perhaps fame), wealth, opportunities for enjoyment and improvement, physical health and capability, and, indeed, life itself, that is, being alive and *compos mentis*.

Now take physical health. This is clearly something that objective list theories can disagree and have disagreed about—some treating it as merely an instrumental good, others as intrinsically (or noninstrumentally) good. To that extent, I think intuitions vary and are not as strong as in other cases, with the result that this candidate for intrinsic good status can be said to be a "don't care."

Now "don't cares" are precisely those things that theory can gerrymander in the name of overall systematizing or simplification. As I mentioned earlier, Chomsky's "colorless green ideas sleep furiously" is just one good example, where theory—in this instance the theory of syntax—can make different judgments about the grammaticality of a given sentence *depending on the other things the theory needs or wants to say*. Chomsky and others have gone back and forth, over the years, on the question of the grammaticality of sentences like that just mentioned, and it is all right for this to happen, I think, just because this sentence and others like it really are "don't cares." They engage with our grammatical intuitions less strongly than most other sentences and yield disagreements that are less pressing or important than other cases where intuitions are more strongly felt.

I want to say the same thing about health and cultural opportunities and life. These are "don't cares," and if our theory rules them out as intrinsic personal or human goods, that shouldn't be considered a problem. Indeed, to the extent the theory itself seems strong, that gives us a reason to gerrymander or place these items where the theory tells us to, gives us a reason to think: well, we didn't know how to categorize these things previously, but given the explanatory power of our theory and its intuitive strength about cases we are surer of, we now have a proper answer to a question or questions that intuition left to itself couldn't help us with.

So I would urge that we now have some reason to exclude most of the items mentioned just above from our list; they are, most of them, "don't cares," and we can, therefore, let the present theory determine their status. I am slightly more reluctant to treat power and wealth in this way, however, because I think in their case there is a stronger tendency to ascribe intrinsic goodness than one finds, say, about cultural opportunities not taken advantage of, about physical health, and about being alive *compos mentis*. And I must admit to having some doubts myself about whether we should rule out power (everything we shall now say about power can be said *mutatis mutandis* about wealth). But I think those doubts in fact stem from *moral* hypotheses or possibilities that are very much at odds with the view of morality subscribed to in these pages, so that, in all consistency, the present approach should *want* to rule out power (and wealth) as a fundamental human good.[9]

---

9. Actually, there is a difference between intrinsic (or noninstrumental) goodness and status as a fundamental good that I should briefly mention, though little hangs

When we are moved toward thinking of power as a basically good thing, I think we are also (more or less consciously) inclining toward skepticism about our obligations to care about others, near or distant. A thirst for power over others is inconsistent with the kinds of humane and intimate caring I have defended here, and anyone with a moral allegiance, therefore, to such forms of caring won't see power over others as a desirable personal goal. It is only, I think, when we are skeptical a bit about morality or about a caring morality, only when we find ourselves tempted toward some sort of egoistic or Nietzschean morality or ethic of power, that we see power as an important good (for us). So in connection with power, we have a real choice: if we want to urge it as a basic personal or human good, we really should give up on the ethic of caring and embrace something more Nietzschean or at least egoistic, but alternatively, and by the same token, if we are sure, really sure, that morality, the morality that really applies to us, requires caring concern for people, then the attractions not only of power but of the idea of treating it as a basic human good must to a large extent fade. So in the end, I think we should reject power (and for the same reasons wealth) as a human good because it doesn't fit with a total picture of morality-cum-rationality-cum-welfare that has a good deal going for it, and certainly, at any rate, more going for it than the total ethical picture we get from Nietzsche or egoism.[10]

---

on it for present purposes. If *the good life* is built up out of the kinds of intrinsic human goods we are talking about here, then we can say having a good life is intrinsically good, but that goodness is composed or constructed (in a complex way, no doubt, that there is no need at present to enter into) out of other elements, so to speak. So although a good life and, say, wisdom are both intrinsically or noninstrumentally good (for people), the latter is fundamental, an atomic or "building-block" good, whereas the former is derivative, molecular, or structural.

10. Perhaps I should slightly expand what I have just said, however, because in many, but hardly all, cases, power is something achieved, not merely possessed. So even if having power over others isn't a good according to the present theory, the perseverance-requiring *achievement* of power may count as a good. Indeed, because the view I am defending is much less globally moralistic than Aristotelian elevationism and claims that achievement goods require only the virtue of perseverance, not the virtues that correspond to and ground *other* goods like civic friendship, that view allows even "immoral" achievements to count as personal goods. (Cf. what we said earlier in Chapter 6 about immoral pleasures.)

Finally, let me mention capability, whose status as a basic good has been defended at considerable length and in several places by Amartya Sen.[11] This is or was a novel suggestion, and I believe that that is in part because many philosophers have been or would be inclined to think of capability as a purely instrumental good, something that gets us the things we want in life. But it is interesting to note where this candidate for good status might fall within the theory I have defended. For most capabilities are acquired or learned—from tying one's shoes to political savvy—and so from the standpoint of the present theory, it seems reasonable to classify most or all capabilities under the rubric of achievements, as good to the extent they can be seen in that light. This doesn't give Sen everything he wants or has wanted, but I wonder whether it represents anything in the way of a serious rift between his views and my own and am inclined to think that it does not.

This, then, completes our main articulation and defense of a hyper-agent-based account of (basic) human good(s). But, of course, I haven't yet said anything about how such goods as the account allows combine or interact in determining how good someone's life is overall, and a hyper-agent-based (or elevationist) theory needs (eventually) to be able to deal with such issues in its own terms. Thus in a recent article, David Velleman has argued (roughly) that smaller goods or facts become relevant to the overall goodness of life through being brought together and subsumed under categories of human good like wisdom and achievement.[12] Since these are two goods the present theory also accepts as such, Velleman's discussion suggests that matters of overall structural good can be assimilated to issues already being considered (by us here) at the atomic or micro level.

But although this would simplify the larger tasks of hyper-agent-basing, I am not entirely convinced. In the book chapter to which Velleman's piece is a reply, I mentioned some reasons for thinking that the importance of a good to a life can sometimes depend on sheer temporal factors ("all's well that ends well" isn't entirely an exaggeration), and I don't think every case where timing seems in-

---

11. See, e.g., Amartya Sen, *Commodities and Capabilities* (North Holland: Elsevier Science, 1985).

12. See his "Well-Being and Time," *Pacific Philosophical Quarterly* 72, 1991, pp. 48–77.

tuitively to make a difference to a life's overall goodness is assimilable to factors such as achievement and wisdom.[13] So we need at this point to consider whether, for reasons of simplicity or unity, we should *throw out* the cases not thus assimilable or whether we should insist on making a place, an intelligible place, for them within a hyper-agent-based account of overall good lives. (Also, one doesn't have an ideal life overall if one hates one's life, but our theory allows for this because it builds positive attitudes like satisfaction, caring, and purpose into its specification of particular goods and because anyone who hates a life full of goods like love and achievement presumably lacks the positive attitude and central good of self-esteem.)

One (further) loose end, moreover, is the fact that we have had nothing to say about the concept of a good state of affairs (Kant's *das Gute*). But I am inclined to think that the main purposes of ethics can be accomplished without that concept, and, indeed, this merely reiterates what certain previous virtue ethicists (notably, Philippa Foot)[14] have said about this concept. If morally good action and just law can be accounted for without this concept, then our intuitions about the goodness of states of affairs can perhaps be left to themselves, as epiphenomena that have no real work to do in articulating our best and most coherent sense of moral demands and ethical ideals.

Moreover, even if one insists on the ethical importance of those intuitions, it seems possible to take them into account in hyper-agent-based terms. The two most prevalent theories of good/just/ deserved states of affairs are those offered by utilitarianism and by Kantian ethics, and they involve understanding that cluster of notions in terms, respectively, of aggregate (or average) well-being and of proportionality or comparative fit between people's moral merits/ virtue and their well-being. Since both moral merit and well-being have here been understood in hyper-agent-based terms, there is no reason in principle why the kind of approach I have taken couldn't

13. See my *Goods and Virtues* (Oxford: Clarendon Press, 1990), ch. 1.

14. See Foot's "Immoralist," reviews of *Nietzsche: The Man and His Philosophy* by R. J. Hollingdale, and *Nietzsche as Philosopher* by A. C. Danto, *New York Review of Books* 6/2 (Feb. 17, 1966), pp. 8–10; and her "Utilitarianism and the Virtues," reprinted in S. Scheffler, ed., *Consequentialism and Its Critics* (Oxford: Oxford University 1988), pp. 224–42.

be extended to deal with issues of desert and good overall states of affairs.[15] But as I suggested above, it might be better to keep this effort in reserve until we see whether, given everything else that can be done in hyper-agent-based terms, the effort is really necessary.

2. General Conclusion

By way of overall conclusion, then, let me say just a bit more about the historical antecedents of agent-basing. There hasn't been much agent-basing either recently or in the past, but the approach taken here does have significant roots in the moral sentimentalism of the eighteenth century (and, further back, in the Christian ideal of compassion and agapic love, which itself constituted a background to and strong influence on sentimentalism's emphasis on universal benevolence). As I noted earlier, Francis Hutcheson considered universal benevolence, in itself and without considering its actual consequences, to be the morally best of motives, but at the same time advocated one of the earliest versions of the principle of utility. That is, Hutcheson evaluated motives "intrinsically," but by and large evaluated actions in terms of their consequences. Utilitarianism as a mature theory eventually developed out of the moral sentimentalism of Hutcheson, Hume, and others; and utilitarianism certainly results if one begins with the "hybrid" theory of Hutcheson and alters it so that motives as well as actions end up being assessed in terms of their consequences.

But it is also possible to alter the hybrid character of Hutcheson's theory in just the opposite direction. If, like Hutcheson, one evaluates motives intrinsically and independently of their consequences, one can also start assessing actions in terms of their inherent motivation rather than by reference to their (actual or expected) consequences, and this precisely yields an agent-based view, in particular, morality as universal benevolence. This is in actual historical fact the "road not taken" from moral sentimentalism, and perhaps it has required a considerable revival of virtue ethics even to see it as a possibility. But what I have been suggesting in this book is that that

---

15. Cf. Foot's "Utilitarianism and the Virtues," where the goodness of states of affairs is understood in terms of the virtues.

possibility may be preferable to what actually, historically, happened, because (as we have already seen) warm or sentimentalist agent-basing has a number of conspicuous advantages over utilitarianism.[16]

Even an impartialistic agent-based theory like morality as universal benevolence has such advantages, but if one takes moral sentimentalism in a partialist direction, then there are additional advantages that I have also been at pains to spell out in these pages. Moral sentimentalism has lately begun to move (once again) in the direction of virtue ethics,[17] and the present book has sought to show, in particular, that an agent-based virtue ethics based (largely) on (partialistic) caring gives moral sentimentalism its greatest potential relevance to the issues and debates of contemporary ethical theory.

16. In *An Introduction to the Principles of Morals and Legislation* (chs. 1 and 2), Bentham treats it as an advantage of utilitarianism that it offers an external criterion of right and wrong action—namely, (the production of) pleasure/pain. (Some of) the views he is critical of anchored morality in moral intuitions and institutions that are not external to morality (or moral opinion) in the requisite sense and thus (according to him) beg some critical moral questions. But Bentham himself relied on intuition, I think, more than he seems to have believed. His argument(s) for example against asceticism and the principle of producing pain rather than pleasure rely on common opinion and common intuition, if one examines them closely enough, so I think utilitarianism lacks any real advantage over agent-based views that rely on our intuitions about (the fundamental or intrinsic moral character of) motives.

17. Here, I am thinking of the work of Noddings and others who work on the ethics of caring; but also, e.g., of Annette Baier, "What Do Women Want in a Moral Theory?" in *Moral Prejudices* (Cambridge, Mass.: Harvard University Press, 1994), pp. 1–17; Jorge Garcia, "The New Critique of Anti-Consequentialist Moral Theory," *Philosophical Studies* 71, 1993, pp. 1–32; Roger Crisp, "Modern Moral Philosophy and the Virtues," in *How Should One Live? Essays on the Virtues* ed. R. Crisp, (Oxford: Oxford University Press, 1996), esp. pp. 13f.; and David Wiggins, "The Artificial Virtues in Hume," in *How Should One Live?*, pp. 131–40. Compare too Linda Trinkaus Zagzebski's *Virtues of the Mind* (Cambridge: Cambridge University Press, 1996).

INDEX

Caring (motive/ethic/morality of)
(*continued*)
184–90, 193, 196, 200, 202n.,
209, 211
balanced, 66, 69–79, 87–90, 97–
101, 121, 137, 187
humanitarian/humane, ix, 47n.,
64–66, 69–72, 76n., 77–78, 89–
90, 93–94, 97, 98n., 100, 116–
17, 137n., 186–88, 200–201
intimate, 64–66, 70–72, 76n., 77–
78, 89–90, 93–94, 100, 187,
200–201
"inverse-care law," 65–66, 74–
75
Chomsky, N., 162, 205–206
Cicero, 176n.
Cohen, G. A., 119n.
Cohen, J., 131n.
Conscientiousness, ix, 37, 49–62,
63n., 110, 195
Consequentialism, vii–viii, 4, 10–
11, 26–28, 48, 67, 72–73, 75,
85–86, 96, 135n., 170, 172–
73, 178, 183, 189
Contract Theory (Contractarianism/
Contractualism), 48, 50, 93,
106, 111, 121
Crisp, R., 211n.

Darwall, S., 41n., 49n., 58n., 202n.
Das, R., 72n.
Dennett, D., 187
Deontic terms/values, 4
Deontology, 28, 68n., 78–87, 96–
97, 115–16
Driver, J., 71n.
Dworkin, R., 95

Egoism (ethical), 22, 52, 189n.,
192–96, 207
Elevation(ism), 145–68, 198–99,
202

Epicureanism (Epicurean ethics), 4,
142, 145–51, 166
Eudaimonia, 6–7

Finlay, J. N., 51n.
Foot, P., viii, 209, 210n.
Frankena, W., 9
Free will, 16, 61n.

Garcia, J., 20, 134, 137n., 211n.
Gauthier, D., 170, 182n., 189
Gelfand, S., 77
Gilligan, C., 29, 48, 92
Goodman, N., 159
Griffin, J., 204n.
Grotius, H., vii
Gutmann, A., 132n.

Hedonism, 18–19, 162, 185, 198
Held, V., ix, 32n., 65n.
Hill, T., Jr., 106n., 203n.
Hoffman, M., 110n.
Hooker, B., 204n.
Hume, D., vii–ix, 8, 20, 41, 121,
159, 169, 185, 210
Hurka, T., 164n., 186n., 199n.,
202n.
Hursthouse, R., viii, 6–8
Hutcheson, F., vii–viii, 9, 20, 41n.,
49n., 54n., 71n., 85, 169, 210
Hyper-agent-basing, 141, 197–210

Impartial benevolence. *See*
Universal benevolence

Justice (Fairness), x, 23, 29, 32,
48, 67, 68n., 92–113, 114–15,
118–23, 125n., 134–36

Kagan, S., 90n., 164n.
Kamm, F., 73n.
Kant (Kantian Ethics/Kantianism),
vii–viii, 9–10, 23, 35n., 36,